AN INTRODUCTION TO THE BOOKS OF THE APOCRYPHA

BY

W.O.E. OESTERLEY

the apocryphile press
BERKELEY, CA
www.apocryphile.org

apocryphile press
BERKELEY, CA

Apocryphile Press
1700 Shattuck Ave #81
Berkeley, CA 94709
www.apocryphile.org

First published in 1935 by the Society for Promoting
Christian Knowledge. Apocryphile Press Edition, 2006.

Printed in the United States of America
ISBN 1-933993-22-7

PREFATORY NOTE

THIS book is in no sense a new edition of *The Books of the Apocrypha : their Origin, Teaching and Contents* (1914). It is from beginning to end a new and wholly independent work. Since the earlier volume appeared, twenty-one years ago, much new literature on the Apocrypha generally, and on its individual books, has been published; and the present writer has had, during these years, opportunities for studying a good deal, at any rate, of this new material, besides paying attention to the older literature. It may, therefore, be hoped that this book will be found to be a considerable improvement on the former.

The work consists of two parts, the earlier of which is perhaps the more important, as it deals with subjects of wider interest than the necessarily more technical introductions to the several books.

Part I, Prolegomena to the Apocrypha, has for its object to show the interest and importance of this neglected body of literature from the literary, historical, doctrinal, and New Testament points of view; while Part II deals with the usual subjects of introduction necessary for the study of the individual books.

That my friend Theodore Robinson has not seen his way to collaborate with me in this work is a matter of much regret to me. I had hoped that he would have done so; but he pleaded that inasmuch as during the many years of reading and teaching in preparation for the books we have written together, he had concentrated more particularly on the earlier periods of the religion, history, and literature of the Hebrews, he did not feel competent to deal with the literature belonging to this late period.

I wish to express my warm thanks to Dr. H. H. Rowley for having read through my manuscript and the proof-sheets, and for many valuable suggestions.

It should be added here that the large number of quotations from the books of the Apocrypha given in full, instead of mere references, was thought advisable because most people are less familiar with the text of these than with that of the canonical Scriptures.

The text of the Septuagint used is that of Swete; but reference should be made also to Rahlfs' edition, which is marvellously cheap and beautifully produced.

W. O. E. OESTERLEY.

February 1935.

CONTENTS

CONTENTS

PART I
PROLEGOMENA TO THE APOCRYPHA

CHAPTER I

THE BOOKS OF THE APOCRYPHA

I. THE TERM "APOCRYPHA"

THE subjects of the Canon of Holy Scripture and of the origin and meaning of the term Apocrypha have been dealt with in *An Introduction to the Books of the Old Testament*; [1] it will suffice, therefore, if we summarize what has been said there.

As a technical term used in reference to the Scriptures the word "Canon" is Christian, appearing in this connexion for the first time, so far as is known, towards the end of the fourth century A.D.[2] In the Jewish Church the process whereby the books of the Old Testament, as we now know it, were finally marked off from all other books was a long one. The need of such differentiation first began to be felt owing to the rise of Greek culture and the growth of Greek literature, with the resultant spread of many books which were deemed harmful by the Jewish religious leaders. But the more immediate cause, which was in part, however, an indirect outcome of this, was the appearance of apocalyptic books among the Jews.

The idea of forming a collection of holy books standing on a plane different from and higher than all others, began to take concrete shape, in all probability, towards the end of the second century B.C.; but the actual formation of what we now understand as the Canon of Holy Scripture did not take place until about 100–120 A.D.; [3] and while, during this period, veneration for the books of the Old Testament, and especially the Pentateuch, prevailed and

---

[1] By Oesterley and Robinson, pp. 1 ff. (1934).
[2] By Amphilochius, Archbishop of Iconium.
[3] On the opposition of the Jewish Church to the Septuagint as being the Bible of the Christians and the consequent exclusion of the books of the Apocrypha from the Canon, see Chap. ix. below, pp. 122 f.

went on increasing, they could not be spoken of as
" canonical " in our sense of the word. The contention
that the formation of a Canon of the Old Testament went
through three stages, first the canon of the books of the
Torah or Law, then that of the prophetical books, and
finally that of the " Writings," rests on no adequate evidence.
Even after the Canon of the Old Testament, as we understand it, was formed, in one act as it were, at the Council of
Jamnia (about 90 A.D.), as is usually held, disputes arose,
and continued for some time, as to whether or not certain
books [1] should be regarded as " defiling the hands," the
Rabbinical equivalent for " canonical."

As to the term " Apocrypha," this was used, in the first
instance, of books containing hidden teaching not to be
disclosed to ordinary people. The Greek word *apokryphos*,
in its technical sense, " is derived from the practice, common
among sects, religious or philosophic, of embodying their
special tenets or formulæ in books withheld from public
use, and communicated to an inner circle of believers." [2]
In reference to Jewish books this is well illustrated by what
is said in our Apocryphal book, II Esdr. xiv. 44–47:

> So in forty days were written fourscore and fourteen
> books.. And it came to pass, when the forty days were
> fulfilled, that the Most High spake unto me, saying, The
> first that thou hast written publish openly, and let the
> worthy and unworthy read it; but keep the seventy
> last, that thou mayest deliver them to such as be wise
> among the people; for in them is the spring of under-
> standing, the fountain of wisdom, and the stream of
> knowledge.

The first twenty-four books here refer to the canonical
books of the Old Testament, the seventy last to apocalyptic
books; the passage shows that in certain Jewish circles at
the beginning of the second century A.D. the latter were
held in higher esteem than the canonical books.

---

[1] i.e. *Esther, Ecclesiastes, Song of Songs* ; the controversy did not cease until
about 120 A.D.

[2] James in *Encycl. Bibl.* i. 249.

A second stage in the history of the term " Apocrypha " is reflected in Origen's use of it; he distinguishes between books read during public worship and those which he calls " apocryphal "; [1] by this word, however, he does not mean the books of what we call the Apocrypha, but those which we designate *Pseudepigrapha*. But Origen is not consistent in his use of the term, because elsewhere he applies it to heretical books.[2]

A third stage, which we find in the fourth century in the Greek Church, is that in which a distinction is made between canonical books and books read for edification; by the latter are meant the books of our Apocrypha, while the word " apocryphal " was still applied to those which we call *Pseudepigrapha*.

Finally, Jerome distinguished between *libri canonici* and *libri ecclesiastici*, the latter referring to the books of our Apocrypha, which were then called " apocryphal " in a new sense. By degrees this use of the term came to be generally accepted,[3] and this has continued to the present day.

II. The Greek Canon

We use the expression Greek Canon for convenience' sake; strictly speaking, there never was a Greek Canon; books were added to the Greek Version of the Scriptures, but they were not " canonized."

This Greek translation of the Old Testament Scriptures, the Septuagint,[4] contains all the books of the Hebrew Bible, and in addition almost all the books of our Apocrypha; these latter, with two exceptions, are interspersed among the canonical books, though their positions vary in the different MSS.[5] In the great uncials BA they are placed thus: *I Esdras* follows *Chronicles* (in Cod. A it comes after *Judith*);

---

[1] *Comm. in Matt.* x. 18, xiii. 57.
[2] *Prolog. in Cant. Cantic.* (Lommatsch xiv. 325).
[3] Augustine, however, continues to use " apocrypha " in the earlier sense (*De Civ. Dei*, xv. 23).
[4] So called because of the tradition (contained in the *Letter of Aristeas*) that this translation was the work of seventy, strictly seventy-two, Jewish elders in the reign of the Egyptian king Ptolemy II Philadelphus (B.C. 285–246).
[5] The order of the canonical books also varies in the Greek MSS.

Judith and *Tobit* follow *Esther*; the *Additions to Esther* (*i.e. The Rest of Esther*), to *Jeremiah* (*i.e. Baruch* and the *Epistle of Jeremy*), to *Daniel* (*i.e.* the *Song of the Three Holy Children,* the *History of Susanna,* and *Bel and the Dragon*), all form integral parts of the canonical books, respectively; *Wisdom* and *Ecclesiasticus* are added after the other Wisdom books (but in Cod. A all the Wisdom books come together at the end of the whole list); *I, II Maccabees* do not occur in Cod. B, but in Cod. A they come after the Esdras books and before the Wisdom books. The two exceptions are: *II Esdras,* which does not appear in any MS. of the Septuagint; and the *Prayer of Manasses,* which figures among the canticles appended to the *Psalms.*

Thus, except for some parts of *I Esdras,* no book of our Apocrypha is found in the Hebrew Old Testament, but all, with the exception of *II Esdras,* belong to the "Greek Canon."

Although the Septuagint was a Greek translation of the Hebrew Scriptures originally undertaken for the benefit of the Jews of the Dispersion (primarily that of Egypt), the books of the Apocrypha were never recognized as forming part of the Holy Scriptures by the Jewish Church; but that many of them were read as books for edification is probable from the fact that most of them were originally written in Hebrew. In the Christian Church—at any rate in the Western Church—all the books of the Apocrypha, with the exception of *II Esdras,* were included in the Canon (see further chap. ix).

The Septuagint Version of the Hebrew Scriptures was made in Egypt, as already indicated; but the work does not belong to any one period; it was begun in the third century B.C., but was not concluded until about B.C. 100, perhaps even somewhat later.

The books of the Apocrypha were added at different times, but it is impossible to say at what times, for in the oldest MSS. of the Septuagint they are all included (excepting *II Esdras*), and the earliest extant MSS. belong to about 350 A.D. The dates of the books themselves are in some cases uncertain, and some time must have elapsed between their first appearance and their inclusion in the "Greek Canon."

Since the Septuagint *in its original form* consisted only of books contained in the Hebrew Scriptures, it may well be asked how it came about that the Jews, with their veneration for their sacred books, should have mixed up with them books not recognized as holy? How, in other words, are we to account for the existence of uncanonical writings, added by Jews, interspersed among those marked off as sacrosanct? In plain language, how did the books of our Apocrypha ever get into the Greek Bible? In reply to this we cannot do better than quote Swete's hypothesis:

A partial explanation of the early mixture of non-canonical books with canonical may be found in the form under which the Greek Bible passed into the keeping of the Church. In the first century the material used for literary purposes was still almost exclusively papyrus, and the form was that of the roll.[1] But rolls of papyrus seldom contained more than a single work, and writings of any length, especially if divided into books, were often transcribed into two or more separate rolls.[2] The rolls were kept in boxes (κιβωτοί, κίσται, *capsae*, *cistae*),[3] which served not only to preserve them, but to collect them in sets. Now, while the sanctity of the five books of Moses would protect the *cistae* which contained them from the intrusion of foreign rolls, no scruple of this kind would deter the owner of a roll of Esther from placing it in the same box with Judith and Tobit; the Wisdoms, in like manner, naturally found their way into a Solomonic collection; while in a still larger number of instances the two Greek recensions of Esdras consorted together, and Baruch and the Epistle seemed rightly to claim a place with the roll of Jeremiah. . . .[4]

[1] See Kenyon, *Palaeography of Greek papyri*, pp. 24, 113 ff. (1899).
[2] *Ibid.*, p. 132.
[3] Thompson, *Greek and Latin Palaeography*, p. 57 (1894).
[4] *An Introduction to the Old Testament in Greek*, p. 225 (1900). As to the linguistic character of the Septuagint, see Swete, *op. cit.*, pp. 289 ff., and R. R. Ottley, *A Handbook to the Septuagint*, pp. 159 ff. (1920).

B

III. CHARACTER AND GENERAL CONTENTS OF THE APOCRYPHA

The collection of writings comprised in the Apocrypha offers an interesting illustration of Jewish literary versatility during the last two or three centuries B.C.; the variety of subject-matter is amazing; here we have, in the books of the *Maccabees*, history, recounting tales of heroism (*e.g.* I Macc. vi. 43 ff.), descriptions of battles (I Macc. ix. 1 ff. and elsewhere), examples of brilliant generalship (*e.g.* I Macc. iv. 1 ff.), information regarding party divisions among the Jews (I Macc. i. 11–15, ii. 45–47), stirring accounts of the valiant struggles of the Jews in defence of their religion (I Macc. ii. 14 ff. and often elsewhere), diplomatic correspondence between the Jews and foreign nations (I Macc. viii. 22 ff., xi. 32 ff. and elsewhere)—to mention but a few of the topics of historical interest. Then we have romance, as in the book of *Tobit*; myth in the story of *Bel and the Dragon*; midrash in *I Esdras*; abundance of Wisdom writing in *Ecclesiasticus* and *Wisdom*; philosophy in the first part of *Wisdom*, numerous instances of folklore (*e.g.* Tob. vii. 16, 17; Bar. ii. 24); manifold pictures of social life in all its phases, in *Ecclus.* Then, in the religious domain, almost every book gives dogmatic teaching in one form or another; further, there is prophecy in *Baruch*; visions in *II Esdras*; prayers, psalms, religious poetry, and liturgical pieces in different books; also eschatology and apocalyptic in *II Esdras*. This does not by any means exhaust the riches of subject-matter, but it will have given some insight into the variety of topics dealt with.

Naturally enough, this material is not all of equal value or importance; as with the books of the canonical scriptures, so with those of the Apocrypha; in the former it must be recognized that in a few cases there are writings which are of less value than the great majority; this would apply to the *Song of Songs*, *Ecclesiastes*, and *Esther*; not that these are without their use and value; but their content seems hardly to be of the same high order as the rest of the Old Testament

Scriptures. In the same way, while most of the books of the Apocrypha are altogether worthy of their place, the *Epistle of Jeremy*, the *Story of Susanna*, and *Bel and the Dragon*, which have doubtless certain points of interest, are nevertheless of greatly inferior value in comparison with the rest of the books.

No classification of the books of the Apocrypha is satisfactory, because in the case of almost every one, into whatever class it is placed from one point of view, it will belong to another class from some other point of view; if, for example, the *Prayer of Manasses* is, rightly of course, classified under " Additions to canonical books," it is also liturgical; if *II Esdras* is classified under " Pseudepigrapha," it is also apocalyptic; if *Tobit* is classified under " Legendary writings," it is also a romance; if *II Macc.* is classified under " Authentic writings," it is also, in part at any rate, legendary—and so on.

Similarly, it is only in a somewhat doubtful and partial way that one can classify the books as " Palestinian " and " Hellenistic "; Schürer, who adopts this classification, is careful to point out that he does this only for the want of a better method; " it must be expressly emphasized," he says, " that the division between the two groups is a fluid one, and the designation must, in any case, be taken *cum grano salis.*" He is dealing with the whole body of extant Jewish literature belonging to the period B.C. 200 onwards, of which the Apocrypha forms a part only, so that what he says applies only in a limited degree to our collection:

By the Palestinian–Jewish literature we are to understand that which in essentials—but only in essentials— represents the standpoint of Pharisaic Judaism as this had developed in Palestine; by hellenistic–Jewish literature is meant that which either in form or content, exhibits in any marked degree hellenistic influence.[1]

[1] *Geschichte des jüdischen Volkes* . . . , iii. pp. 188 f. (1909).

IV. Hellenistic Influence Observable in the
Apocrypha

In the case of the books of the Apocrypha it is primarily
in the book of *Wisdom* that hellenistic influence is seen.
Thus, in vii. 24 it is said: "For Wisdom is more mobile
than any motion, yea, she passeth and goeth through all
things by reason of her pureness"; and in viii. 1: "But
in full might she reacheth from end to end, and doth order
all things properly." That we have here a reflection of
Stoic philosophy is evident; Zeller, in describing the doctrine
of the Stoics, says:

But all the powers operating in the world come from
one original power, as is proved by the unity of the world,
the combination and harmony of all its parts. Like all
that is real, this also must be corporeal, and is regarded
more precisely as warm vapour (πνεῦμα), or fire, for it is
warmth which begets, enlivens and moves all things.
But, on the other hand, the perfection of the world and the
adaptation of means to ends, and more especially the
rational element in human nature, show that this final
cause of the world must, at the same time, be the most
perfect reason, the kindest, most philanthropic nature—
in a word, the Deity. It is this just because it consists
of the most perfect material. As everything in the world
is indebted to it for its properties, its movement and life,
it must stand to the universe in the same relation as our
soul to our body. It penetrates all things as the πνεῦμα,
or artistic fire (πῦρ τεχνικόν), enlivening them, and
containing their germs in itself. It is the soul, the spirit
(νοῦς) the reason (λόγος) of the world. . . .[1]

Again, Stoic influence is observable in the enumeration
of the four cardinal virtues (viii. 7): temperance (σωφροσύνη),
prudence (φρόνησις), justice (δικαιοσύνη), manliness (ἀνδρεία).[2]
The influence of Platonic philosophy is to be discerned

[1] *Outlines of Greek Philosophy*, pp. 239 f. (Engl. transl. 1909); more fully in
Die Philosophie der Griechen, iii. 271 f. (1881).
[2] Cp. the stoical writing *IV Maccabees*, where these find frequent mention.

in such passages as viii. 19, 20, where the pre-existence of the soul is taken for granted: " Now I was a goodly child, and a good soul fell to my lot; nay, rather, being good, I came into a body undefiled "; and ix. 15, which teaches the corruptibility of the body: " For a corruptible body weigheth down the soul, and the earthly frame oppresseth the mind that museth upon many things." To quote Zeller again, where he discusses the Platonic philosophy:

The soul of man is in its nature homogeneous with the soul of the universe, from which it springs. Being of a simple and incorporeal nature, it is by its power of self-movement the origin of motion in the body; inseparably connected with the idea of life, it has neither end nor beginning. As the souls have descended from a higher world into the earthly body, they return after death, if their lives have been pure and devoted to higher objects, to this higher world, while those who need correction in part undergo punishments in another world, and in part migrate through the bodies of men and animals.[1]

The intellectual part of man is eternal, the corporeal is perishable. It need hardly be insisted that this teaching is wholly different from the Jewish doctrine of the resurrection of the body.

With regard to *Ecclesiasticus*, although this is a distinctly Jewish–Palestinian book, there are, nevertheless, traces of Greek influence; but these are to be found

in general conception rather than in definite form; for example, the identification of virtue with knowledge is a distinct Hellenic *trait*, and is treated in the book as axiomatic; in the past, human and divine wisdom had been regarded as opposed, whereas owing to Greek influence, in *Ecclesiasticus*, as well as in the Wisdom literature generally, it is taught that Wisdom is the one thing of all others which is indispensable to him who would lead a godly life.[2]

[1] *Outlines* . . . , pp. 152 f.
[2] See the present writer's *The Wisdom of Jesus the son of Sirach, or Ecclesiasticus*, p. xxv. (Cambr. Bible, 1912).

Other books of the Apocrypha which may be classed as Jewish–hellenistic are *I Esdras*, the *Additions to Esther* and the *Additions to Daniel*, the book of *Baruch* and the *Epistle of Jeremy*; these are undoubtedly predominantly orthodox-Jewish, but slight indications of hellenistic influence may be discerned here and there in each of them.

It is, however, necessary to repeat what was implied above, that while Greek influence is to be detected in some of the books of the Apocrypha, they contain nothing that would have offended orthodox Judaism of those days; it is simply that the Greek atmosphere which permeated the world was breathed in unconsciously by the writers and manifested itself at times in their writings.

As to those Jewish–Palestinian writings in which hellenistic *traits* are rarely, if ever, to be discerned—*Tobit, Judith I, II Maccabees, II Esdras*, and, in the main, *Ecclesiasticus* (see above)—we need not discuss their Judaism here, as this will be gone into fully below (chap. vii).

CHAPTER II

THE APOCRYPHA AS LITERATURE

In a collection of writings of such various authorship as the Apocrypha, and in which the purposes of the writings are so different, it is natural enough that the standard of literary merit should not be the same in all. With one exception, we have no knowledge of the personalities of the writers, apart from a few exiguous hints to be gleaned from their books, and therefore as to their claims to be regarded as *littérateurs*. The compiler of *I Esdras* was nothing more than a compiler who shows but little skill in piecing together the fragments which he had collected; one piece, at least, has distinct literary value; true, the compiler has somewhat marred the original symmetry, but he makes up for it by adding a fine piece of his own; to this we shall return (p., 15). The writer of *II Esdras* was an apocalyptist who had no faith in humanity, and his pessimism colours his writing, but his sympathy for his fallen brethren and his deep piety are beautiful *traits*; more than one writer has contributed to the book, but of this later; taken as a whole it has much that is of value from a literary, as well as from other points of view. The authors of *Tobit* and *Judith* are both fine story-tellers; the latter book, especially, is of high literary excellence. The author of *Wisdom* was a cultured man with some knowledge of Greek literature; the earlier part of his book is superior to the latter from the literary point of view; it is not by any means certain that both parts belong to one author. The book has been described as " perhaps the finest work in the whole range of Apocryphal literature "; [1] taking it as a whole, that may be true, but it applies to the former rather than to the latter part. The writer of *I Maccabees* has left to posterity a work of the greatest value;

---

[1] Fairweather and Black, *The First Book of Maccabees*, p. 15 (1908).

as his object was to set forth nothing but historical events, it cannot be said that the simple narrative prose is of great literary worth; nevertheless, the writer is sometimes moved to pen some fine rhetorical passages, and some exciting episodes are realistically portrayed. Of greatly inferior ability is the writer of *II Maccabees*; but he does not profess to do more than give a digest of the historical work of Jason of Cyrene. He cannot be said to have done his work well, whatever the reasons may be; he often leaves gaps in the history, and the whole presentation is much wanting in unity; his own additions, prompted no doubt by the best of motives, are not always in good taste. Of the *Rest of Esther* and the *Additions to Daniel* there is little to be said from the literary point of view. The three pieces included under the *Song of the Three Holy Children* all have their points of merit. That the *Prayer of Manasses* should have been incorporated in the early Church liturgy can be readily understood; as a penitential liturgical piece it would be difficult to find its equal. In *Baruch* we have, in the later portions (iii. 9–v. 9), some highly edifying literary pieces of the "Wisdom" type. We have purposely left to the end the great figure of Ben-Sira and his book; of his personality we know more than that of any other writer of the books of the Apocrypha, and his book is, we believe, by far the most important from most points of view, literary and other, of all those classed under this misleading title. This grand old Sage gives us in his book (*Ecclesiasticus*) quite a lot of information about himself—not purposely, for he is anything but an egotist, but incidentally and by implication. He was a Wisdom-scribe, learned in the Scriptures, a teacher and public lecturer; he had travelled, and had experienced much among his fellow-creatures; he had thus gained a wide knowledge of the world; a careful observer of human nature, his insight into the weaknesses of men, as well as of their virtues, was deep; gifted with a keen sense of humour, he could with biting sarcasm penetrate the armour of egotistic self-esteem, and without malice scourge those who deserved his censure. But dominating his entire outlook there was a depth of religious conviction to which everything

was subordinated.   It will, therefore, readily be understood
why his book stands out as the brightest gem of the collection,
and why it has been the most highly treasured by the thoughtful
in all ages.   As pure literature it may not reach the standard
of the first part of the book of *Wisdom*, but it has compensating
excellences which make it of higher value.

We will now offer a few illustrations showing some of the
literary characteristics of these writings.

As an example of the art of narration we may mention
the " Story of the Three Pages," in I Esdr. iii. 1–iv. 63.
This tells of how three young men of the bodyguard of
Darius I undertook an intellectual contest as to which of
them could describe in a single wise sentence the strongest
thing in the world; the king and the three princes of Persia
were to be the judges.   Each writes down his sentence, on a
piece of papyrus (presumably): they run: " Wine is the
strongest "; " The king is strongest "; " Women are the
strongest."   Here, however, an element is brought in which
quite obviously does not belong to the original story, but
which is interjected for the special purpose which the
compiler of *I Esdras* had in view; after the sentence,
" Women are strongest," the entirely irrelevant words are
added: " But above all things Truth beareth away the
victory."   That, however, by the way.   The story goes
on to narrate how the king and his courtiers assembled to
hear the young men read out their sentences, and to set
forth the reasons whereby each was justified.   This done, the
king and his nobles take counsel; it is unanimously decided
that the champion of women has won the day, and the
king pronounces the verdict in the words: " O sirs, are not
women strong? "   Now, in the original story it is highly
probable that the virtues of woman were lauded; but here,
be the reason what it may, the writer goes off on to a panegyric on Truth.   The winner is suitably rewarded by the
king.   There is no doubt that as a piece of popular literature
the story is told with great skill, for the reader's interest,
gripped at the start, is arrested all through.   With the
origin of the story we are not here concerned, but the compiler has made good use of it; his own addition on the

praise of Truth is, from the literary point of view, the best part of the story as it now stands, and is worth quoting:

> Great is the earth, high is the heaven, swift is the sun in his course, for he compasseth the heavens round about, and fetcheth his course again to his own place in one day. Is he not great that maketh these things? Therefore great is Truth, and stronger than all things. All the earth calleth upon Truth; and the heaven blesseth her; all works shake and tremble, but with her is no unrighteous thing. Wine is unrighteous, the king is unrighteous, women are unrighteous, all the children of men are unrighteous, and unrighteous are all their works—all such-like; and there is no truth in them; in their unrighteousness also they shall perish. But Truth abideth, and is strong for ever, she liveth and conquereth for evermore. With her there is no accepting of persons or partiality; but she doeth the things that are just, away from all unrighteous and wicked things, and all men have pleasure in her works. And neither in her judgement is aught unrighteous, and hers is the strength, and dominion, and power, and majesty, of all ages. Blessed be the God of Truth. And he ceased speaking. Then all the people shouted and said: "Great is Truth and of exceeding power!" [1] (iv. 34–41).

To illustrate the literary style of Ben-Sira is a little difficult because the choice is so great; his book is much longer than any other in the collection. As he writes throughout in parallels, or their development, it will be best to give the quotations in this form. A beautiful piece is the poem on the Fear of the Lord: [2]

The fear of the Lord is glory and exultation,
  And gladness and a crown of joy.
The fear of the Lord delighteth the heart,
  And giveth gladness, and joy, and length of days.
For him that feareth the Lord it shall be well at the last,
  And in the day of his death he shall find grace.

---

[1] Μεγάλη ἡ ἀλήθεια καὶ ὑπερισχύει = *Magna est veritas et praevalet* (there is no good manuscript authority for *praevalebit*).
[2] From the Greek; the Hebrew is not extant.

The beginning of wisdom is to fear God,
    And with the faithful she was created in the womb;
With men of truth she is established for ever,[1]
    And with their seed her love abideth.[1]
Satiety of wisdom is the fear of the Lord,
    And she intoxicateth with her fruits.
She filleth all her house with desirable things,
    And her garners with her produce.
A crown of wisdom is the fear of the Lord,
    Making peace to flourish and healthful healing.
A strong staff is she and a glorious stay,[2]
    And everlasting honour for those who take hold of her.[2]
The fear of the Lord is the root of wisdom,
    And her branches are length of days.
                    (Ecclus. i. 11–20.)[3]

Our next illustration is translated from the Hebrew; the English translation from the Greek is familiar to many, but it will be seen that the Hebrew differs from this in many particulars. The illustration is taken from the famous " Praise of the Fathers of old "—that is the title given in the Hebrew[4]—(Ecclus. xliv. 1–15):[5]

Let me now sing the praises of pious men,
    The fathers in their generations.
Great glory did the Most High allot them,
    And great were they from the days of old.
They held dominion on earth in their royalty,
    Renowned for their mighty deeds,
Counsellors with discernment,
    Seers all by prophecy.
Rulers of the Gentiles through their craft,
    And leaders through their insight.

---

[1] On the basis of the Syriac; the Greek text is corrupt.

[2] From the Syriac; the Greek text is corrupt.

[3] The Syriac adds twelve distichs in continuance of the same theme which, in all probability, represent the original Hebrew; see Smend, *Die Weisheit des Jesus Sirach*, pp. 13 f. (1906).

[4] The Greek Version has the title: " Hymn of the Fathers."

[5] In a few cases the rendering is somewhat free in order to bring out the sense of the Hebrew.

Wise in speech through scribal learning,
    Uttering the sayings of tradition;
Composers of psalms according to rule,
    And authors of written proverbs;
Men of ability, possessing wealth,
    And living at ease in their homes.
All these were honoured in their generation,
    And in their day had honour.
Some of them have left a name,
    That men might tell their praise;
And some of them have no memorial,
    And they rested, even as they rested;
They were as though they had not been,
    Even as their children after them;
Yet were they men of piety,
    Good fortune abode with them.
With their seed their goods remained secure,
    And their inheritance to their children's children.
Their posterity held fast to the covenant,
    So, too, their children for their sakes;
Their memory abideth for ever,
    Their righteousness shall never be forgotten;
Their bodies were buried in peace,
    But their name liveth unto all generations.
The assembly recount their wisdom,
    And the congregation declare their praise.

In the story of Tobit there is a pathetic episode when Tobit misjudges his wife, in consequence of which she taunts him with being lacking in charity; not content with this, she wounds him to the quick by telling him that all his pious acts and almsgiving are nothing but hypocrisy, and that all the world knows it. This grieves Tobit to such an extent that he pours out his soul in bitterness to God, and prays that he may die. Our next illustration shall be Tobit's prayer, expressing as it does with such poignancy the bitterness of a sensitive soul; especially noteworthy also is his conviction that he is suffering for the sins of his fathers:

O Lord, thou art righteous, and all thy works are mercy and truth, and thou judgest true and righteous judgement for ever. Remember me, and look on me; take not vengeance on me for my sins and mine ignorances, and the sins of my fathers, which sinned before thee; for they disobeyed thy commandments; and thou gavest us for a spoil, and for captivity, and for death, and for a proverb of reproach to all the nations among whom we are dispersed. And now, many are thy judgements, true are they; that thou shouldest deal with me according to my sins and the sins of my fathers; because we did not keep thy commandments, for we walked not in truth before thee. And now deal with me according to that which is pleasing in thy sight, command my spirit to be taken from me, that I may be released, and become earth; for it is profitable for me to die rather than to live, because I have heard false reproaches, and there is much sorrow in me; command that I be now released from my distress, and go to the everlasting place; turn not thy face away from me (Tob. iii. 2–6).

An illustration from the book of *Judith* might have been given, but that it would involve a somewhat lengthy quotation, the narrative form of the book would demand this; as an instance, however, of the arresting literary style we may refer, for example, to x. 10–23, describing Judith's daring entry through the hostile camp into the tent of Holofernes; this, like many another passage in the book, reveals a remarkably high standard in the art of story-telling; no detail is without point; the course of the narrative is here and there held up with the purpose of whetting the reader's appetite, arousing the feeling of the need to go on in order to see what happens; and the *dénouement* does not disappoint; the climax in the story is terribly dramatic, one might say tragic, were it not that the heroine wins the day (xvi. 1–17).

In *I Maccabees*, owing to the subject-matter, passages of artistic literary excellence are hardly to be looked for; yet there are some realistic battle descriptions which rivet

the attention; in vi. 39–46, for example, we have a stirring
account of an act of individual heroism during a battle
in which the Syrians had brought up thirty-two elephants
trained for warfare:

> Now when the sun shone upon the shields of gold and
> brass, the mountains shone therewith, and blazed like
> torches of fire. And a part of the king's army was spread
> upon the high mountains, and some on the low ground,
> and they went on firmly and in order. And all that
> heard the noise of their multitude, and the marching
> of the multitude, and the rattling of the arms, did quake;
> for the army was exceeding great and strong. And
> Judas and his army drew near for battle; and there fell
> of the king's army six hundred men. And Eleazar, who
> was called Avaran, saw one of the beasts armed with
> royal breastplates, and he was higher than all the beasts,
> and the king seemed to be upon it; and he gave himself
> to deliver his people, and to get him an everlasting name;
> and he ran upon him courageously into the midst of the
> phalanx, and slew on the right hand and on the left,
> and they parted asunder from him on this side and on
> that. And he crept under the elephant, and thrust him
> from beneath, and slew him; and the elephant fell to the
> earth upon him, and he died there.

Sometimes the writer bursts forth into a poetic strain
(*e.g.* iii. 1–9, 45; vi. 10–13), showing that the war-chronicler
could also express himself in poetry.[1]

In the last three chapters of the book of *Baruch* we have a
collection of poems among which are several addressed to
Jerusalem personified; the last three speak of comfort to
the bereaved " mother," for her children are coming back
to her. One of these runs thus:

> O Jerusalem, raise thine eyes to the east,
> And behold the joy that cometh to thee from God.

---

[1] Assuming, that is, that such passages are from the hand of the writer
himself, which is not certain, see below, p. 302.

Lo, thy children are coming,
Whom perforce thou didst send away, they are coming,
Gathered from the east to the west,[1]
Rejoicing in the glory of God.
Put off, O Jerusalem, the garment of thy mourning,[2]
And put on the ornament of the glory of God.[3]
Cast about thee the robe of the righteousness of God,
Set a diadem on thine head of the glory of the Everlasting.
For God will show thy brightness to all the earth under
    heaven,
For thy name shall be called by God:
" The peace of righteousness " and " The glory of god-
    liness."

                                        (Bar. iv. 36–v. 4.)

If we had the Hebrew original of this beautiful little poem,
we should doubtless find the unevenness which occurs here
and there smoothed away.

One of the most striking pieces of its kind, and probably
unparalleled elsewhere, is the heart-searching confession
of sin in the *Prayer of Manasses*; and one can fully understand and appreciate the reason for its having been put to
liturgical use in the Church. It is too long to quote in full
but part of it may find a place here:

. . . For thou art the Lord Most High, o great compassion, long-suffering, and abundant in mercy, and dost
grieve [4] at the evils of men. Thou, O Lord, according
to thy great goodness, hast promised repentance and
forgiveness to them that have sinned against thee; and
of thine infinite mercies hast appointed repentance unto
sinners, that they may be saved. Thou, therefore, O
Lord, that art the God of the just, hast not appointed
repentance to the just, to Abraham, and Isaac, and
Jacob, which have not sinned against thee; but thou
hast appointed repentance unto me that am a sinner.

---

[1] The words; " at the word of the Holy One " are a later addition.
[2] The words: " and affliction " are a later addition.
[3] The words: " for ever " are a later addition.
[4] Lit. " dost repent of."

For I have sinned above the number of the sands of the sea. My transgressions are multiplied, O Lord, my transgressions are multiplied, and I am not worthy to behold and see the height of heaven for the multitude of mine iniquities. I am bowed down with many iron bands, that I cannot lift up my head by reason of my sins, neither have I any respite, for I have provoked thy wrath, and done that which is evil before thee. I did not thy will, neither kept I thy commandments. . . . Now, therefore, I bow the knee of my heart, beseeching thee of grace. I have sinned, O Lord, I have sinned, and I acknowledge mine iniquities; but I humbly beseech thee, forgive me, O Lord, forgive me, and destroy me not with mine iniquities. . . .

Many other illustrations could be given to show the manifold richness of this literature; one last one we cannot refrain from giving, even though it is probably the best-known passage in the whole of the Apocrypha; it is from Wisd. iii. 1–9:

But the souls of the righteous are in the hand of God,
And, in truth,[1] no torment shall touch them.
In the eyes of the foolish they seemed to have died,
And their departure was accounted a misfortune,
And their going from us their destruction;
But they are in peace.
For even if in the sight of men they suffered punishment,
Yet was their hope full of immortality;
And having been chastened a little, they shall be greatly
    blessed,
For God tried them,
And found them worthy of himself.
As gold in the furnace did he prove them,
And as a whole burnt-offering he accepted them.
And in the time of their visitation [2] they shall shine forth,

---

[1] Added to express the emphatic negative of the Greek.
[2] *I.e.* the Day of Judgement.

And as sparks among stubble shall they run to and fro.[1]
They shall judge nations, and have dominion over peoples,
And the Lord shall reign over them for ever.
They that trust in him shall understand truth,
And the faithful shall abide in him in love;
For grace and mercy are for his elect,
And he will graciously visit his sanctified ones.

These few illustrations will, it may be hoped, give some
idea of the literary value of the books of the Apocrypha.

[1] Cp. Enoch civ. 2: " Ye shall shine as the lights of heaven, ye shall shine,
and ye shall be seen."

C .

CHAPTER III

THE BOOKS OF THE APOCRYPHA IN THEIR CHRONOLOGICAL ORDER

THE order in which the books are placed in the Revised Version of the Apocrypha is not a chronological one; but it is necessary that we should at the outset determine, so far as this is possible, the periods, at any rate, to which the various books belong, respectively. Exact dates it is impossible to give; but to indicate approximate dates will be sufficient for practical purposes. It must, however, be recognized that, even so, we are confronted with difficulties. In the first place, opinions differ in a number of cases as to the dates of books, and the arguments for and against a particular date are, as often as not, inconclusive; the subject is further complicated by the fact that some of the books are of composite authorship, the component parts being, in all probability, of different dates; and here, too, opinions differ both as to authorship and date. And, once more, inasmuch as it may be regarded as certain that a number of these books, as we now have them, are translations, the question arises as to the relative dates of the original and the translation. Regarding this last point, however, reference must be made to the respective introductions; we are concerned here with the dates of books in their original form.

It will be understood, then, that we do not wish to be dogmatic in the matter of the dates here given; at the same time, it will be found that they have the support of many, probably the majority of competent scholars.

In the following chronological table the books are assigned to the three periods: pre-Maccabæan, Maccabæan, and post-Maccabæan, closer, approximate, dates being added:—

Pre-Maccabæan: *I Esdras, circa* B.C. 300.
      Tobit, circa B.C. 200.
      Ecclesiasticus, B.C. 200–180.
      The Hymn in the *Song of the Three Holy Children* probably belongs to this period.

Maccabæan: The Prayer in the *Song of the Three Holy Children, circa* B.C. 168.
      Judith, circa B.C. 150.
      Additions to Esther, circa B.C. 140–130.

Post-Maccabæan: *I Maccabees, circa* B.C. 90–70.
      II Maccabees, circa B.C. 50.
      Susanna, B.C.?
      Bel and the Dragon, B.C.?
      Wisdom, circa 40 A.D.
      Baruch, after 70 A.D.
      II Esdras, circa 100 A.D.
      Prayer of Manassès?

For further details and the arguments in favour of these dates, see the introductions to the respective books.

CHAPTER IV

A SURVEY OF THE HISTORICAL BACKGROUND

THE outside limits of the period with which we are concerned may be roughly dated from about B.C. 300 to 100 A.D. The history of this period undoubtedly influenced its literature, and is not infrequently reflected, or directly referred to, in it; hence the need of taking a historical bird's-eye view of these centuries, and, without going into details, to lay emphasis on those more outstanding events which affected the destiny of the Jewish people. For, since the literature with which we shall be concerned is Jewish, the historical background is, in the present connexion, of interest and importance mainly in so far as the Jewish nation was concerned.

These centuries fall, mainly, within the Greek period which may be roughly reckoned as beginning with the conquests of Alexander the Great; for the intensive propagation of Greek culture was due to him.[1] For his love of Greek culture Alexander, as is well known, was indebted to Aristotle, who made him wholly Greek in intellect. With his brilliant achievements, both as general and statesman, we are not here concerned; suffice it to quote the words of his most recent biographer:

> We see the greatness of Alexander as a whole, only when we contemplate the effects of his life-work in successive periods of history. In the few years of his reign he actually put the ancient world on a new basis. The subsequent course of history, the political, economic, and cultural life of after times, cannot be understood apart from the career of Alexander.[2]

[1] Greek culture was, of course, being spread abroad to a varying extent long before the fourth century B.C.; fragments of Greek pottery have been discovered in Ras Shamra belonging to the fourteenth and thirteenth century B.C.; and Greek influence continued beyond our period.

[2] Wilcken, *Alexander der Grosse*, Eng. transl., p. 265 (1932).

What Josephus says about his dealings with the Jews [1]
cannot all be regarded as reliable history; but it affords,
at any rate, an illustration of Alexander's ideal of spreading
peace and good-will among peoples, so far as this lay in his
power. His attitude towards them was undoubtedly
friendly.

When Alexander died, in B.C. 323, not yet thirty-three
years old, the problem arose as to what was to become of
his world-wide empire; for, in the nature of things, the
rulers of the many lands which he had subdued saw in the
disappearance of their conqueror the opportunity of regaining independence. His empire was " an artificial creation
of a purely military kind, in which the disruptive forces
were stronger than those which made for unity; but his
personality was indispensable to its continuance "; [2] and
here was the Macedonian army by means of which the
master-mind had been able to carry out its will. To the
minds of Alexander's generals it seemed clear that to him
who could obtain command of this invincible army the
prospect of becoming world-ruler was no idle dream. But
among these generals there was not one of sufficiently outstanding character and individuality to play this leading
rôle; instead, they fought among themselves, the ambition
of each seeking to gain the unattainable. After many
years of conflict a settlement was reached, when, at the
battle of Ipsus, in Asia Minor, Antigonus was defeated by
two of the allied armies of other generals who were rulers of
provinces, namely Lysimachus of Thrace, Seleucus of Babylonia, and Cassander of Macedonia. This occurred in B.C.
301. The undivided empire of Alexander was thus a
thing of the past; it became split up into several
kingdoms.

We are concerned with only two of these: that of Ptolemy
of Egypt, which was the first to be established, and that of
Seleucus, with Antioch in Syria as one of the royal resi-
dences. As between these two, of central importance for

[1] *Antiq.* xi. 313-338.
[2] Rostovtzeff, *A History of the Ancient World*, I. The Orient and Greece,
p. 353 (1926).

present purposes was their struggle for the possession of Palestine. After the battle of Ipsus this land was annexed by Ptolemy I Soter, not without protest from Seleucus, who regarded it as belonging to his share of the division of provinces. His protest did not go beyond words; nevertheless, the seed of future dissension was thus already sown. With the details of the struggle, lasting for a century, between the Seleucids and the Ptolemys for the possession of Palestine it is unnecessary to deal; but what is of prime importance from the present point of view is the final phase of that struggle. This can be described in a few words: the first step was taken by Antiochus III, the Great, in B.C. 217, when he invaded Palestine; but in the battle of Raphia, which followed, he was defeated by Sosibius, the Egyptian commander-in-chief. In consequence, Antiochus gave up, for the present, his design of conquering Palestine, especially as revolts in the eastern parts of his empire demanded his attention elsewhere; these occupied him for a number of years. His second attempt was made in B.C. 202; this time he was partially successful, for he pushed down to the south of Palestine as far as Gaza; but in the following year he was driven northwards again by the Egyptian army, now under Scopas. The Egyptian success was, however, short-lived; and at the battle of Panion Antiochus gained an overwhelming victory over Scopas; by B.C. 198 the whole of Syria was finally incorporated in the empire of the Seleucids. Antiochus' treatment of the Jews was friendly, following herein the example of the Egyptian rulers. He fell in battle against an enemy in the east, in B.C. 187, and was succeeded by his son Seleucus IV. It was during the reign of this king that the episode recorded in II Macc. iii took place. Heliodorus, his chief minister, attempted to seize the Temple treasure, but was prevented from doing so by what is described as supernatural means. The kernel of the story, viz. the attempt to appropriate the Temple treasure, is doubtless historical. Seleucus was murdered by Heliodorus in B.C. 175,[1] and soon after, with the accession of his brother, Antiochus IV Epiphanes, in

---

[1] Appian, *Syr.* xlv.

the same year, we enter upon the period of the Maccabæan wars. Here it is necessary to insist that the initiative in the attempt to stamp out orthodox Judaism and to hellenize the Jews was not taken by Antiochus, but by the influential body of hellenistic Jews, as is clear enough from what is said in I Macc. i. 11–15, 34–40; the ground was thus well prepared before Antiochus appeared as the protagonist in this attempt.

Into the details of the Maccabæan struggle we cannot enter here; suffice it to summarize thus: Judas Maccabæus, Jonathan, and Simon, the three sons of Mattathias, the priest of Modein, in turn championed the cause of those of their brethren who clung to the faith of their fathers. The first of these (B.C. 166–160) gained religious freedom for his people; the second (B.C. 160–159 to 142–141) secured considerable territorial additions for the country; and the third (B.C. 142–141 to 135–134) succeeded, to all intents and purposes, in throwing off Syrian suzerainty, though it was not until some few years later that this was definitely and finally achieved. Still more important was the fact that Simon was the real founder of the combined High-priestly and princely dynasty of the Hasmonæans,[1] since he was the first of this house to become the fully recognized High-priest in addition to his being civil ruler of his people.[2] "The yoke of the heathen," it is said in I Macc. xiii. 41, 42, "was taken away from Israel. And the people began to write in their instruments and contracts, In the first year of Simon the great High-priest and Captain and Leader of the Jews." Soon after this the Citadel of Jerusalem, which had for so long been in the hands of the Syrian soldiery, was evacuated, and the Jews entered it in triumph "with praise and palm branches, and with harps, and with cymbals and with viols, and with hymns and with songs, because a great enemy was destroyed out of Israel" (I Macc. xiii. 51).

[1] Asmonæus, or Hashmon according to the Hebrew form, was the ancestor of the Maccabæan family, see Josephus, Antiq. xii. 265.
[2] See I Macc. xiv. 25–49. Jonathan had been appointed High-priest by Alexander Balas (I Macc. x. 15–17), but he was not recognized as such by the people in the way that Simon was (see I Macc. xiv. 46, 47).

On the death of Simon, who was treacherously murdered,[1] in B.C. 134, his son John Hyrcanus I became High-priest; he was the first of the Hasmonæans to assume the royal title.[2]

At the beginning of his reign a great disaster overtook the Jewish people. A vigorous king, Antiochus VII Sidetes, once more raised the Syrian kingdom from the helpless state into which it had fallen. He invaded Judæa, and captured Jerusalem after a year's siege. John Hyrcanus had to submit once more to Syrian suzerainty. It seemed as though the Jewish State were doomed again to vassalage; and that may well have been its destiny had Antiochus VII not fallen in battle against the Parthians (B.C. 129); he had been called to the eastern parts of his empire owing to the menace of this warlike people. As a result, the Jewish State once more regained its freedom, which it retained for a period of sixty-six years.

The reign of John Hyrcanus was of special importance for several reasons: he extended very considerably the borders of his dominions; he conquered Idumæa and forced the inhabitants to become Jews; this was destined to have momentous consequences in later days; he subdued the Samaritans, and destroyed their temple on Mount Gerizim; he broke with the Pharisees (the *Chasidim* of earlier days), with whom he had at first been on friendly terms, and who had for some time previously been the most influential party among the Jews; instead, he supported the party of the Sadducees; and, finally, during his reign arose the pronounced popular hatred of the Hasmonæan rulers, owing mainly to the incongruity of the pursuit of worldly aims on the part of him who held the High-priestly office;[3] this assumed serious dimensions in course of time owing to Pharisaic influence.

John Hyrcanus died in B.C. 104. He was succeeded by his son Aristobulus I, who reigned for less than a year; but one important event during his reign demands attention:

[1] See I. Macc. xvi. 16, 17.
[2] For the justification of this statement see Oesterley and Robinson, *A History of Israel*, ii. 285 f. (1933).
[3] Cp. Josephus, *Antiq.* xiii. 288.

he carried the Jewish frontier farther north by subduing part of what was known as Galilee of the Gentiles, the *Region* of the Gentiles, the part inhabited by the Ituræans. These, like the Edomites, were forced to embrace Judaism, and Aristobulus was thus the creator of that Galilee which we know in our gospels—a region whose population was Jewish in belief and practice, but Gentile to a large degree in descent.[1]

At the death of Aristobulus I, his brother Alexander Jannæus succeeded him. He further greatly extended the frontiers of Palestine, and during his reign the Jews were, for the time being, the most powerful people in the land; but, probably, a more barbarous ruler never held sway over the Jewish people; and although he was a successful fighter, the ravages of war left the country in a disastrous condition. Personally, he was a man of repulsive character, cruel, bloodthirsty, and immoral. The antipathy of the Pharisees towards the Hasmonæan rulers, which had shown itself during the two preceding reigns, reached a climax during that of Jannæus; his utter unfitness for the High-priesthood so scandalized them and their great following among the people, that ultimately civil war broke out. Although Jannæus conquered here too, and took a most barbarous revenge on the Pharisees, he realized towards the end of his life that their power, owing to their influence over the bulk of the people, made it politic to conciliate them; and he adjured his wife Alexandra (Salome), as Josephus tells us, who was to succeed him, to " put some of her authority into the hands of the Pharisees . . . for they had power among the Jews, both to do hurt to such as they hated, and to bring advantages to those to whom they were friendly disposed "; he went on to say that " it was by their means that he had incurred the displeasure of the nation. . . . Promise them also," he concluded, " that thou wilt do nothing without them in the affairs of the kingdom." [2]

---

[1] Edwyn Bevan, *Jerusalem under the High-priests*, pp. 115 f. (1904).
[2] Josephus, *Antiq.* xiii. 400–404.

He died in B.C. 76, and his advice was followed by his
widow, Alexandra, who succeeded him; to quote Josephus
again; he tells us that " she restored those practices which
the Pharisees had introduced, according to the tradition of
their forefathers, and which her father-in-law, Hyrcanus,
had abrogated. So she had, indeed, the name of Regent,
but the Pharisees had the authority."[1] Unfortunately, the
Pharisees abused the power thus placed in their hands, and
fell foul of the Sadducæan party who were the aristocratic
upholders of the Hasmonæan High-priesthood. Alexandra,
being a woman, could of course conduct only the civil
power, and that, as we have seen, only nominally; the
High-priesthood devolved upon her elder son, Hyrcanus II,
but—and here we see the complicated state of affairs—
Hyrcanus, a man of weak character, but otherwise a good
man, was more in sympathy with the Pharisees than with
the Sadducees, who were the supporters of the Hasmonæan
High-priesthood; in consequence, the Sadducees regarded
their nominal representative with disfavour. But further;
Hyrcanus' younger brother, Aristobulus, a vigorous but
unscrupulous personality, aspired to the kingship, and
succeeded in gaining the support of the military element
which, under Jannæus, had been the dominating power.
To complicate matters still farther, while the enmity between
the two brothers was reaching a critical point, Alexandra
died, in B.C. 67. A battle was fought between the brothers,
in which Aristobulus was victorious; thereupon an agreement was reached between them, according to which
Aristobulus was to be king and High-priest, while Hyrcanus,
much to his liking, was to be permitted to retire into private
life. The younger brother thus ruled as Aristobulus II.
That, one might suppose, would have been a settlement
favourable to both parties; and so it would have been,
as far as one can see, had it not been for the appearance
of a new character upon the scene.

We have seen that John Hyrcanus had compelled the
Idumæans to accept the Jewish religion, so that from that
time Idumæa had become a province of Judæa. The

[1] See *Antiq.* xiii. 408, 409; *Bell. Jud.* i. 110, 111.

Governor of this province was at this time one Antipater (the father of Herod the Great), an enemy of Aristobulus II, but the friend of Hyrcanus, upon whom he had a profound influence. He persuaded Hyrcanus not to submit to the terms which had been agreed upon by the two brothers. Consequently war broke out again between them, the details of which we cannot enter into now. The ʋvent of prime importance was the intervention of Rome. Aristobulus withstood the Roman army; but Hyrcanus, under the influence of Antipater, allied himself with Rome. Pompey besieged Jerusalem in B.C. 63, the city fell, Aristobulus II was taken by Pompey a prisoner to Rome, together with some thousands of Jews, and Hyrcanus was made High-priest with the title of ethnarch. Judæa was thus no longer a kingdom, but a division of the Roman province of Syria.

Hyrcanus was, however, only nominal ruler, the real power being wielded by Antipater, the Idumæan. Thanks to the crafty statesmanship of Antipater, Hyrcanus was able to maintain his position in spite of the tumultuous unrest in the outside world. Not that Judæa was unaffected by the civil war and its consequences which had been ravaging the Roman state; but the troubles which beset Hyrcanus in his own land were not of his own making, nor yet the fault of Antipater. They were of three kinds: great unrest was caused by several attempts on the part of the Hasmonæan family to oust Hyrcanus from his position; in the second place, misrule on the part of the proconsuls of Syria brought the whole country into a grave state of anarchy; an act of injustice and great folly, for example, was the plundering of a large part of the Temple treasury, which naturally inflamed the already burning hatred of the Jews for Rome; and thirdly, there was the inveterate contempt felt towards Antipater owing to his being an Idumæan; to be virtually ruled by one who was not a real Jew rankled in their hearts.

During the High-priesthood of Hyrcanus, though neither he nor Antipater was in any way the cause of this, the proconsul Gabinius deprived the former of all his civil power, leaving him only religious functions, and divided his land into five administrative districts; this latter action was probably undertaken in order to facilitate the collection of tribute.

But in spite of all, and owing to the clever, but not always very laudable action of Antipater, Hyrcanus managed to retain the High-priesthood. In B.C. 43 Antipater was murdered; but he was avenged by his son Herod, who also upheld Hyrcanus. The friendship between the two latter was cemented by the betrothal of Herod to the grand-daughter of Hyrcanus, Mariamne; in this way Herod became related to the ruling house—a matter of importance for the subsequent history.

Hyrcanus continued to hold his office until B.C. 40; in this year the Parthians, who were the inveterate enemies of Rome in the east, over-ran Syria, captured Hyrcanus, the friend of Rome, mutilated his ears so as to incapacitate him from holding the High-priestly office, and made Antigonus, the son of Aristobulus II, both High-priest and king; on his coins he described himself as both "king Antigonus" and "Mattathiah the High-priest" (Mattathiah was his Jewish name).

In opposition to him Herod was proclaimed king of the Jews by the Romans. It took a few years for Herod to make good his claims; but in B.C. 37, supported by a Roman army, he besieged Jerusalem and captured the city; Antigonus was beheaded by the Romans.

· Into the details of the reign of Herod the Great we cannot enter now. From the point of view of Jewish history the facts of paramount importance may be briefly summarized: first, and most ominous, to be noted was the hatred entertained towards him by his Jewish subjects; there were several reasons for this; one of his first acts was to put to death a number of influential citizens who had sided with Antigonus; this served to embitter the feelings of the people who had an initial cause of hatred for him owing to his being an Idumæan; then there was the fact that he had displaced a Hasmonæan prince, for bitterly opposed as the people had been in past days to the

Hasmonæans, they had in course of time come to regard them as their legitimate rulers. A cause of even deeper hatred was that Herod was the friend and *protégé* of Rome. Further, owing to Herod's constant need of money, the people were severely taxed, and this caused much bitterness. There were, therefore, ample reasons for the unhappy relations between Herod and his Jewish subjects, and this lasted throughout his reign.

Of sinister importance for the later history was the rift between the party of the Zealots, who originated in Galilee, and the Pharisees; they had been associated at first, but the cause of the break was that the Pharisees were content to acquiesce in Roman overlordship, represented in the person of Herod, while the Zealots refused to recognize any earthly king. Ultimately the Zealots, with the direst consequences, gained the bulk of the people to their side. On the other hand, owing to his friendship with Rome, Herod's dominions became greatly enlarged, and his kingdom was of greater extent than that of the Hasmonæans had ever been. With the exception of Ascalon, it included the whole coast-line of Palestine, to the east, Batanæa, Trachonitis, and the Hauran, extending up to the source of the Jordan.

Again, Herod's love of architecture, of which the rebuilding of the Temple was the outstanding feature, conferred great benefit on his people, and was much to his credit. He rebuilt the city of Samaria, which had been destroyed by Hyrcanus I, and to which he gave the name of Sebaste; he also built a city on the site of Strato's Tower, which he named Cæsarea, where great harbour works were constructed jutting out into the sea, so that the city became for some time the chief port of Palestine. In addition, he built temples in various cities: in the two just mentioned, in Panium and Rhodes, besides less important buildings in other cities.

Of his deplorable family quarrels we need not speak, as these affected the history of his times but indirectly.

Herod died in B.C. 4; his dominions were divided among his sons as follows: Archelaus received Judæa and Samaria, as well as Idumæa, with the title of ethnarch—the evidence of the coins is against his ever having received the royal title. Antipas was appointed tetrarch of Galilee, Peræa on the east of Jordan, together with such other districts on the east of Jordan which were inhabited by Jews. Philip was made tetrarch of the more northerly parts on the east of Jordan, Batanæa, Trachonitis, and Auranitis.

We are concerned mainly with Judæa. Unfortunately, Archelaus was the least fitted of Herod's sons to be a ruler; we have but little information regarding his reign of ten years; the outstanding fact about him was the estrangement between him and his people; his tactless and tyrannical behaviour resulted in an appeal by the Jews to Cæsar to displace him. He was banished to Gaul; and henceforth Judæa was governed by a Roman procurator who ruled to a large extent independently of the Syrian legate.

The history of Judæa under the procurators during the next thirty years is a deplorable record of misgovernment, with the inevitable consequence of ever-growing resentment on the part of the Jews, together with increasing resistance to constituted authority. For the brief space of seven years (37–44 A.D.) the rule of procurators ceased; during these years, owing to his friendship with the emperor Cäligula, Herod Agrippa I, a grandson of Herod the Great, reigned as the king of Judæa, the last to hold that office.

On his death, in 44 A.D., he was to have been succeeded by his son, also named Agrippa; but he did not receive the title of king of Judæa; he was only a lad of seventeen years, and continued to live at the court of the emperor Claudius, where he had been brought up. Judæa was again placed under the rule of procurators. But Agrippa was given the little kingdom of his uncle Herod of Chalcis, a small domain bordering on the Libanus; this occurred in 50 A.D.; on the death of his father he was, further, permitted to have the oversight of the Temple, and to appoint the High-priest.

Agrippa was a faithful upholder of the Roman power; at the same time, he tried to conciliate his Jewish subjects, though with but small success.

In the meantime, the tension between Rome and the bulk of the people continued to grow; at last, in 66 A.D. the Jews openly rebelled, and the actual beginning of the great war with Rome took place.

This war lasted from the spring of 66 A.D. until the late summer of 70 A.D., and even after the fall of Jerusalem sporadic fighting went on for nearly three years more in the country districts; the last stronghold of the Jews, Masada,[1] fell in the spring of 73 A.D.

The war may be roughly divided into four periods:—

(1) The immediate occasion for the outbreak, which had long been simmering, was a comparatively insignificant occurrence, namely a raid on the Temple Treasury by the procurator Florus for the purpose of appropriating seventeen talents; but this had the effect of rousing the masses in Jerusalem to fever heat, and they resisted the attempt of Florus with success. This seemed to be the signal for an anti-Gentile rising all over the country; the High-priest, aided by the Pharisees, sought in vain to calm the people; ultimately, the peace-party had to resort to arms in the endeavour to curb the insensate folly of the masses; but this, too, was without avail; the revolutionaries gained the upper hand in many cities of Palestine, especially in Galilee. By the end of the year 66 A.D. the whole country was ablaze.

(2) The second stage was the subjugation of Galilee; many months of terrible bloodshed ensued, and it was not until the end of the year 67 A.D. that Galilee was finally subdued by the Romans.

(3) The third stage was a long-drawn-out preparation for the siege of Jerusalem; various causes in the outside world contributed to the postponement of the actual siege; it was also felt by the Roman military leaders that the fighting among the Jewish parties in Jerusalem would, by being permitted to run its course, so weaken the defence of the city that it would fall an easy prey to the besieging forces; this did not, however, prove to be the case. More than two years elapsed before the city fell.

---

[1] See Schulten, *Masada* . . . , pp. 172 ff. (1933), where details are given.

(4) The final phase, which began early in 70 A.D., was the actual surrounding and siege of Jerusalem; in spite of appalling bloodshed, both through the internecine struggles among the Jews themselves, and by the attacks of the Romans, the city did not fall until the late summer of 70 A.D.

In looking back upon the history of these centuries it would not, at first sight, suggest itself as a period during which literary activity would be likely to flourish. It was a time of great unrest, for, as we have seen, there was the continual internal discord among the Jews themselves; the bitter opposition between the orthodox and the hellenistic parties was not restricted to the strife of tongues, but issued not infrequently in violence and bloodshed. Then there came the terrible upheaval of the Maccabæan wars, the land being constantly overrun by foreign soldiery, with insecurity for life and property, incessant turmoil, anxiety for what the next day might bring forth. A little later there were further internal dissensions among the Jews, this time between the Pharisees, followed by the great mass of the people, and the Hasmonæan rulers. Then came the ceaseless fighting during the reign of Alexander Jannæus; particularly ominous was his use of mercenary troops who would care little what damage they might do to Jewish homesteads; to have had this foreign soldiery constantly spreading itself over the countryside must indeed have been a cruel hardship. Later there arose a renewed cause of unrest owing to opposition of the Hasmonæan party to Hyrcanus II; thus, again, internal dissension, with its baneful excitement, affecting everybody in the land. Added to this there was the misrule of the Roman procurators, the grinding down by unconscionable taxation of all who had anything to be robbed of, with the consequent reaction on the poorer classes which would take various forms—less trade, less charity, less food—all this aroused fierce anger. As though these internal troubles were not enough, there occurred presently the Parthian incursions into Palestine; thus, foreign troops again overran the country; troops, too, of a particularly fierce nature; it is true, no details are recorded of their doings during these incursions, but it does not require much imagination to picture the kind of thing that would go on when armies of a powerful, semi-civilized people were let loose upon a centre of a more advanced civilization, with but little to restrain lawless passions and the lust of plunder. Once more, there was the struggle between Herod and Antigonus, and the bitter hatred on the part of the Jews for Herod, which caused continual unrest. Nor must it be forgotten that the detestation of the Roman power resulted in ever-increasing mutual distrust and antagonism; it was, as it were, the ground-swell presaging the advent of tempest. And, finally, there was, largely in consequence of Roman misrule, the rise of the Zealots which brought such appalling disasters on the whole Jewish nation.

Such a condition of affairs, then, extending over nearly three centuries, would not seem to have been conducive to literary activity. And yet during this period, as we have seen, a considerable amount of literature was produced. There is a two-fold explanation of this. Although the period, as a whole, was one of great unrest, there were, nevertheless, times of respite, sometimes of an appreciable number of years; this offered opportunities for those who felt impelled by the events of the times to put forth messages to the people to undertake their task. Thus, *e.g.*, after the battle of Panion (B.C. 198), as a result of which Antiochus III brought Palestine under Syrian suzerainty, there were fully ten years of comparative quietude for the Jews; this was followed, moreover, by a period of peace for them during most of the reign of Seleucus IV (B.C. 187–175). Again, even during the Maccabæan wars the fighting was not incessant; for example, after the victory of Judas Maccabæus over the Syrian forces in B.C. 164, there were nearly two years of peace; under Jonathan's leadership, when the Syrian general Bacchides withdrew, thinking that his task of subduing the Maccabæans was accomplished, we read that for two years again " the land of Judah had rest " (I Macc. ix. 59); and still later, during approximately five years

D

(B.C. 152–147), there was peace in Palestine owing to the struggle for the Syrian throne of two aspirants.

Similarly during Simon's leadership times of peace intervened.

Tumultuous as this period was, then, opportunities for literary activities were not wanting. But apart from this, it must be recognized that these wars and internal dissensions were in themselves incentives to many to produce writings; this applies more especially to the apocalyptic writers, following herein the prophets of old who wrote [1] particularly during troublous times. The paramount need of the people during those times of stress was to be strengthened and heartened by encouragement and hope—encouragement to trust in their God, and hope that He would help them. This is one of the main themes of the Apocalyptic Literature, of which the Ezra-Apocalypse (*II Esdras*) is an important part; the historical conditions prompted others, such as the attitude of pessimism adopted by the writers owing to the chaotic state, religiously, ethically, and materially, of the world (this applies especially to the Ezra-Apocalypse, towards the end of our period); the conviction of the near approach of the end of the present world-order, described in lurid colouring largely borrowed from extraneous sources; added to these were traditional expectations, both indigenous and foreign, regarding the advent of the Messiah, influenced now by present political conditions. (See further Chap. VI on the Apocalyptic Literature.) Thus, the literature of our period [2] owed its existence, certainly to a large extent, to the very causes which, normally, might have been supposed to stand in the way of it.

[1] Either they or their disciples.
[2] It is not forgotten that a certain number of the canonical books, or portions of them, belong to the Greek period, to which a large part of the times with which we are concerned belongs; thus, to the years B.C. 300 onwards belong *Chronicles, Esther, Job,* many of the *Psalms*; the latest parts of *Proverbs*; *Ecclesiastes*; some sections incorporated in *Isaiah*; *Joel,* and *Jonah,* as well as the latest parts of the Pentateuch P document; in addition, a certain number of the *Psalms,* the book of *Daniel,* and the second part of *Zechariah* (ix–xiv) belong to the Maccabæan era; see on this, Oesterley and Robinson, *An Introduction to the Books of the Old Testament* (1934).

CHAPTER V

THE WISDOM LITERATURE

In *Ecclesiasticus* and *Wisdom* we have two books belonging to the Wisdom Literature, each of which is, in its own way, unique. Details of their subject-matter and the like will be discussed below. Here it is our purpose to say something about the Wisdom literature as a whole; and while restricting ourselves, in the main, to the books of the Hebrews, it is quite necessary that some reference should be made to those of other peoples; for the Hebrew Wisdom literature is only a department of a much larger entity comprising books belonging to Sages of other nations; and when this larger body of literature is examined it is seen that national boundaries offered no obstacles to the interplay of thought between like-minded men who were concerned with matters of general human interest, and between whom there was much mutual sympathy and reciprocal influence. Not that the books of the writers of different countries lack individual distinctiveness; far from that; nothing is more striking than the difference in the presentation of Wisdom as between writers of different nationalities,—differences in conception and modes of thought, of literary form, and so on; but in spite of all such differences, one cannot fail to see an underlying unity of purpose common to all; and it is this, primarily, which compels us to recognize a principle of fellowship among the Sages of the various countries, and therefore to see in the Wisdom literature of the ancients a world-literature. Our first concern, however, is with the Wisdom literature of the Hebrews.

I. The Hebrew Wisdom Literature

The books of Hebrew Wisdom constitute a body of literature in regard to which the distinction, so far as the

books of the Old Testament and the Apocrypha are concerned, between canonical and uncanonical books, may be
ignored; for to make such a distinction is unscientific, and
was originally, in part at any rate, due on the one hand,
to misconception, and on the other, to arbitrariness;
misconception as to what should constitute canonicity,
arbitrariness as to the conception of inspiration.

Just as in the Old Testament, so in the Apocrypha, there
are, in addition to those books which are wholly concerned
with Wisdom in its various forms, single wise sayings, sometimes whole sections, found elsewhere, which are of a Wisdom
character; the former were current proverbs, the latter
may possibly have been taken from some specifically Wisdom
book, or they may be isolated compositions purposely added
by the writer of books belonging otherwise to a different
category. Thus, for example, proverbs are quoted, in I Sam.
xxiv. 13 : "Out of the wicked cometh forth wickedness";
"Let not him that girdeth on (his armour) boast himself as
he that putteth it off" (I Kgs. xx. 11); "They that sow the
wind shall reap the whirlwind" (Hos. viii. 7); "Do
they plough the sea with oxen?" (Am. vi. 12, emended
text); "The fathers have eaten sour grapes, and the
children's teeth are set on edge" (Ezek. xviii. 2), and
others. Of isolated compositions, though of quite limited
extent, we have, for example, such a piece as Jotham's
parable of the trees (Judg. ix. 8–15), and a shorter one on the
thorn and the cedar in II. Kgs. xiv. 9. Further, Wisdom
compositions are incorporated in collections of psalms
belonging to different periods; the earlier ones are xxxii.
8–11, xxxiv. 11–22 (12–23 in Hebr.), xxxvii, xlix, lxxiii,
cxxvii, cxxviii, cxxxiii ; of later date are i, xix. 7–14 (8–15 in
Hebr.), xciv. 8–23, cxi, xcii, cxix; in addition, there are
numerous Wisdom sayings interspersed elsewhere among the
psalms.[1] Similarly in the Apocrypha, apart from the
specifically Wisdom books, there are sections containing
Wisdom material, viz. I Esdr. iii. 1–iv. 63, Tob. iv. 5–19, xii.
6–11, Bar. iii. 9–iv. 4, iv. 5–19.

[1] See Gunkel-Begrich, *Einleitung in die Psalmen*, pp. 381 ff. (1933); Fichtner,
Die altorientalische Weisheit in ihrer israelitisch-jüdischen Ausprägung, pp. 9, 90 ff.
(1933).

All these, both in the Old Testament and in the Apocrypha, must be regarded as belonging to the Wisdom literature in addition to the Wisdom books proper: *Proverbs, Job, Ecclesiastes, Ecclesiasticus,* and *Wisdom.* For completeness' sake we may add the four following writings which belong to the Hebrew Wisdom literature, though not included either in the canonical or deutero-canonical collections: *The Letter of Aristeas* [1] 187–294, *IV Maccabees,*[2] *Pirke Aboth,*[3] and the *Poem of Phokylides.*[4]

II. EXTRA-ISRAELITE WISDOM LITERATURE

Since, as already remarked, the Hebrew Wisdom literature forms part of a world literature, it will be well to enumerate briefly the various non-Israelite writings which are known and have been published.

The Wisdom literature of Egypt must at one time have been very extensive; the writings which have so far come down to us have for the most part been collected and translated into German by Erman, *Die Literatur der Ägypter* (1923); they are as follows: *The Teaching of Ptahhotep* (pp. 86 ff.); *The Teaching of Kagemni* (pp. 99 f.); *The Teaching for King Merikare* (pp. 109 ff., the most important of the older Egyptian Wisdom writings); *The Teaching of King Amenemhet* (pp. 106 ff.); *The Teaching of Duauf* (pp. 100 ff.); *The Wisdom of Anii* (pp. 294 ff.).[5] The most recently discovered Egyptian Wisdom book is *The Teaching of Amenemope;* this writing is of deep interest and importance for the study of the Hebrew Wisdom literature on account of its influence on parts of the book of *Proverbs;* [6] of later date are the tomb inscriptions containing *The Teaching of Petosiris,*[7] and *The Insinger Papyrus,* which has

---

[1] Thackeray, *The Letter of Aristeas* (Engl. transl. 1917); Greek text in Swete, *Intr. to the O.T. in Greek,* pp. 519–574 (1900).

[2] Emmet, *The Third and Fourth Books of Maccabees* (Engl. transl. 1918); Greek text in Swete, *The O.T. in Greek* iii. pp. 729–762 (1899).

[3] Taylor, *Sayings of the Jewish Fathers* (Hebr. text and Engl. transl. (1897)); Oesterley, *The Sayings of the Jewish Fathers* (Engl. transl. 1919).

[4] Bernays, *Über das phokylideische Gedicht* (1856).

[5] The respective pp. in the Engl. ed. are: 54, 66, 75, 72, 67, 234.

[6] See Lange, *Das Weisheitsbuch des Amen-em-ope* (German transl. 1925); Ranke, in Gressmann's *Altorientalische Texte zum Alten Testament,* pp. 38 ff. (1926); and the present writer's *The Wisdom of Egypt and the Old Testament* (1927), for further literature.

[7] Lefèbvre, *Tombeau de Petosiris* (Service des Antiquités de l'Égypte, Le Caire, 1923 f.).

a number of religious and moral precepts; [1] this last is as late as the first century A.D. There are, further, a few other writings of a quasi-Wisdom character which should be noted; these are also included in Erman's work mentioned above: *The Controversy of One Tired of Life with his Soul* (pp. 122 ff.); *The Sorrows of the Peasant* (pp. 157 ff.); *Monitions of an Egyptian Sage* (pp. 130 ff.); *The Plaint of Cha-cheper-re-seneb* [2] (pp. 149 ff.); *The Song of the Harpist* (pp. 177 f.).[3]

Babylonian Wisdom literature, so far as its writings have come down to us, is represented in a far less degree. A collection of *Babylonian Proverbs* is given by Meissner in *Babylonien und Assyrien*, i. 21–29 (1920). Another collection of *Wisdom Sayings* is published in a German translation by Ebeling in Gressmann, *op. cit.*, pp. 291 ff.; see also Langdon, *Babylonian Wisdom*, p. 89 (1923). The most interesting writing is *The Story of Aḥiḳar*, containing the *Proverbs of Aḥiḳar* (Chap. ii), and the *Parables of Aḥiḳar* (viii. 1–41).[4] Further, there is the so-called *Babylonian Job*; [5] the *Bilingual Book of Proverbs*, also called the Babylonian *Koheleth*; [6] and *A Sage's Plaint over the Wickedness of the World.*[7]

The many points of contact between these Egyptian and Babylonian Wisdom books with those of the Hebrews are sufficient to show that all three collections form parts of a cosmopolitan whole. And it is well to emphasize the fact that the Old Testament writers fully recognized the existence of Wisdom teachers, outside their own borders, from quite early times. Thus, in Num. xxii. 5 it is said that messengers were sent " unto Balaam the son of Beor, to Pethor, which is

---

[1] Boeser, *Transcription und Übersetzung des Papyrus Insinger* (1922).
[2] *I.e.* " Cha-cheper is in good health " (Erman).
[3] On all the Egyptian Wisdom books see also Humbert, *Recherches sur les sources Égyptiennes de la Littérature Sapientale d'Israël*, pp. 5–16 (1929).
[4] See Harris, Lewis, and Conybeare, in Charles, *Apocrypha and Pseudepigrapha of the O.T.*, ii. 653–784; Sachau, *Aramäische Papyrus . . .*, pp. 148 ff. (1911); Cowley, *Jewish Documents of the time of Ezra*, pp. 81–95 (1919), Engl. transl.
[5] This is not the title, which the writing does not possess; but this name has been given to it because it deals with problems similar to those in the *Book of Job*; Engl. transl. by Ball, in *The Book of Job*, pp. 12–30 (1922); Germ. transl. by Ebeling, in Gressmann, *op. cit.*, pp. 273 ff.
[6] There is no title; it is so called because it shows affinities of thought with *Ecclesiastes* (*Koheleth* in Hebr.); see Langdon, *op. cit.*; Ebeling, *Ein Babylonischer Koheleth* (1924), and in Gressmann, *op. cit.*, pp. 287 ff.
[7] There is no title, that given is descriptive of its contents, see Ebeling, in Gressmann, *op. cit.*, pp. 284 ff.

by the River, to the land of the children of his people ";
this is done by Balak, the king of Moab, for the purpose of
procuring a diviner to curse the Israelites; instead of this
he utters wise prophecies concerning Israel. Whatever may
lie behind this, it is clear that the writer recognized in the
alien from Babylonia a speaker of wise sayings. Another
reference to extra-Israelite wisdom occurs in II Sam. xx. 18,
where it is said: "They were wont to speak in old time,
saying, They shall surely ask counsel at Abel "; this place
is to be identified with Abel-beth-Maacah (see II Sam. xx.
14; II Kgs. xv. 29), and was situated on the slopes of the
Hermon, in Syria therefore. Again, in I Kgs. iv. 30, 31
(10, 11 in Hebr.), we read that "Solomon's wisdom excelled
the wisdom of all the children of the east, and all the wisdom
of Egypt. For he was wiser than all men, than Ethan the
Ezrahite, and Heman, and Calcol, and Darda, the sons of
Mahol." By the "children of the east" are meant Arabians
and Edomites, as the context shows, and also doubtless
Babylonians. The tradition of the wisdom of Edom is
referred to in Jer. xlix. 7, where Edom is spoken of in the
words: "Is wisdom no more in Teman? is counsel perished
from the prudent? is their wisdom vanished?" Moreover,
"the wise men of Edom" are spoken of in Obad. 8. And
once more, in Job ii. 11 the names of Job's friends show that
they were non-Israelite—and this book makes it clear that
these men are represented as Wisdom teachers; thus,
Teman, where Eliphaz came from, was in Edom; Bildad
the Shuhite was a native of Shuah in Assyria; in the case of
Zophar the Naamathite, it is probable that he was thought of
as an Edomite, because although Naamah lay to the south-
west of Judah, the clan which settled in Naamah, namely the
Calebites (see I Chron. iv. 5, where Naam is the same as
Naamah), was of Edomite extraction. It is also possible
that in the corrupt text of Prov. xxx. 1, "The words of Agur
the son of Jakeh, the oracle," we should read for the last
word (in Hebr. *Massa*, "oracle") "the Massite," *i.e.*, an
inhabitant of Massa (see I Chron. i. 30), or one belonging to
the tribe of Massa, which was, according to Gen. xxv. 14,
an Arabian tribe. Even apart from this last reference, it is

quite clear that the Israelites were acquainted with the
wisdom of Babylon, Egypt, Syria, Arabia and Edom; and so
far as Babylonia and Egypt are concerned, we have seen that
material of the Wisdom type, with which the Hebrew Sages
were doubtless familiar, must have been abundant in these
two countries.

III. Purposes and Characteristics of the Hebrew Wisdom Literature

In one of his essays Emerson writes: " Nature makes fifty
poor melons for one that is good, and shakes down a tree full
of gnarled, wormy, unripe crabs, before you can find a dozen
dessert apples; and she scatters nations of naked Indians,
and nations of clothed Christians, with two or three good heads
among them." [1] Somewhat over-stated as these words are,
they nevertheless reflect what must often have been in the
minds of the Hebrew Wisdom writers; for it is evident from
their writings that they regarded the great majority of mankind as lacking sense. One is led to this conclusion by
observing how frequently they address themselves to
" fools." These " fools " are of various types. Thus, there
is the type designated *Pethi*; this denotes one who is not
necessarily wicked in the worst sense, but one who is simple-
minded, stupid; but stupidity is regarded by the Wisdom
writers as wrong in God's sight; indeed, stupidity is sin
because out of harmony with the mind of God. It is worth
noting that the word *Pethi*, in its root-meaning, is " to be
open "—which indicates the type; for the idea of being open
here applies in the first instance, to the literal opening of the
lips:

He that goeth about as a tale-bearer revealeth secrets;
Therefore meddle not with him that openeth wide his lips.
(Prov. xx. 19.)

Such a one was in the mind of Ben-Sira when he wrote in his
blunt, yet pointed way:

[1] In the Essay: " Considerations by the Way."

Hast thou heard a thing? Let it die with thee;
Be of good courage,—it will not burst thee.
(Ecclus. xix. 10.)

But besides the meaning of the literal opening of the lips,
Pethi has the further metaphorical sense of being " open " to
every influence; this marks the weakness of character of this
type of " fool."

A somewhat worse type, and the one most frequently
dealt with in the Wisdom literature, is the *Kesîl*. His
foolishness is shown, first and foremost, in his hatred of
knowledge (Prov. i. 22), so that he is incapable of appreci-
ating what is good (Prov. xviii. 2). He is further characterized by his want of self-control; he cannot, for example,
contain himself when he is angry:

A fool (*Kesîl*) uttereth all his anger,
But a wise man keepeth it back and stilleth it.
(Prov. xxix. 11.)

He takes a delight in doing what is wrong (Prov. x. 23); he
is quarrelsome and contentious (Prov. xviii. 6); he is also
deceitful (Prov. xiv. 8); and therefore must be regarded as
altogether a dangerous person:

Let a bear robbed of her whelps meet a man
Rather than a fool (*Kesîl*) in his folly.
(Prov. xvii. 12.)

The third type of " fool " is the *Evîl*; this kind is always
described as morally bad; about him there is something
worse than stupidity or wantonness because he is one who is
intent on sin, as though it were the business of his life; the
inured habit of sin has made him a hardened sinner:

Though thou bray a fool (*Evîl*) in a mortar,
Yet wilt thou not make his foolishness to depart from him.
(Prov. xxvii. 22.)

And lastly, there is the worst type of all, the *Lêtz*, translated " scorner " in the Revised Version. The underlying
idea of this word is that of being not " straight." As in
the case of the *Evîl* this type takes a delight in wrong-doing,
but he is worse in so far that he has his wits thoroughly

about him. Not only does he refuse to listen to better counsels, but he retaliates if reproved:

He that correcteth a scorner getteth to himself shame
                                        (Prov. ix. 7);

and he is incapable of discipline:

Reprove not a scorner lest he hate thee (Prov. ix. 8),

implying that he will do an injury to anyone who rebukes him. Moreover, he is proud, haughty, and arrogant (Prov. xxi. 24), the overbearing person whom men abominate (Prov. xxiv. 9); even the simple-minded *Pethi* is frightened into sense when he sees how the scorner is punished:

When the scorner is punished the *Pethi* is made wise.
                                        (Prov. xxi. 11.)

Thus, one of the main purposes of the Wisdom literature is that of redeeming fools from folly. Yet however hard the Wisdom teachers hit their victims, to their honour be it said that they realized the potentialities for good in every type of " fool "; and that is, clearly enough, the reason why so much of their teaching was addressed to them: they despaired of none,—the simpleton, the " stupid idiot," the thoughtless, the " jackass," the hypocrite, the churl, the credulous, the irrepressible chatter-box, the quarrelsome, and all the rest of them; none is irreclaimable; it only wants the art of knowing how to touch the right spot; and the Hebrew Sages cultivated that art and sought to gather in the most unpromising; to quote once more from Emerson's essay: " Nature is a rag merchant who works up every shred and ort and end into new creations; like a good chemist whom I found, the other day, in his laboratory, converting his old shirts into pure white sugar." That was the kind of metamorphosis which the Hebrew Sages sought to bring about in that somewhat unpromising material composed of the " fools " of humanity.

But, obviously, many as may be the " fools " of humanity, there were numbers of men, young and old, who could not be classed among such; and the Wisdom literature is full

of precepts and words of guidance for those who want to do
what is right if told how. The Wisdom writers, naturally
enough, assume a general familiarity with a certain norm
of right conduct, which does not require definition, and to
which men ought to conform; and they give many precepts
of direction, which, if followed, will enable this to be done.
This norm of right conduct applies to every action and to
every kind of calling and occupation of men in everyday
life; it applies, moreover, not only to individual men
regarding themselves, but also to their relations with their
fellow-creatures, *e.g.*:

Reprove a friend that he do no evil,[1]
And if he have done anything, that he do it not again.
> (Ecclus. xix. 13.)

Before thou diest do good to him that loveth thee,
And according as thou has prospered, give to him.
> (Ecclus. xiv. 13.)

Failure to live according to the norm of right conduct
inevitably results in retribution, so the Wisdom writers teach,
while right living brings prosperity:

Evil pursueth sinners,
But the righteous shall be recompensed with good.
> (Prov. xiii. 21.)

From the son of the unrighteous dominion shall be
wrenched away,[2]
And want shall ever abide with his seed.[3]
> (Ecclus. xli. 6.)

Vanity is man concerning his body,
But the name of the pious shall not be cut off.[4]
> (Ecclus. xli. 11.)

That practical experience of life showed this to be
erroneous did not disconcert those to whom this was a
dogma, for it was affirmed that if a man who seemed to be

[1] So the Syriac; the Hebrew is not extant.   [2] So the Hebrew.
[3] So the Syriac; the Hebrew is not extant.
[4] This verse is extant in Hebrew.

righteous was in adversity it meant that he was, nevertheless, guilty of some sin known to God and himself, but not to others, for which he was suffering (Job viii. 6), or owing to some sin he had forgotten, or which was perhaps unrecognized owing to self-deception (Job xv. 2–5). If, on the other hand, the incongruity presented itself of a wicked man being in prosperity, the answer was, in effect, that his time would soon come (Job xx. 4 ff.).

This doctrine of retribution, which plays a prominent part in the Wisdom literature, and which clearly touches upon the religious domain, leads us to say something further upon the religious element in this body of literature.

It has sometimes been felt that in the Wisdom literature, as a whole, the religious element has had to suffer at the expense of that which is merely ethical. Here it must, however, be borne in mind, that to the Hebrew Sages, Wisdom, whatever its form, was a divine gift, an attribute to God Himself (Prov. viii. 22–31; Ecclus. i. 1, 8), and therefore in its nature had a religious element about it; in some of its forms, of course, more developed than in others (see further below); it follows that everything that the Wisdom writers wrote about Wisdom had for them an underlying religious content. It is perfectly true that there are many passages, especially in *Proverbs* and *Ecclesiasticus*, which, as they stand, seem to be entirely devoid of any religious content; a few illustrations may be offered:

He that is surety for a stranger shall suffer for it,
But he that hateth suretyship is sure.
(Prov. xi. 15, cp. Ecclus. xxix. 18.)

A wicked messenger causeth a man to fall into evil,
But a faithful envoy is profitable.
(Prov. xiii. 17.)

The appetite of a labouring man laboureth for him,
For his mouth urgeth him thereto.
(Prov. xvi. 26, cp. Ecclus. xxxi. 3.)

The rich man's wealth is his strong city,
And as a high wall in his estimation.
(Prov. xviii. 11, cp. Ecclus. xiv. 11.)

Sayings of this kind, of which there are many, might well be thought to be of a purely secular character; but such a judgement would not be just to the writers; for all utterances of the Wisdom writers have, from the point of view of these Sages, an underlying religious motive. It is perfectly true that passages such as those quoted, apart from their context, could be explained as expressing such commonplace truths as that ordinary caution in money-matters should be observed; that it is wise to employ a messenger who is reliable; that the labourer must work to obtain his food, and that wealth is often an effectual protection. These are all things of common sense which appeal to any man of the world, to whom they appear without any religious signification; and in themselves they certainly have not necessarily anything to do with religion. But if understood and interpreted from the point of view of the Wisdom writers, and in the light of their intention, they *have* a religious content; for, according to them, prudence and reliability are God-given forms of Wisdom; the hunger which forces a man to work belongs to the divine economy; wealth is a good thing, but it entails responsibilities to God and man. This, at any rate, is the way in which the Wisdom writers envisaged these things; at the back of their minds there was always a God-ward thought and impulse which, in their eyes, hallowed worldly wisdom and common sense. This must be borne in mind if we would rightly estimate the purpose and intention of what the Hebrew Sages taught.

But while in its early phases the teaching of Wisdom, whether by oral instruction or, somewhat later, in written form, was addressed to ordinary men, whether of the " fool " types or those of more estimable character, in course of time some of the Wisdom teachers thought and wrote for those more exceptional thinkers who pondered upon the deeper problems of life. This is not to say that the more popular form of teaching was neglected; far from that; being always called for, it was supplied in all ages, both in oral (cp. Ecclus. li. 23 ff.) and in written form. The more profound form of teaching did not begin until the Greek period (*circa* B.C. 300 onwards), when the problems of life were more fully realized and solutions were sought, and when, consciously or unconsciously, the minds of the deeper thinkers were influenced by Greek culture which more and more permeated the mental atmosphere of the world; hence the appearance of such writings as *Job, Ecclesiastes, Ecclesiasticus,* and later, *Wisdom.* To deal with the first two would be out of place here; for the last see pp. 196 ff.

IV. The Hebrew Conception of Wisdom[1]

A large variety of meanings are expressed by the root from which the Hebrew word for Wisdom, *Ḥokma,* comes; it is used in the sense of the " skill " of the workman (Isa. iii. 3, Jer. x. 9); of proficiency in mourning ceremonies (Jer. ix. 16); in the art of spinning (Exod. xxxv. 25); in fighting (Isa. x. 13); in the administration of affairs (Isa. xxix. 14; Jer. xlix. 7); of the skill of magicians (Isa. xlvii. 10); of shrewdness (II Sam. xx. 22; Jer. ix. 22); of craftiness (II Sam. xiii. 3); even of the intelligence of animals (Prov. xxx. 24). So that in its earlier sense, though this is not excluded from its later usage, wisdom meant the faculty of distinguishing between what was useful and what harmful; its ethical meaning belongs to later times when also a directly religious sense was connected with it. In the Wisdom literature generally it is never used of pure knowledge. In the teaching of the Sages, as we have seen, wisdom has a religious content; whatever form it assumes the saying always applies: " The fear of the Lord is the beginning of Wisdom." The Hebrew word for " beginning " has the twofold sense of the " earliest " and the " last," in the sense of chief;[2] so that the saying can be applied to the earlier forms of wisdom, as well as to its most developed form; it is certain, at any rate, that the Wisdom writers regarded the "fear of the Lord " as the basis and condition, and at the same time, as the fullness, the zenith, of Wisdom.

The developed conception of Wisdom is met with first in Prov. viii. 22–ix. 12, upon which, no doubt, Ecclus. xxiv. 1–34 was based; and, later, in the book of *Wisdom.* As a

---

[1] See also pp. 218 ff.
[2] For the meaning of " beginning " see, *e.g.* Job viii. 7, in reference to early life; for that of " chief," as the most important, *e.g.* Am. vi. 1.

rule, in this later literature Wisdom is treated as something abstract, but in each of these three books striking passages occur in which Wisdom is personified. In discussing this subject it is necessary to keep the mean between two extremes; refraining, on the one hand, from reading into words which speak of the personification of Wisdom a meaning which they were not intended to bear; and, on the other, seeking to explain away altogether the meaning which they *were* intended to bear. When in modern speech things, whether abstract or concrete, are spoken of as personalities the words are used metaphorically without the remotest intention of really imputing personality to them; but it is extremely doubtful whether that can always be postulated in the case of ancient Jewish writers. There are some passages in all three books mentioned which, so far as the nature of Wisdom is concerned, suggest a parallel with some other personifications, or at least quasi-personifications, of divine attributes which appear in early post-Christian Jewish writings; they occupy, to state it moderately, an intermediate position between personalities and abstract beings. While, on the one hand, they are represented as being so closely connected with God as to appear as parts of Him, or His attributes, they are, on the other hand, so often spoken of as undertaking individual action that they must be regarded, in a real sense, as separate from Him.[1] This is suggested by such a passage as Prov. viii. 22–31, which seems to express something more than merely figurative language:

The Lord possessed me in the beginning of his way,
    Before his works of old.
I was set up from everlasting, from the beginning,
    Or ever the earth was.
When there were no depths I was brought forth;
    When there were no fountains abounding with water . . .
When he established the heavens I was there;
    When he set a circle upon the face of the deep;
When he made the firm skies above;
    When the fountains of the deep became strong;

[1] These are dealt with in Oesterley and Box, *The Religion and Worship of the Synagogue*, 2. ed. pp. 195–221 (1911).

When he gave to the sea its bound,
  That the waters should not transgress his commandment;
When he marked out the foundations of the earth;
  Then was I by him, as a master workman . . .

With the thought of Wisdom being utilized by God in creating the world ("Then was I by him, as a master workman"), one thinks of what is said about God having created the world through His Word; this thought is already adumbrated in such a passage as Ps. xxxiii. 6: "By the word of the Lord were the heavens made" (cp. Ps. cxlviii. 5; Ecclus. xlii. 15; Wisd. iv. 1; II Esdr. vi. 38); these words were interpreted in later times to mean that the whole creation, as described in *Genesis*, was accomplished through the Word of God, the "Word" (*Memra*) having become, in the meantime, a quasi-personality like Wisdom.[1] Ben-Sira, though influenced by Prov. viii. 22 ff., has his own way of expressing the same thought:

I came forth from the mouth of the Most High,
And as mist I covered the earth.
In the high places did I fix my abode,
And my throne was in the pillar of cloud.
Alone I compassed the circuit of heaven,
And in the depth of the abyss I walked
  (Ecclus. xxiv. 3–5, Greek; the Hebrew is not extant).

We come very near to a hypostatization of Wisdom in a passage like this; and the same is true of Wisd. ix. 9–11:

And with thee is Wisdom which knoweth thy works,
Being also present (with thee) when thou madest the world,
And understandeth that which is pleasing in thine eyes,
And what is right in thy commandments.
Send her forth out of the holy heavens,
And speed her from the throne of thy glory. . . .

But the most striking passage on the nature of Wisdom is Wisd. vii. 22–viii. 1; the passage is too long to quote, but it is admirably summarized by Gregg:[2]

[1] Especially in the Targums; for the relevant passages see Weber, *Jüdische Theologie* . . ., p. 183 (1897).
[2] *The Wisdom of Solomon*, p. xxxv (1909).

Her functions and attributes mark her out as being very near to God Himself, and the writer accumulates such expressions as breath, effluence, effulgence, mirror, image (vii. 25, 26), in order to assert her divineness without attributing to her deity. She is pictured as a "solar energy, emanating from the focus of power, and though exerting characteristic influences on every variety of object, yet never breaking loose into separate existence, or violating the indissoluble unity of her source." With this central source she is one; yet, though possessing all that God has to give, she does so only by derivation. . . . No better summary could be offered than the words of Drummond: "Wisdom is a self-adaptation of the inviolable spirituality of God to material conditions, an assumption of the necessary community of nature, in order to bring the infinite and eternal into those relations of space and time which are implied in the creation and government of the world of sense." [1]

Surveying the whole ground, it may be said that Hebrew Wisdom was primarily empirical, rather than speculative, and essentially pragmatic. In so far as it was speculative, the speculation was not about the nature of reality, or the being of God, or the end of life, but on the nature of Wisdom itself; and that speculation is the climax, not the starting-point of Wisdom thought. It was only after Greek influence began to be felt that the deeper speculation arose, and even then the severely limited field of speculation among the Hebrew Wisdom writers, as compared with the Greeks, must be recognized. It must also be again emphasized that the Hebrew Wisdom writers approached everything from a fundamentally religious standpoint and this was in striking contrast to the Greeks.

[1] Drummond, *Philo Judaeus, or the Jewish-Alexandrian Philosophy in its development and completion*, i. 225 (1888).

E

CHAPTER VI

THE APOCALYPTIC LITERATURE

I. Eschatological and Apocalyptic Elements in the Prophetical Literature [1]

As the Apocrypha comprises one of the most important books of the Apocalyptic literature, some detailed consideration of this·literature as a whole is called for.

When we speak of the "Apocalyptic literature" we mean the body of writings belonging approximately to the period B.C. 200–100 A.D. which deals with the subjects of the end of the present world-order and the nature of the world to come. To restrict the expression "Apocalyptic literature" to this body of writings is, however, not, properly speaking, correct; for there is a certain amount of apocalyptic literature in the Old Testament, quite apart from the *Book of Daniel*; and inasmuch as this is *one* of the roots from which the later Apocalyptic literature grew, it would be a mistake to study the later growth without considering that from which it issued. Stress is laid on the words "*one* of the roots," for, as we shall see later, there is much in the Apocalyptic literature which is independent of anything occurring in the Old Testament, and for which a different origin must be sought. It is therefore essential that, before we deal with the Apocalyptic literature in the more restricted sense, we should take a glance, though it be but a slight one, at the apocalyptic elements in the Old Testament; they all occur in the prophetical books— *Daniel* is excluded because that belongs to the body of the Apocalyptic literature in the generally accepted sense— in fact, it was only under a misapprehension that *Daniel* was admitted into the Canon.

[1] Eschatology deals with the subject of the end of the present world-order, and after, while Apocalyptic describes certain phenomena which will take place then, and which have been revealed beforehand.

In a number of passages in the prophetical books [1] there occur prophecies regarding the "last times" (אַחֲרִית הַיָּמִים), frequently spoken of as "that day," or, more specifically, "the day of Yahweh." These prophecies are of two orders: on the one hand, they speak of the "last times" as those of judgement and punishment, *i.e.* they are prophecies of woe; on the other hand, there are prophecies full of hope and happiness, and these present the "last times" as full of joy and peace, *i.e.* they are prophecies of bliss. The important point to bear in mind is that there is no thought of a future life here in a heavenly sphere; whatever happens in those "last times" is to take place on this earth. True, the moral element comes in, though by no means always; woe is for the wicked, bliss for the righteous, but not infrequently it is simply that the "last times" are described as a period of terror, or a period of prosperity, without mention of either the righteous or the wicked; and, in any case, the idea of a future life, in the generally accepted sense, does not come in at all.

We have, thus, in the prophetical literature an eschatology of woe, and an eschatology of bliss; and, at first sight, there may appear something incongruous in these opposed ideas occurring together; so that it cannot occasion surprise that this incongruity of both conceptions finding expression in one and the same prophetical writing has led some scholars to deny the authenticity of prophecies of bliss in pre-exilic writings; and this gains point when it is remembered that, as these scholars rightly maintain, it was both the duty and object of pre-exilic prophecy to denounce sin and to proclaim coming judgement; for the pre-exilic prophets, therefore, to hold out hopes of coming bliss was outside their province. Only prophecies of woe, it is held, belong to the

---

[1] Am. v. 16–20; ix. 11–15. Isa. xxiv–xxvii, original portions xxiv, xxv. 6–8; xxvi. 20–xxvii. 1, 12, 13; later insertions xxv. 1–5, 9–11; xxvi, 1–19; xxvii. 2–5, 6–11. Further, Isa. xxxiii, xxxiv. 1–4. Joel i. 15; ii. 1–11, 20; iii. 1–5 (E.V. ii. 28–32); iv. 1–8 (E.V. iii. 1–8); iv. 9–21 (E.V. iii. 9–21). Zeph. i. 14–18; iii is of later date. In Nah. i. 2–10 there are the remains of a psalm in which apocalyptic *traits* are adapted and applied to the historical situation; Mal. iii. 19–24 (E.V. iv.). Zech. xii. 1–9; xiii. 1–6; xiv. Ezek. xxxviii, esp. verses 8–12, 14–23; xxxix; and probably elsewhere in this book. Possibly there are some other passages.

pre-exilic prophets; but after the Exile, regarded as a punishment of the nation for its sins, prophecies of bliss were
appropriate, for the people had by the Exile been punished
for their sins; they had been " refined as silver," and their
sins had been atoned for (Isa. xl. 2). Therefore it is held
that prophecies of bliss belong only to post-exilic times.[1]
There is a great deal to be said in favour of this view;
but it involves much cutting out of prophetical utterances, for since no prophecy of bliss can belong to a
pre-exilic prophet, everything which speaks of this in a
pre-exilic writing is declared to be a later post-exilic
insertion.

Among those scholars who oppose this view we may
mention, e.g., Gressmann;[2] he instances, to mention but
one point, Isaiah's doctrine of the remnant (cp. the name
Shear-jashub, " a remnant shall return," which the prophet
gives to his son, Isa. vii. 3); this necessarily presupposes
the thought of an eschatology of bliss in the prophet's mind;
and Gressmann brings forward many other passages witnessing to the same truth. About one thing, however, all
scholars are agreed, and that is that eschatology of woe is
predominant in pre-exilic prophecy.

Whichever view be held on this subject, and it is confessedly
a complicated one, it may be asserted with confidence that,
quite apart from anything that the prophets taught, belief
in an eschatology of bliss was ingrained in the *popular conception* long before the Exile; in support of this it is sufficient
to point to Am. v. 18, which nobody would claim as post-
exilic; here the prophet says: " Woe unto you that desire
the day of Yahweh! Wherefore would ye have the day of
Yahweh? it is darkness and not light," showing clearly
that in the popular conception an eschatology of bliss was
believed in.[3] Here a question naturally arises as to how

---

[1] See, e.g., von Gall, Βασιλεια του θεου esp. pp. 37 ff. (1926); others, before
him, had also held this view, e.g. Hühn, *Die messianischen Weissagungen* (1899).
[2] *Der Ursprung der israelitisch-jüdischen Eschatologie*, pp. 178 ff., 234, 242 f.
(1905).
[3] This is differently interpreted by von Gall, *op. cit.*, pp. 24 ff. Hölscher,
Geschichte der israelitischen und jüdischen Religion, p. 105 (1922), holds that the
" Day of Yahweh " has nothing to do with eschatology; there is an element
of truth in this, but Hölscher restricts the expression overmuch.

this conception arose in the popular mind; and this brings us to the important subject of the origin of Old Testament eschatology, whether of woe or of bliss.

II. THE ORIGIN OF OLD TESTAMENT ESCHATOLOGY

Was eschatology indigenous in Israel, or was it due to extraneous influences? Here again opinions differ, but it must be recognized that such scholars as Gunkel,[1] Gressmann,[2] and others, have fully demonstrated that the prophets made use of extraneous traditional material in their prophecies concerning the " last times."

A convincing preliminary argument which bears this out is the fragmentary character of the eschatological picture presented in the prophetical writings. Had the eschatology of the prophets been evolved within Israel itself the picture presented would have been more complete, and constructed as a consistent whole, instead of what we now find, namely, a number of isolated *traits* lacking logical connexion. It is only after laborious archæological investigation, as Gressmann truly remarks, that the fragments can be identified and their original connexion ascertained; for

> the mythical background still visible to the practised eye, is faded and blurred, and cannot be detected by a merely superficial glance. What is intelligible alternates with what can be only partly understood, or else what is wholly incomprehensible; current history is mixed up with mythical elements . . .[3]

This fragmentary character of prophetical eschatology can be accounted for only on the assumption that it originated outside of Israel, and was adapted as occasion served; and a fact of significance in this connexion is that the later Apocalypses (taken as a whole) present us with a full and complete eschatological picture; that which in the pro-

---

[1] *Schöpfung und Chaos in Urzeit und Endzeit* (1895).
[2] In the work referred to above (p. 58 note 2).
[3] *Op. cit.*, pp. 246 f.

phetical descriptions is only touched upon or hinted at appears in these Apocalypses as a clear and consistently connected whole; so far as the eschatology of bliss is concerned, there is—apart from the preliminary signs and the world conflagration—a new heaven and a new earth and the return of Paradise in all its original beauty, following upon the resurrection; all the parts are thus joined into a completed whole; in the case of the eschatology of woe, there is likewise a completed whole.[1] That in the different Apocalypses one element in the drama here and another there is more emphasized is merely due to the idiosyncrasy of the different writers; but the main consistent scheme is as outlined. Is it likely, asks Gressmann, that this well-constructed edifice, presented in these later Apocalypses, should have been put together with the fragments scattered about in the writings of the Old Testament? The problem can only be solved, he maintains, by assuming a twofold entry into Palestine of the same extraneous material. In the first instance, it came in early pre-prophetical times from Babylonia, the last traces of it being visible in the prophetical writings. The second flooding of the land with extraneous eschatological ideas occurred much later; it was at the time when the melting into one another of the religions of the East began; that period of religious syncretism which owed its origin to the cosmopolitanism brought about, in the first instance, by the conquests and policy of Alexander the Great.

One important point regarding the " second flooding " should be added here; the great influence exercised by Persian eschatology on that of the Jews has in recent years received notable attention;[2] the question is: when did this influence begin to assert itself? Opinions differ here, and naturally enough, for the evidence is inconclusive;

---

[1] We must emphasize again that we are referring to the Apocalyptic literature as a *complete whole*; the individual Apocalypses are by no means always consistent with one another; one writer stresses certain aspects of the eschatological drama which another writer passes over lightly or omits altogether.

[2] See Böklen, *Die Verwandtschaft der jüdisch-christlichen mit der persischen Eschatōlogie* (1902); Scheftelowitz, *Die altpersische Religion und das Judentum*, pp. 158 ff. (1920); Oesterley and Robinson, *Hebrew Religion*, pp. 342 ff. (1931). Bousset, *Die Religion des Judentums im späthellenistischen Zeitalter*, pp. 202 ff., 502 ff. (1926). Meyer, *Ursprung und Anfänge*, passim (1901).

that it began during the Persian period would seem likely enough; the silence of our records—and it is not certain that they are as silent on the subject as many believe, would not necessarily disprove the existence of that influence; in the Apocalypses it is glaringly in evidence, and it is wholly within the bounds of possibility that Persian eschatological beliefs were current in certain Jewish circles, and had become stereotyped, even prior to the Greek period, before having been put into literary form. However, it is granted that we are on uncertain ground here.

While, then, the Apocalyptic literature is not dependent, or only so in part, on the Old Testament for its eschatology, there is no sort of doubt that the Apocalyptists utilized the Old Testament; that is very evident; and a great deal of what they say is coloured by Old Testament ideas. That is the reason why we have devoted a section to Old Testament eschatology before coming to deal with the Apocalyptic literature itself.

III. THE APOCALYPTIC LITERATURE

The eschatological picture which we have in the various apocalyptic books is not a uniform presentation; all the elements are there, but the presentation is not uniform; the descriptions of the revelations regarding the events which are to take place at the end of the present world-order and after, often differ in detail. The traditional eschatological material is handled differently by the various writers of this literature; some elements are emphasized by one writer more than by another, while others are not mentioned at all by other writers.

The development of eschatological ideas is a matter of individual treatment; one writer develops an idea in one way, another in a different way; while yet another writer will merely embody traditional material without developing it. These are factors to be taken into consideration when studying the Apocalyptic literature; and they account in large measure for the lack of uniformity in the presenta-

tion of the material; they are also in part, but only in part,
an explanation of many of the contradictions which occur.
For these, however, there is a more deep-seated reason;
and here we come to a matter of fundamental importance.
The Eschatology of the Apocalyptic literature is of two
kinds, and these are irreconcileable with one another;
this can be set forth in the following way:

(1) There is the ancient expectation of a political re-
establishment of the Israelite nation to a freedom and power
hitherto undreamt-of; a time of absolute well-being and
prosperity, as well as supremacy over the nations of the
world.   This re-establishment at the end of the times of the
nation is to be brought about by God's specially anointed
one, the Messiah, who will be of the seed of David; an
earthly Messiah, therefore, and a temporal rule, of which
Palestine is to be the scene; his advent will be preceded by
all · kinds of fantastic occurrences in the natural world.
The Messiah will annihilate all the enemies of Israel, for
they are also the enemies of God.

That is one presentation of what is to occur when the
Day of Yahweh comes.   But alongside of this there is a very
different presentation:

(2) There is, first, an altogether higher conception of the
nature of the "good time" to come; material benefits
which figure so prominently in the other presentation, are
not thought of; for that time will be one of *spiritual* ascendancy; we have here a religious development in a universalistic transcendental direction.   No more a Jewish overlordship of all the nations of the earth; but, first the destruction
of all evil and all anti-religious elements, spiritual as well
as material; and then the coming into existence of a new
world of goodness and true happiness.   *The whole idea of
Jewish nationalism has disappeared.*   Instead of the traditional
antagonism between Israel and the Gentiles, the antithesis
is between God and the supernatural powers of evil; and,
following that, between good and evil men, which brings
to the fore a pronounced *Individualism.*

In addition to this there are two entirely opposed conceptions of the Messiah; there is, on the one hand, an

earthly Messiah, purely human, who dies like all men; on the other, and more frequently, we have the figure of a transcendental Messiah who has existed from all time, from before the creation of the world.

One or two illustrations may be given; and here it must be pointed out that the dates of the writings from which these are taken are immaterial, because the writers all use the same eschatological traditions which go back to periods long before their time.

First, as to an earthly kingdom of the Israelite nation in the " last time." For this we may turn to the 17th of the *Psalms of Solomon* (middle of the 1st cent. B.C.); it is too long to quote in full, but a few of the verses are as follows:

Behold, O Lord, and raise up unto them their king, the son of David . . .
. . . And he shall gather together a holy people whom he shall lead in righteousness . . .
And he shall have the heathen nations to serve him under his yoke . . .
All nations shall be in fear before him;
For he will smite the earth with the word of his mouth for ever.
He will bless the people of the Lord with wisdom and gladness,
And he himself will be pure from sin, so that he may rule a great people . . .
He will be mighty in his works, and strong in the fear of God,
He will be shepherding the flock of the Lord faithfully and righteously. . . .

(vv. 23 ff.)

As an illustration of the spiritual kingdom of the Messiah we may quote *Enoch* xlv. 3-5 (early 1st cent. B.C.):

On that day mine Elect One shall sit on the throne of glory, and shall try their works, and their places of rest shall be innumerable. And their souls shall grow strong within them when they see mine elect ones, and those who have called upon my glorious name. Then will I cause mine Elect One to dwell among them; and I will transform the heaven and make it an eternal blessing and light. And I will transform the earth and make it a blessing; and I will cause mine elect ones to dwell upon it; but sinners and evil doers shall not set foot thereon.

Then as to an earthly Messiah; in the *Ezra Apocalypse* (II Esdr. [end of 1st cent. A.D.]) vii. 29, 30 it is said:

After these years shall my son the Messiah die, and all that have the breath of life. And the world shall be turned into the old silence seven days, like as in the beginning; so that no man shall remain.

Similarly in the *Test. of the XII Patriarchs*, Judah xxiv. 1 ff. (early 1st cent. B.C.):

And after all these things shall a star arise to you from Jacob in peace, and a man shall arise like the sun of right-eousness, walking with the sons of men in meekness and righteousness. And no sin shall be found in him. . . . Then shall the sceptre of my kingdom shine forth; and from your root shall arise a stem; and from it shall grow a rod of righteousness to the Gentiles, to judge, and to save all that call upon the Lord.

Finally, a couple of passages illustrating the belief in a transcendental Messiah; Enoch lxii. 7 ff.:

For from the beginning the Son of Man was hidden,
And the Most High presented him in the presence of his might,
And revealed him to the elect . . .
And all the kings and the mighty and the exalted and those who rule the earth, shall fall down before him on their faces,
And worship and set their hope upon that Son of Man,
And petition him and supplicate for mercy at his hands . . .

Similarly in the *Sibylline Oracles* v. 414 ff. (circa 150 B.C.):

For there has come from the plains of heaven a blessed

man with the sceptre in his hand which God has committed to his clasp. . . .

Many more quotations would be required to illustrate to the full the immense contrast between these two wholly differing eschatological pictures; but the whole position may be summed up thus:

Opposed to the expectation of Jewish political ascendancy in a kingdom of hitherto undreamt-of prosperity, established in Palestine, or else over the whole earth, we find, first of all, great emphasis laid on the contrast between this world and the world to come; the evil of the present world is such that its utter annihilation is the necessary prelude to a new earth, and also a new heaven (to discuss this latter point would take us too far afield); the new age of bliss, of which, according to the traditional expectation, Palestine —sometimes the whole earth—was to be the scene, is now transferred to Paradise, or as some of the Apocalyptists teach, to Heaven itself. In place of the destruction of Israel's enemies, the enemies of God, there is to be a *universal* Judgement; all alike, Jews as well as Gentiles, will stand before the Judgement seat; Jews as well as Gentiles will be punished if found among the wicked; and Gentiles as well as Jews will enter into bliss if found among the righteous; for in the world to come there is a place for the righteous and a place for the wicked. The Judgement is, thus, to be a universal one, but inasmuch as each man singly will be judged it is also an *individual* judgement. Further, in the world to come righteous men will be transformed into angel-like beings; they will be partakers in the resurrection; there will be an end of death, and instead, everlasting life. According to the traditional teaching the enemies of Israel are God's enemies and will therefore be destroyed; but according to this other view the enemies of God are Satan and his hosts, *i.e.* spiritual enemies. And finally, as we have seen, the personality and nature of the Messiah has undergone an overwhelming change.

How fundamentally irreconcileable the differing points of view on all these matters are will be fully realized!

and yet there is a constant intermingling of them in the Apocalyptic literature. How is this to be explained? Probably, to put it quite baldly, because the Apocalyptists were, in a sense, cosmopolitan Jews. True, they all have as their central theme the future re-establishment of Israel; and, naturally enough, they could not shake off their ingrained traditional, nationalistic Jewish attitude; since their primary object was to strengthen the faith of their people, to hearten them with hope in the surroundings of an unkind world, they could not ignore the time-honoured expectations in which their people had been reared from childhood. How could they have gained the ear of those to whom they were attached, and whose spiritual welfare lay so close to their hearts, if they had represented all those cherished ideas as chimerical? It seems hardly possible to believe that the Apocalyptists, with their wider spiritual horizon, could themselves have had any faith in those narrow nationalistic expectations so dear to the bulk of their people; but expediency demanded that they should mention them in their writings. That will account for the orthodox Jewish element (so far as this subject is concerned) in the apocalyptic writings.

But on the other hand, the Apocalyptists show by their writings that they were steeped in extraneous eschatological ideas; how did this come about? To answer this we must again take a glance at the religious condition of the world in general during the third and second centuries B.C. One of the most striking results of the conquests of Alexander was the breaking down of the barriers between the nations and a great intermingling of peoples. The fuller knowledge of one another gained through this intercourse resulted, among other things, in a loosening of the ties whereby men had been attached to the religion of their country; [1] that was inevitable when they began to realize the variety of religious beliefs and practices in the world of their sur-

---

[1] What Hecatæus of Abdera (B.C. 306–283) wrote a century before this time is applicable to this period: " Under the later rule of the Persians and of the Macedonians, who overthrew the empire of the former, many of the traditional customs of the Jews were altered owing to their intercourse with aliens."

roundings. Religious unrest arose in all the countries of
the Mediterranean sea-board. The religious ideas of East
and West intermingled owing to widespread borrowing and
interchanging; hence arose universalistic tendencies in
religion. It is not to be denied that, as a whole, the Jews
withstood, to a great extent, these tendencies; but the
different parties which existed among the Jewish people is a
factor not to be overlooked. The hellenistic Jews formed a
powerful party in the land, and how strong their influence
was is clearly shown in *I Maccabees*—let alone the Jews of the
Diaspora whose liberal views cannot have been altogether
without effect on their kinsmen in Palestine. The chaotic
condition of Jewish parties in Palestine during the second
and first centuries B.C. must also be taken into consideration;
the hellenistic Jews were opposed by the nationalists, headed
by the Maccabæan leaders; but it was not very long before
the orthodox party, originally nationalistic, found themselves
in opposition to the Hasmonæan High-priesthood and those
attached to it, on account of their worldly ambitions and
their lax observance of the Jewish religion. Then, belonging
to neither of these were the Apocalyptists, who stood aloof
from the hellenistic Jews, but were repudiated by the
orthodox party. Under these bewildering conditions it can
occasion no surprise that non-Jewish extraneous influences
in the religious, as well as in other spheres, should have
made themselves felt.

In the case of the Apocalyptists, with whom we are specially
concerned, these influences are to be observed in their
literature. To illustrate these influences properly we should
have to give a large number of quotations both from non-
Jewish literature wherein are described the various eschatological ideas which, it may be confidently asserted, influenced
the Jewish Apocalyptists, and also from the Apocalyptic
literature itself in order to compare the two. But for this
the special works already referred to must be consulted.
In some respects Babylonian influence may be discerned,
but that of ancient Persia is far more striking; it is in connexion with such subjects as dualism, the final judgement,
and the world-conflagration, the combat between the

spiritual powers of good and evil, the triumph of good
and the end of evil, the new world, and the resurrection,
as well as some minor matters, that Iranian influence may
be seen.

The question may be asked what reasons there are for
maintaining that Jewish eschatology has been influenced
by Iranian beliefs, and not *vice versa*; the question is the more
justified in that some notable scholars, though few in number,
deny this influence of ancient Persia on the Jews; an attempt
to answer it is therefore called for.

It should first be pointed out, however, that the denial of
Iranian influence has been based on the uncertainty of the
date of the *Avesta*, the sacred Scriptures of the Persians;
but this no longer holds good, for " it can be proved from
Greek, Latin, and other writings, that the tradition of the
wisdom of Zoroaster lived on during the long period between
Alexander and the rise of the house of Sāsān in the third
century A.D.";[1] the tradition of this wisdom which includes
eschatological teaching must therefore have been in existence
before B.C. 300, a date prior to the rise of Jewish Apocalyptic
in the developed sense.   Besides, it is granted, even by such
a strong opponent of those who insist on Persian influence
as Söderblom, that the *Gāthās, i.e.* the songs or psalms, which
constitute the oldest as well as the most important part of
the *Avesta*, and which contain eschatological material,
belong, at any rate in part, to the seventh century B.C.

More worthy of consideration is Söderblom's objection
on the ground of the striking *differences* between Jewish and
Persian eschatology.[2] But, as Bousset has forcibly protested,
it is a one-sided proceeding to emphasize all the differences
while passing over the many striking similarities.[3] Moreover, we have this obstinate fact, from which no amount
of special pleading can get away, that among all the various
eschatological systems of antiquity there is nowhere any
approach to the degree of relationship such as exists between
the Iranian and the Jewish.   The fact of that relationship

---

[1] Williams Jackson, in Hastings' *ERE*, ii. 270 *b*.
[2] *La vie future, d'après le mazdéisme*, pp. 301 ff. (1901).
[3] *Op. cit.*, p. 509.

is fully recognized by every investigator of the subject; it is only a question of which has influenced the other. For anyone who approaches the subject with an open mind there would hardly seem to be room for doubt. The plea that both might be indebted to some earlier common source is excluded because there is nothing to show that such an earlier source ever existed, for neither Egyptian nor Babylonian [1] eschatology offers an analogy here.

There is, further, another consideration; it is *a priori* probable that Jewish religious beliefs in this domain should have been affected by Persian thought. From the beginning of the Medo–Persian empire the relations between the Jews and the suzerain power were of a friendly character; the Old Testament makes that clear enough. The very existence of the post-exilic Jewish community was, in the first instance, due to Cyrus; and there is every reason to believe that as long as the Persian empire lasted, the Jews were, in general, left in peace to develop their religion and culture unmolested. Further, that as a result of the Exile many Jews had become attached to their new home in which they settled down permanently, *i.e.* under Persian rule, is well known; there is also evidence that there was constant intercourse between the Jews of east and west, so that there was plenty of opportunity for the Jews of the eastern Diaspora to exchange thought with their western brethren. It is impossible not to believe that the Jews, living in the heart of the Persian empire and coming into daily contact with their Persian neighbours, were affected in many directions, including religious ideas. While, on the one hand, the Exile had the result of narrowing the religious thought of the Jews, it is certain, on the other, that among some circles the living in a foreign land had the effect of widening their mental horizon; that is clear from Deutero–Isaiah.

Eschatology was more or less neutral ground, so that in this domain beliefs could be taken over or adapted by the Jews without necessarily involving any disloyalty to their ancestral faith. And, as we have seen, the soil was ready,

---

[1] An exception is perhaps the idea of world epochs, but that does not touch the really fundamental subjects of the eschatological drama.

for the roots of Jewish eschatology reach back far into pre-exilic times.

In addition to what has been said, it is also worth pointing out that in some other respects the influence of Persian on Jewish belief is generally recognized. The immense development of Angelology and Demonology in Judaism, for example, was largely due to this influence; and the Jewish conceptions concerning superhuman intermediaries between God and men show the influence of the teaching about divine hypostases in the *Gāthās*.

Finally, attention may be drawn to a national Jewish *trait*, which, in spite of rigid tenacity in all that concerned the fundamental tenets of their faith, has always been characteristic of the Jews; namely, their receptivity, together with a genius for absorbing and adapting whatever seemed worthy of acceptation in other religious systems. This national characteristic should not be lost sight of in connexion with the subject we have been considering.

It will, thus, be granted that the *a priori* probabilities of the case must incline the impartial investigator to expect to see some signs of Persian influence on Jewish eschatology.

IV. THE APOCALYPTISTS AND THEIR TEACHING

Reference has been made to certain inconsistencies in the teaching of the Apocalyptists, but we merely touched upon their teaching, and did not deal with the manifold messages which they felt impelled to convey; so that a brief examination of their characteristic doctrines is called for.

There is, as already pointed out, no uniform system in the eschatological teaching set forth by the individual writers; certain fundamental truths are common to all of them, but the relative stress laid on these varies in the mind of the Apocalyptists when they deal with details; each individual writer feels at liberty to treat of these in his own way.

But one conviction common to all the Apocalyptists is that the end of the present world-order is to be expected in the near future; a great deal of what they have to say, therefore, is concerned with the events which will occur when the end approaches, and with what will happen thereafter. Their outlook is, therefore, wholly other-worldly; their references to this world-order merely emphasize its transitoriness and its approaching end, and to describe the occurrences which will bring about its destruction. All these things are hidden from ordinary mortals; they were known to the great national heroes of the past, Enoch, Noah, Abraham, Moses and others, having been revealed to them by angels while they were yet alive, or else in heaven after they had gone hence; and now the Apocalyptists have been made partakers of these divine secrets. One of the main purposes, therefore, for which the Apocalyptists wrote was to make known to their fellow-men the things which should come to pass, and thus to prepare them for the end.

In this respect the Apocalyptists may be regarded as the successors of the prophets of old; like them, they never tire of denouncing the wicked for their evil ways, and of proclaiming the coming doom upon the enemies of God; and, like the prophets, they have words of comfort and hope for the godly who in this world of iniquity are suffering for their loyalty to God.

In another direction, moreover, the Apocalyptists show themselves to be in the following of the prophets. These latter had taught that, in accordance with the divine fore-knowledge and plan, the destruction of the Israelite nation was, on account of its wickedness, predetermined. This conception is taken over by the Apocalyptists and greatly developed; indeed, their doctrine of Determinism is at times carried to extreme lengths. In II Esdr. iv. 36 f., e.g., it is said: "For he hath weighed the world in the balance; and by measure hath he measured the times, and by number hath he numbered the seasons; and he shall not move nor stir them, until the said measure be fulfilled," see also Enoch xciii. 1 ff.; all things are predetermined from the beginning of the world. It seems highly probable that this exaggerated Determinism was due to Iranian influence.[1]

---

[1] See, for detailed evidence, Bousset, *op. cit.*, pp. 502 f.

F

Further, it is characteristic of all the Apocalyptists that their outlook was pessimistic; this was undoubtedly due in large measure to the chaotic political conditions of the world in general in their time. Then, too, as the Apocalyptists saw, the world was wicked; and this, not only because of widespread vice of every kind, but also because there was no true belief in God. As to their own nation, the outlook was desperate; trodden down under the heel of tyrants, their position was hopeless; there was nothing to look for in this world; and among their own people, too, evil was in the ascendant; most men, as the apocalyptic writings show, were steeped in sin. The pessimistic attitude of the Apocalyptists was, therefore, comprehensible. But there was something else which was, in part at any rate, responsible for this pessimism. The predominance of evil was an incontrovertible fact; but why was this, and whence came all this evil among men? In answer to this question, one of the great problems with which the Apocalyptists were confronted, they were forced into holding a form of Dualism. The world was a world of wickedness opposed to which were the righteous who hated it: " They have hated and despised this world of unrighteousness, and have hated all its works and ways in the name of the Lord of Spirits " (Enoch xlviii. 7); on one side " the generation of light," on the other those " born in darkness " (Enoch cviii. 11, 14), representing respectively the kingdom of God and the kingdom of the Evil one. The antagonism was not only between good and evil men, but between angels and demons, between God and Satan. Thus the Apocalyptists, though they never seem to realize what it ultimately involved, held a form of Dualism.[1] But, so far as this world was concerned, the battle certainly seemed to have been won by the powers of evil; hence the pessimistic attitude of the Apocalyptists.

One other matter may be briefly referred to. Although orthodox Judaism, with its centre of gravity on the Law, had little sympathy with the apocalyptic movement, it must

[1] That Persian influence is to be discerned here cannot be doubted; the religious system of Mazdaeism centres in the perennial warfare between the two opposing powers Ahura Mazda and Angra Mainyu, and their innumerable retinues.

not be thought that the Apocalyptists were unorthodox;
in certain respects they did not, it is true, see eye to eye with
Pharisaism, but in all fundamental beliefs they were loyal
Jews. This applies also to their observance of the Law;
probably they did not in all respects observe the Law in the
strict Pharisaic sense; but that they honoured it highly is
certain. In Jub. ii. 33, *e.g.*, it is said: " This law and
testimony was given to the children of Israel as a law for
ever unto their generations " (see also vi. 17 ff.). In
II Esdr. ix. 37 the seer says: " The Law perisheth not,
but remaineth in honour " (see also v. 27; vii. 20, 21, 133;
ix. 30, 31, etc.); and in other writings similar ideas are
expressed.

These, then, are the more outstanding characteristics of the
apocalyptic writers; [1] some further details regarding their
teaching will be found in chapter VII: " The Doctrinal
Teaching of the Apocrypha."

[1] For their universalistic outlook, see above, pp. 62, 65.

CHAPTER VII

THE DOCTRINAL TEACHING OF THE APOCRYPHA[1]

I. The Doctrine of God

In the Apocrypha belief in God is identical with that of the
Old Testament in its most highly developed form. Here
attention must first be drawn to the conception of God as
One who reveals Himself. Throughout the books of the
Apocrypha the Old Testament doctrine of the self-revelation
of God is fundamental and taken for granted; but a difference is often observable in the former in so far as the revelation of the divine will is communicated through the agency
of an angel. This is by no means always the case, but it
occurs sufficiently often to show that the belief in the method
of divine self-revelation was undergoing a change; and it .
was a change which in later Jewish theology became more
pronounced. A fine passage in *Ecclesiasticus* describes the
revelation of God in Nature (xlii. 15–xliii. 33). In Wisd. x.
1 ff., and elsewhere God reveals Himself through Wisdom.
All through the book of *Tobit* the divine will is revealed by
means of an angel (cp. also Sus. verse 59). Speaking generally, there is a certain contrast between the two books of the
Maccabees; while the subject-matter of the first does not
offer much scope for dealing with the doctrine of God,
here and there a passage occurs in which we see a direct
approach to God to reveal His will (*e.g.* iii. 50 ff.); but in
II Maccabees intermediate agencies play an important part
in indicating and fulfilling His purpose (*e.g.* iii. 22 ff.; xi.
8 ff.; on the other hand, see xii. 41 f.). In the visions in
II Esdras the divine messages come to the Seer at times
directly, at other times through the medium of an angel;

[1] It will be readily understood that the illustrations to be given are very
far from being exhaustive.

74

indeed, the distinction is not always made. In iii. 3 ff., *e.g.*, the Seer addresses himself directly to God; but when he concludes his words to the Almighty, he continues: " And the angel that was sent me to . . ."

But all through the books of the Apocrypha there is the belief in God's self-revelation to men, whether it is directly, as normally in the Old Testament, or indirectly, through the medium of an angel.

In the next place, we have the constantly recurring emphasis on the *Unity of God*, an affirmation which the true believer would love to express for his own satisfaction, but which was also a necessary witness in the midst of a poly-theistic environment; there is no doubt, moreover, that it was at times specially called for owing to the weakening belief of some of the Jews in Gentile surroundings. Thus, Ben-Sira prays: " Save me, O God of all, and cast thy fear upon all nations. . . . That they may know, even as we know, that there is none other God but thee " (Ecclus. xxxvi. 1–5 Hebr.; see also xlii. 21). Similarly in the *Song of the Three Holy Children*, Azarias prays that the enemies of his people may know " that thou art the Lord, the only God, and glorious over the whole world " (verse 22). In Wisd. xii. 13 it is said: " For neither is there any God but thee, who carest for all."

The *Creative Activity* of God is very often spoken of; but the two outstanding passages, too long to quote, are Ecclus. xlii. 15–xliii. 33, and The Song of the Three Holy Children, verses 35–68 (the *Benedicite*); in most of the other books God as Creator is commemorated: " Lord of the Heavens and of the earth, Creator of the waters, King of all thy creation, hear thou my prayer " (Jud. ix. 12); " For thou hast made heaven and earth, and all the wondrous things that are beneath the heaven; and thou art the Lord of all " (Rest of Esther xiii. 10, 11); see also Wisd. xiii. 1–9, II Esdr. iii. 4 ff., vi. 1–6, 38–55; II Macc. i. 24.

The *Fatherhood of God* is spoken of in Tob. xiii. 4: " He is our Lord, and God is our Father for ever." Ben-Sira prays: " O Lord, Father, and Master of my life . . ." (xxiii. 1), and elsewhere.

The Divine Attributes find expression again and again throughout the books; we can do no more than merely enumerate them with one or two references in each case: *Eternity,* "Thou art the Lord the Eternal God" (Ecclus. xxxvi. 17, see also xviii. 1 ff.; *Benedicite* 89, 90; II Esdras viii. 20). *Holiness* (Tob. iii. 11; Ecclus. iv. 14, xxiii. 9, etc.; Bar. iv. 22: "Joy is come unto me from the Holy One"). *Omnipotence*: Ben-Sira, after his description of the divine activity in Nature, concludes with: "And the sum of our words is, He is all" (Ecclus. xliii. 27). In Jud. ix. 14 it is said: "And make every nation and tribe of thine to know that thou art God, the God of all power and might . . ."; in the Rest of Esther xiii. 9–11 there is this beautiful passage in Mordecai's prayer: "O Lord, Lord, thou King Almighty; for the whole world is in thy power, and if it be thy will to save Israel, there is no man that can gainsay thee; for thou hast made heaven and earth, and all the wondrous things that are beneath the heaven; and thou art Lord of all, and there is no man that can resist thee, which art the Lord." The *Divine Omniscience*, again, is fully recognized; Ben-Sira says: "He searcheth out the deep, and the heart (of man), and discerneth all their secrets; for the Lord knoweth all knowledge, and he looketh into the signs of the world, declaring the things that are past and the things that shall be, and revealing the traces of hidden things; no knowledge is lacking to him, and not a thing escapeth him" (Ecclus. xlii. 18–20); see also Rest of Esther xiii. 12, etc. The frequency with which the *Righteousness of God* is proclaimed is a notable witness to the lasting influence of prophetical teaching on this sublime subject; thus, in Tob. iii. 2, Tobit says: "O Lord, thou art righteous, and all thy works are mercy and truth, and thou judgest true and righteous judgement for ever." Azarias praises God in the words: "Blessed art thou, O Lord . . . for thou art righteous in all things that thou hast done; yea, true are all thy works, and thy ways are right, and all thy judgements true" (Song vv. 3–5); similarly in the Rest of Esther xiv. 7; Sus. 60; and in Wisd. xii. 15 it is said: "For being righteous, thou rulest all things righteously"; see also

Bar. ii. 18; II Esdr. viii. 36, and often elsewhere. The righteous *Justice of God* occurs, *e.g.* in the words: ". . . and our God and the Lord of our fathers, which punisheth us according to our sins and the sins of our fathers . . ." (Jud. vii. 28). Ben-Sira says: "Delay not to turn unto him, and put it not off from day to day; for suddenly doth his indignation come forth, and in the time of vengeance thou wilt perish" (Ecclus. v. 7; see also ix. 12, 13, xvi. 6 ff.); among other passages where this is dealt with, see Tob. xiii. 9; Bar. i. 21 ff.; II Macc. ix. 5, 6; Wisd. xi. 17–20; II Esdr. vii. 3 ff., etc. More frequent, however, is the mention of the divine *Mercy and Longsuffering*: "Therefore is the Lord longsuffering toward them, and poureth out his mercy on them . . . the mercy of man is upon his neighbour, but the mercy of the Lord is upon all flesh, reproving, and chastening, and teaching, and bringing back as a shepherd his flock. He hath mercy on them that accept chastening and that diligently seek after his judgements" (Ecclus. xviii. 11–14); among the many other passages of similar import reference may be made to Tob. vi. 17; Wisd. xi. 21 f.; Bar. ii. 35, iii. 12; iv. 5–v. 9; II Esdr. vii. 132 ff., Prayer of Man. 7, 8.

In the next place it is necessary to draw attention to another prophetical tenet in the doctrine of God, assimilated by the writers of these books, namely that God is the *God of History*. Whatever difficulties may suggest themselves in regard to this—and with these we are not here concerned—it is quite clear that the writers of these books shared the prophetical teaching. Ben-Sira, in saying that "His indignation driveth out nations" (Ecclus. xxxix. 23), implies, as the context shows, that just as all natural occurrences are the outcome of God's will, so the happenings in the world's history are ordained by Him. This is expressed in fuller detail by the same writer in xxxvi. 1–9 (in the Greek xxxiii. 1–9): "Save us, O God of all, and cast thy fear upon all the nations. Shake thine hand against the strange people, that they may see thy power. As thou hast sanctified thyself in us before their eyes, so sanctify thyself in them before our eyes; that they may know, as even we know, that there is none other God but thee. Renew the signs, repeat the wonders; make glorious thy hand and thy right arm. Awake wrath, and pour out indignation; subdue the foe, and drive out the enemy." Similarly in the prayer of Judas Maccabæus (I Macc. iv. 30–33): "Blessed art thou, O Saviour of Israel, who didst quell the onset of the mighty man by the hand of David, and didst deliver the army of the strangers into the hands of Jonathan, the son of Saul, and his armour-bearer; shut up this army in the hand of thy people Israel, and let them be ashamed for their host and their horsemen; give them faintness of heart, and cause the boldness of their strength to melt away, and let them quake at their destruction; cast them down with the sword of them that love thee, and let all that know thy name praise thee with thanksgiving." Further quotations are unnecessary; in most of the books the same thought is either expressed or implied (*e.g.* Jud. xvi. 3; II Esdr. iii. 9 ff.; I Macc. i. 64; iii. 18, etc.).

An important element in the doctrine of God, though this does not apply to all the books, is the tendency to avoid the direct mention of God. In Tob. iii. 16, *e.g.* it is said: " And the prayer of both was heard before the glory of the great " (*i.e.* God); xii. 12: "I did bring the memorial of your prayer before the Holy One " (see also iii. 11; viii. 5; xi. 14). This is especially characteristic of *I Maccabees*, in which the name of God is never directly mentioned. The writer frequently uses instead the second or third person (ii. 21; iii. 22, 60; iv. 10, 24); sometimes " heaven " is used for the direct mention of God (iii. 18, 19, 50, 60; iv. 10, 24, 40, 55; v. 31; ix. 46; xvi. 3). This idiosyncrasy on the part of the writer must be owing to reverential reasons, for there is not a similar reticence in other books of this period; but it may, on the other hand, point to the growth of the transcendental view of God which existed in the last century B.C.

It must be said, in conclusion, that, in reading through this literature, one cannot fail to be impressed by the reality, and sincerity, and depth of belief in God among these writers; that belief is a part of their very being. Their conviction that God is ever present, ever guiding, and ever active among those who are faithful to Him is very inspiring. This alone should make the books of the Apocrypha dear to all.

II. THE LAW

As a whole, this literature represents the Pharisaic standpoint regarding the Law; in some books this is more evident than in others; though in a few instances words are uttered which suggest that the writers did not feel themselves bound by the strict rules and outlook of the Pharisees; but, speaking generally, it may be said that the Pharisaic conception of the Law predominates.

It will be instructive to discuss this subject under the three following heads:

I. *Utterances of a general character concerning the Law.*

The eternity of the Law from all time to all time, and that its observance is life, is thus expressed:

This is the book of the commandments of God,
And the Law that endureth for ever;
All they that hold it fast (are appointed) to life;
But such as leave it shall die (Bar. iv. 1, 2).

This identification of the Law, or *Torah*, with Wisdom[1] re-echoes the opening words of the section:

Hear, O Israel, the commandments of life,
Give ear to understand Wisdom (Bar. iii. 9).

This conception of the Law finds full expression in *Ecclesiasticus*, and both writers are likely to have been indebted for it to Prov. iv. 1–9, viii. 22–31. Ben-Sira brings it out, *e.g.*, in xxiv. 23: "All these things (*i.e.* utterances of Wisdom) are the book of the Covenant of God Most High, the Law which Moses commanded (as) an heritage for the assemblies of Jacob" (see also xv. 1; xix. 20; xxi. 11; xxxiv. 8). The eternity of the Law is expressed in II Esdr. ix. 36, 37: "For we that have received the Law shall perish by sin,

---

[1] This is the theme of the whole section iii. 9–iv. 4.

and our heart also which received it. Notwithstanding, the
law perisheth not, but remaineth in its honour."

That men should die rather than be unfaithful to the Law
appears in several places; in I Macc. ii. 29–38 it is told
how many of the Jews, including women and children,
suffered death rather than break the Law of keeping the
Sabbath holy; " Let us die all in our innocency; heaven
and earth witness over us, that ye put us to death without
trial . . . and they died, they and their wives and their
children, and their cattle, to the number of a thousand souls."
Judas Maccabæus, in a somewhat similar strain, exhorts his
followers " to contend nobly even unto death for laws, temple,
city, country, commonwealth " (II Macc. xiii. 14). The
seer, in II Esdr. vii. 20 likewise exclaims: " Yea, rather, let
many that now live, perish, than that the law of God that is
set before them be despised."

ii. *Non-Pharisaic conceptions of the Law.*

A few instances, and they are exceptional, of an attitude
towards the Law which would not have met with Pharisaic
approval, are worth mentioning; for they illustrate the
fact that there were circles of faithful Jews who were, nevertheless, not wholly orthodox in some particulars; this would
apply more especially to the Apocalyptists; but there were
also hellenistic Jews whose views were less restricted than
those of the thoroughgoing Pharisees, but who would have
resented the imputation of unorthodoxy. Of these latter
we have a representative in the writer of the second part of
the book of Wisdom, in xviii. 4 he says: " . . . through
whom (*i.e.* the children of Israel) the incorruptible light
of the Law was to be given to the world "; here we have, in
effect, the view that the Law was originally meant for the
whole world, not merely for Israel. This is more pointedly
expressed by the apocalyptic writer in II Esdr. vii. 20, 21:
" Yea, rather, let many that now live, perish, than that
the law of God that is set before them be despised. For
God straitly commanded such as came (*i.e.* into the world),
when they came, what they should do to live, and what they
should observe to avoid punishment." It is clear that

humanity in general is here contemplated, not Israel exclusively (cp. the preceding verses). The traditional contention was that the Law was given to and for Israel alone; but the universalistic attitude here taken up shows that this rigid particularism was giving way, and this was doubtless due to the missionary activities of the Jews during the last two centuries B.C. onwards. In later times, as Schechter [1] has pointed out, this idea that the Law was not originally intended to be Israel's exclusive possession was often insisted upon.

Another, and more directly un-Pharisaic, conception about the Law is its inadequacy to redeem the sinner: " For we that have received the law shall perish by sin, and our heart also which received it " (II Esdr. ix. 36, cp. iii. 22). It needs no words to show that such an idea of the impotency of the Law to save would not have commended itself to the Pharisees.[2]

Once more, quite un-Pharisaic is the teaching in *II Esdras* that " it is the *acceptance* of the Law as the standard by which men must be judged at the last, not the *observance* of it. It is true that on strict legal principles the Law, having once been given, ought to have been observed. But so far is this from being the case that very few, if any, even in Israel, have lived up to the divine requirements as set forth in the divinely given Law: ' For in truth there is none of the earth-born that has not dealt wickedly, and among those that exist that has not sinned ' " (II. Esdr. viii. 35).[3]

These points show, then, that among the writers of the books of the Apocrypha were some who did not see eye to eye with the Pharisees. This was worth drawing attention to; but it was exceptional, as we shall now see.

iii. *The Pharisaic standpoint regarding the Law.*

In his " Praise of the Fathers of old," Ben-Sira writes thus of Moses: " And he (God) placed in his hand the commandment, even the Law of life and discernment; that he might

---

[1] *Some Aspects of Rabbinic Theology*, pp. 131 ff. (1909). See further, Volz, *Die Eschatologie der jüdischen Gemeinde im neutestamentlichen Zeitalter*, p. 67 (1934).
[2] The Pharisaic attitude to the Law may be gathered, *e.g.* by St. Paul's words in Rom. iii. 20, viii. 3, 4; and Gal. iii.
[3] Box, *The Ezra-Apocalypse*, p. xxxix (1912).

teach statutes unto Jacob, and his testimonies and judgements unto Israel " (Ecclus. xlv. 5). In a similar strain it is said in Bar. ii. 27–29: " Yet, O Lord our God, thou hast dealt with us after all thy kindness, and according to all that great mercy of thine, as thou spakest by thy servant Moses in the day when thou didst command him to write thy Law before the children of Israel . . ." And, once more, in II Esdr. ix. 29–31 the seer says: " O Lord, thou didst show thyself among us, unto our fathers in the wilderness . . . and thou didst say, Hear me, thou Israel, and mark my words, O seed of Jacob. For, behold, I sow my law in you, and it shall bring forth fruit in you, and ye shall be glorified in it for ever."

The orthodox doctrine of the divine origin of the Law, given through the hands of Moses, is thus expressed in the earliest and latest books of the Apocrypha, and is found directly asserted or implied in practically all the others.

Mention of the observance of the Law occurs very frequently: " Let thy converse be with a man of understanding," says Ben-Sira, " and let thy discourse be in the law of the Most High God " (Ecclus. ix. 15, see also xii. 11; xxxii. 15–24, Sus. 3, and often elsewhere). The neglect of it is an act of sin: " Woe unto you, ungodly men, who have forsaken the law of the Most High God " (Ecclus. xli. 8); " We have sinned before the Lord, and disobeyed him, and have not hearkened unto the voice of the Lord our God, to walk in the commandments of the Lord that he hath set before us " (Bar. i. 18, cp. II Macc. iv. 17). " For though ye were officers of his kingdom ye judged not rightly, neither kept ye the law, nor did ye walk according to the counsel of God " (Wisd. vi. 4 f.). " Heaven forbid that we should forsake the law and ordinances " (I Macc. ii. 21). It is the stay of man in view of death: " Remember corruption and death, and abide in the commandments " (Ecclus. xxviii. 6); the love of Wisdom, identified with the Law, offers the certitude of immortality: " . . . love for her is the observance of her laws, and the heeding of her is the assurance of incorruption " (Wisd. vi. 18). They who turn to the Law may be assured of divine compassion (II Esdr. vii. 133).

Detailed precepts of the Law are incidentally referred to
again and again; most notable here is the book of *Tobit*:
" Give alms of thy substance; and when thou givest alms,
let not thine eye be envious . . . alms delivereth from death,
and suffereth not to come into darkness. Alms is a good
gift in the sight of the Most High for all that give it " (Tob.
iv. 7–11; see also i. 3, 16). Prayer, fasting, and alms are
mentioned together, especially the latter, in Tob. xii. 8–10,
cp. Jud. iv. 13; the paying of tithes is insisted on in Tob. i. 7,
Jud. xi. 13; the avoidance of eating with Gentiles is emphasized in Tob. i. 10, 11; Rest of Esther xiv. 17; and the
need of purification after touching something unclean
(Tob. ii. 15); also the keeping of the feasts in Jud. viii. 6;
II Macc. i. 8, 9, 18.

In all that has been said the references are merely isolated
illustrations, but they reflect the general attitude towards the
Law of all the writers of the books of the Apocrypha. The
book of *Wisdom* is, as would be expected, the only one in
which the Law receives very scant notice.

III. THE SCRIPTURES

The veneration for the Scriptures and their authoritative
character are emphasized again and again in the books of
the Apocrypha. The Pentateuch, or *Torah*, naturally
enough, stands foremost, as being not only Scripture, but
also the Law;[1] nevertheless, the other parts of the Old
Testament are also frequently referred to or quoted, and
are regarded as of fundamental authority; for example, in
Tob. ii. 6 the action of Tobit is said to be based on Am. viii.
10, which is quoted; a few other passages may be mentioned: Tob. ix. 12; xiv. 8, 9; Jud. iv. 14; viii. 26; and
the whole of Jud. xvi is full of Scriptural reminiscences;

---

[1] It is, however, necessary to remember that while the Pentateuch is often
spoken of as the *Torah* (*e.g.* Ecclus. xv. 1; xvii. 11 and elsewhere) the term
is used also in the sense of " instruction " or the like (*e.g.* Ecclus. xxxiv [xxxi],
8; xxxv. [xxxii.] 1). What Schechter says of later times applies here too:
" The term *Law* or *Nomos* is not a correct rendering of the Hebrew word
Torah. The legalistic element, which might rightly be called the Law,
represents only one side of the *Torah*. To the Jew the word *Torah* means a
teaching or instruction of any kind. It may be either a general principle or
a specific injunction, whether it be found in the Pentateuch or in other parts
of the Scriptures, or even outside the Canon " (*op. cit.*, p. 117).

Sus. verse 62, Bel and the Dragon, verses 33 ff.; Prayer of Man., verse 1; and very often elsewhere. But the most striking illustrations are found in some of the other books; in *Ecclesiasticus*, apart from the Prologue and numberless incidental references, there is in the great section of the " Praise of the Fathers of Old," a kind of summary of the history of Israel, in which the deeds of Israel's great ones are commemorated. In the book of *Wisdom*, apart from viii. 2–ix. 18, where Solomon's wisdom and piety are spoken of, and which is full of Scripture references, there is the account of Wisdom's activity among the heroes of old and among Israel's forefathers (x. 1–21); and in xi. 1–xii. 27 the early history of the nation is recounted in order to show God's mercy and forbearance towards His own people, and His judgement upon the Egyptians. In the early parts of *Wisdom*, too, there are constant references and quotations from Scripture. The love and veneration of the Scriptures is graphically illustrated in I Macc. i. 56, 57, 63; at the command of Antiochus all copies of the Scriptures were to be burned, and anyone found in possession of any book of the Scriptures was threatened with death; but many died that they might not be faithless to the covenant. Finally, in *II Esdras*, there are also many allusions to the Scriptures as authoritative (*e.g.* vii. 106 ff., 127 ff., 132 ff.), in addition to a great many incidental references.

There is only one passage in the Apocrypha in which the Scriptures are not held to be of the highest and final authority, *i.e.* in II Esdr. xiv. 44–47; here it is commanded that seventy secret apocalypses are to be kept from ordinary men, for whom the twenty-four books of the Scriptures are sufficient; but the secret books are to be delivered to the wise among the people. This, however, is wholly exceptional; otherwise the entire Apocrypha is saturated with the spirit and teaching of the Scriptures; they are the source of the religion and faith of all the writers.

IV. SACRIFICES

The sacrificial system is taken for granted; but in some of the books it receives far more attention than in others. Thus, in I Esdras, as is to be expected, sacrifices are frequently mentioned, i. 1 ff.; v. 47 ff.; vii. 7 ff.; viii. 65, 66, and the whole system is regarded as an integral part of Judaism. In *Tobit*, on the other hand, in spite of its otherwise orthodox attitude, sacrifices are barely noticed (i. 6 is an exception); the contents of the book, it is true, offer but little occasion for the subject to be mentioned. It is in *Ecclesiasticus* that a full appreciation is found. Ben-Sira's reverence for the Temple-worship is eloquently expressed in l. 1–24, which is a panegyric on Simon the High-priest. In vii. 31 he says: " Glorify God and honour his priests, and give their portion as thou art commanded, the food of the trespass-offering, and the heave-offering of the hand, the sacrifices of righteousness, and the offerings of holy things " (see also xxxv [xxxii] 1–3, 8–13). But while he thus extols material sacrifices, it is noteworthy that he expresses himself strongly both on the right attitude of the offerer and, more important still, on the efficacy of spiritual sacrifices; in xxxiv. 21–23 [xxxi. 18–19] he says: " The sacrifice of an unrighteous man is a mocking sacrifice, and the oblations of the wicked are not acceptable. The Most High hath no pleasure in the offerings of the ungodly, neither is he pacified for sins by the multitude of sacrifices," see also xxxv. (xxxii.) 14, 15. His view regarding spiritual sacrifices is expressed in xxxv. (xxxii.) 1–5, a very important passage: " He that keepeth the Law multiplieth offerings, and he that giveth heed to the commandments offereth a peace-offering.[1] He that rendereth kindness [2] offereth fine flour, and he that giveth alms sacrificeth a thank-offering. A pleasing thing unto the Lord it is to depart from wickedness, and a propitiation it is to turn away from unrighteousness." The tendency here exhibited increased among certain circles of the people as time went on; " it is beyond doubt that within Judaism

---

[1] Cp. Ps. cxl. 1, 2.   [2] Cp. Matth. ix. 13; xii. 7.

itself, especially throughout the Diaspora, tendencies were already abroad by which the temple cultus, and primarily its element of bloody sacrifices, was regarded as unessential, and even of doubtful validity. . . . With regard to the sacrificial system, the right of abandoning the literal meaning had been clearly made out, as that system had already become antiquated and depreciated in the eyes of large sections of the people." [1] This tendency is also to be discerned in the Song of the Three Children 15–17 (38–40): " Neither is there at this time prince or prophet, or leader, or burnt-offering, or sacrifice, or oblation, or incense, or place to offer before thee, and to find mercy. Nevertheless, in a contrite heart and a humble spirit let us be accepted; like as in burnt-offerings of rams and bullocks, and like as in ten thousand of fat lambs; so let our sacrifice be in thy sight this day . . ." Apart from these passages, however, this tendency does not appear further in the books of the Apocrypha, unless it is to be inferred by the silence regarding sacrifices in some of the books (*Jud.*, though passing references occur in iv. 14; xi. 1; xvi. 16; *Esther, Sus., Bel, Pr. of Manasses, Bar.* once in i. 10). The system is fully recognized and honoured in *I Macc., e.g.* i. 45, iii. 51; iv. 42 ff., 52 ff., and in *II Macc., e.g.* i. 8, 9, 18, 26; x. 3, 6, 7; xiii. 23; xiv. 31. The same is true of *II Esdr., e.g.* iii. 24; x. 19 ff., 46, although the sacrifices had ceased with the destruction of the Temple.[2]

V. The Doctrine of Sin

While the existence and wide prevalence of sin are recognized, more or less, in all our books (*e.g.* I Esdr. viii. 74 ff.; Tob. iii. 3; Song of the Three Children, 5, 6, 14; Jud. xi. 11; Esther xiii. 6; Wisd. xii. 10, 11; Bar. i. 21, 22; ii. 5, 12; Pr. of Manasses 9; but, owing to the nature of their contents, *I, II Macc.* cannot be expected to be occupied

---

[1] Harnack, *The Mission and Expansion of Christianity*, vol. I. pp. 50, 54 (1908).

[2] It is, however, worth pointing out that a prayer in the Jewish Liturgy (the " Eighteen Benedictions ") contains a petition that the sacrifices may be re-inaugurated. This is still used in the daily services of the Synagogue; it contains pre-Christian elements.

with the subject), a real doctrine of Sin is to be found only in *Ecclesiasticus* and *II Esdras*; it is, therefore, with these two books that we shall deal almost exclusively, so far as this subject is concerned.

The writers of both these books deal with what they conceive to be the *origin of Sin*; both trace it to the beginning of the human race, but in different ways. Ben-Sira says: " From a woman was the beginning of sin; and because of her we all die " (xxv. 24). In thus tracing the origin of Sin back to the Fall, and as its result, death, Ben-Sira differs in one respect from what the normal view of Jewish teachers was, namely, that both sin and death originated with *Adam*; but neither draws the conclusion that owing to the Fall sin was inherited by the whole human race. Similarly, the writer of Wisd. ii. 23, 24 says: " . . . Because God created man for incorruption, and in the likeness of his own proper being made He him; but by the envy of the devil death entered into the world . . ."; though not directly mentioned, Sin is obviously implied here. It is not until we come to the later book of *II Esdras* that we meet with the idea that the transmission of sin to the whole human race resulted from Adam's sin; in iii. 21, 22 it is said: " For the first Adam, bearing a wicked heart, transgressed, and was overcome; and not he only, but all they also that are born of him. Thus disease was made permanent; and the law was in the heart of the people along with the wickedness of the root; so the good departed away, and that which was wicked abode still." The seer evidently felt strongly on this, for he says elsewhere: " For a grain of evil seed was sown in the heart of Adam from the beginning, and how much wickedness hath it brought forth unto this time! and how much shall it yet bring forth until the time of threshing come! Ponder now by thyself, how great fruit of wickedness a grain of evil seed hath brought forth. When the ears which are without number shall be sown, how great a floor shall they fill! " (iv. 30–32). And, once more, in vii. 118 it is said: " O thou Adam, what hast thou done? For though it was thou that sinned, the evil is not fallen on thee alone, but upon all of us that come of thee." On the idea of the trans-

G

mission of Sin through the fall of Adam and the connexion between Sin and death, more will be said later;[1] at present we are concerned with the theories of the origin of Sin. Ben-Sira sees the beginning of sin in Eve; *Wisdom* holds that it originated with the devil; and *II Esdras*, while maintaining that it is to be traced back to Adam, is inconsistent, for he says, on the one hand, that Adam bore a wicked heart (iii. 21) and therefore sinned (vii. 118), but, on the other, he says that a grain of evil seed was sown in his heart (iv. 30); he does not say by whom it was sown, but obviously it must have existed before Adam, and he cannot therefore have been responsible for its origin. If this writer thought, with *Wisdom*, that this evil seed was sown by the devil, he apparently did not realize, any more than *Wisdom*, the dualism involved; if he thought, on the other hand, that it was sown by God (and iv. 10, 11 might imply this), then he was, in effect, in agreement with a second theory of the origin of Sin put forth by Ben-Sira, which is this: in his day there were those who directly imputed the origin of evil to God, and this attitude is condemned by Ben-Sira in the words: " Say not thou, It is through the Lord that I fell away, for thou shalt not do the things he hateth. Say not thou, It is he that causeth me to err, for he hath no need of a sinful man " (xv. 11, 12). But then he goes on to say: " God created man from the beginning, and placed him in the hand of his *Yetzer* (*i.e.* a technical term meaning the ' evil tendency '). If thou so desirest, thou canst keep the commandment, and it is wisdom to do his good pleasure " (xv. 14, 15); that is to say, by the exercise of his free-will man has the power to resist the evil tendency of his nature; but Ben-Sira does not seem to realize that if, according to his own statement, God placed man in the hand of the *Yetzer*, which is part of his nature, then the *Yetzer* must have been created by God; thereby unconsciously imputing the origin of evil to God. He says in another passage: " O evil tendency (*Yetzer*), wherefore wast thou created, to fill the face of the world with deceit ? " (xxxvii. 3),[2] thus directly imputing its creation to

[1] See Chap. viii.
[2] Cp. the Hebrew and Greek texts.

God; and equally pointed is xxxiii. 14, 15: "Good is set over against evil, and life over against death; so is the sinner over against the godly. And thus look upon all the works of the Most High; two and two, one against another." Though Ben-Sira combatted this doctrine of the evil *Yetzer* having been created by God, which the logic of his own argument forced him to admit, it is found in somewhat later times put forth authoritatively; for in the Midrash *Bereshith Rabba* xxvii, which has preserved so much ancient material, it is definitely stated that God created the evil *Yetzer*; in the Babylonian Talmud, too, *Kiddushin* 30*b* it is said: "I created the evil *Yetzer* (*Yetzer-ha-ra'*); I created for man (too) the Law as a means of healing. If ye occupy yourselves with the Law, ye will not fall into the power of it" (*i.e.* the evil *Yetzer*).[1]

It is small wonder that Ben-Sira, in his ponderings upon the great mystery, should have been dissatisfied with both these theories of the origin of evil. He has, therefore, a third theory which, for the practical man that he was, may have set his mind at rest on the subject; he says: "When the ungodly curseth Satan, he curseth his own soul. The whisperer defileth his own soul, and shall be hated whithersoever he goeth" (xxi. 27, 28). The words "his own soul" mean "himself"; here "Satan" is synonymous with evil and with the man himself; and taking the two verses together they mean that evil is of man's own making, he is not only responsible for his own sin, but he is himself its seat. In such a case it is not necessary to seek for any other origin of sin. Again, in xvii. 31 it is said: "What is brighter than the sun? Yet this faileth; and an evil man will think on flesh and blood"; the Syriac Version (the Hebrew is unfortunately not extant) reads for the second clause: "Even so man does not curb his inclination (= *Yetzer*), for he is flesh and blood." Tennant paraphrases the passage: "Even the sun darkens itself—the brightest thing in the world; how much more, then, frail man?" and adds that

---

[1] Quoted by Weber, *Jüdische Theologie*, p. 218 (1897). Contrast this view with Isa. xlv. 6, where "I create evil" means I originate physical evil as the instrument for the punishment of moral evil.

if Ben-Sira offers any excuse for man's depravity " it is that of his natural and essential frailty " but " never traced to an external cause." [1] The verse is undoubtedly a difficult one, but it does seem to point to the belief that sin originated in man (by which is not meant Adam); and that this belief was held by others is seen by such a passage as Enoch xcviii. 4: " I have sworn unto you, ye sinners, as a mountain does not become a slave and will not, nor a hill a handmaid of a woman, even so sin hath not been sent upon earth, and man of himself hath created it. . . ." On the other hand, it is true that apparently Ben-Sira thinks of Sin as something external to man: " The lion waiteth for its prey, so sins for them that work iniquity " (xxvii. 10): " Flee from sin as from the face of a serpent, for if thou draw near it will bite thee; the teeth thereof are the teeth of a lion, slaying the souls of men . . ." (xxi. 2, 3); but the probability is that Ben-Sira is using "lion" and "serpent" as metaphors for temptation, from which man must keep away if he would avoid sin.

On the subject of atonement for Sin it is again primarily to *Ecclesiasticus* that we must go; for though every reference to Sacrifices (see above) necessarily implies atonement, and though repentance, so prominent in the *Prayer of Manasses*, is a means of obliterating Sin, no book in the Apocrypha, other than *Ecclesiasticus*, contains definite utterances on the subject. The teaching of Ben-Sira may be briefly summarized thus: Like every orthodox Jew he recognized the atoning efficacy of sacrifices; he says, *e.g.*, that God chose Aaron " to bring near the burnt-offerings and the fat pieces, and to burn a sweet savour and a memorial, and to make atonement for the children of Israel " (xlv. 16, cp. xxxv. 7). But what is specially noteworthy in Ben-Sira is his emphasis on the right spirit in offering sacrifices and their uselessness if offered otherwise: " The sacrifice of an unrighteous man is a mocking sacrifice . . ." (see above, pp. 85 f. where this is quoted in full, and the other passages referred to). Sacrifices, if rightly offered, are, according to Ben-Sira, the chief means of atoning for Sin; there are others, but in considering these we come to the subject of the efficacy of works.

[1] In the *Journal of Theological Studies*, Vol. II. p. 212.

VI. The Doctrine of Works

It is again in *Ecclesiasticus* and *II Esdras* that we get detailed information on this subject; in the other books only incidental mention of it occurs.

On the doctrine of good works atoning for sin we have some striking illustrations in *Ecclesiasticus*: "He that honoureth his father maketh atonement for sins " (iii. 3); similarly in iii. 14, 15 it is said:

Alms given to a father shall not be blotted out,
And it shall stand firm as a substitute for sin;
In the day of trouble it shall be remembered,
Obliterating thine iniquities as heat the hoar-frost.

In Hebrew the word for " alms " is *tzedakah* " righteousness," the two had become synonymous since almsgiving was regarded as righteousness *par excellence*; so, too, in iii. 30:

A flaming fire doth water quench,
So doth almsgiving (*tzedakah*) atone for sin;

in the same way it is said in Tob. xii. 9 that alms " purge away all sin." But though almsgiving is the chief of works which atone for, or obliterate, sins, there are others which are also efficacious; among these is the forgiving of injuries; in Ecclus. xxviii. 1–7 we have a beautiful section on forgiveness in which verse 2 runs:

Forgive an injury (done) by thy neighbour,
And then when thou prayest, thy sins will be forgiven;

at first this looks like a parallel to the petition in the Lord's Prayer; but, in fact, there is a great difference; in the context (verse 5) Ben-Sira, in reference to the man who does not forgive, says:

He being flesh nourisheth wrath,
Who will make atonement for his sins?

The point is that he who does not forgive does not make atonement for his sins, the implication being that he who does forgive thereby makes atonement for sins (see verse 2);

the good work of forgiving atones for sins, and it is a work that man can fulfil, so that by his work his sins are atoned for. But that is very different from sins being forgiven by God; in the one case forgiveness of sin is effected by a work of man, in the other forgiveness is granted by the mercy of God, not in recognition of a work done by man, but because the man has become worthy of God's mercy; it is just the difference between human works and divine grace ("when 'ye shall have done all the things that are commanded you, say, We are unprofitable servants, we have done that which it was our duty to do," Luke xvii. 9).

Forgiveness, according to Ben-Sira, therefore, is a work which atones for sin. Another work of atoning efficacy is fasting; in xxxiv. 31 (26) reference is made to one who fasts "for his sins"; and in xviii. 22 it is said, almost in so many words, that death atones for sins:

Let nothing hinder thee from paying thy vows in due time,
And wait not till death to be justified.

This belief in death being an atonement for sins meets us elsewhere in Jewish literature, *e.g.* in *Sifre* 33*a* (a very early *Midrash* on *Numbers* and *Deuteronomy*) it is said: "All who die are reconciled thereby." It may also be added that in the Jewish liturgy in the service of "Confession on a death-bed," it is said: "O may my death be an atonement for all my sins, iniquities, and transgressions of which I have been guilty against thee." [1]

In II Esdr. viii. 26–30 the idea is expressed of the sins of men being overlooked on account of the good works of the righteous; and in Ecclus. xlv. 23 it is said:

Moreover, Phinehas, the son of Eleazar,
Was glorious in might as the third [*i.e.* after Moses and Aaron],
In that he was jealous for the God of all,
And stood in the breach for his people,
While his heart prompted him,
And he made atonement for the children of Israel.

---

[1] In the Sephardic Ritual this is more fully expressed. Cp. also Rom. vi. 7: "For he that hath died is justified from sin."

As against this idea we have in Bar. ii. 19 the words:
" We do not present our supplications before thee, O Lord,
for the righteousness of our fathers, and of our kings." Such
a difference of opinion between different writers on the
subject of the efficacy of the merits of others we can well
understand; but the inconsistency which we find in such a
passage as II Esdras viii. 26–36 is more striking; and it is
also of great interest as showing how some thinkers were
perplexed about the subject; thus, in verses 26–30 there is
the thought of sins being pardoned because of the good works
of the righteous; in verses 31, 32 it is said that all men are
sinners and have no good works to their credit, for which
reason the divine mercy is appealed to; in verse 33 the
righteous, who have a treasury of good works laid up for
them, can use them only for their own reward; in verses 34,
35 it is said again that all men are sinners, and are not worthy
of thought; and in verse 36 God's mercy is again appealed
to on behalf of those who have no good works to their credit.
It seems unnecessary to suppose that these inconsistencies
arise owing to scribal interference with the text. The
difficulty of the subject is quite enough to explain the writer's
feelings of uncertainty.

Apart from this, however, there is one other point worth
referring to; good works, irrespective of their atoning
efficacy, bring their own reward; on the face of it, this is a
rational, common-sense attitude; but there is an element
here which must not be lost sight of: the two conceptions of
the divine transcendence, and the direct divine action in the
affairs of the world, are by no means necessarily opposed;
but that at times one should be unduly stressed at the expense
of the other, and *vice versa*, is not a thing to be wondered at;
to keep a sane balance in such things is not easy to most.
It can hardly be doubted that Ben-Sira, with his very
practical mind, would be inclined to represent those who
believed, perhaps in an exaggerated way, in the divine action
in the affairs of men (see *e.g.* xxxiii. 13). This would, to
some extent at least, affect men's estimate of the part they
had to play in shaping their destinies; if God's activity in the
world was such as to minimize that of man, then there was

the danger of an exaggerated quietism, as it were, leaving everything to God and, at the most, seeking to incline Him favourably by doing such good works as lay in man's power; in other words, by inducing God, through acts prescribed by the Law, which were pleasing to Him, to grant prosperity. Good works would thus assume the nature of a bribe. Not for itself, but what it can gain, would then be the motive-power behind doing what was right. In Ecclus. xvi. 14–16:

> Every one that doeth righteousness shall receive his reward,
> Yea, every man shall find it before him, according to his works.
> The Lord hardened the heart of Pharaoh who knew him not,
> Whose works were manifest under the heavens.
> His mercies are seen by all his creation,
> And his light and his darkness hath he apportioned unto the children of men.

The last four lines occur only in the Hebrew, not elsewhere, and it is possible that they are a later addition; but even so, it would be quite in keeping with Ben-Sira's view as expressed elsewhere, e.g. xxix. 11, 12:

> Lay up thy treasure according to the commandments of the Most High,
> And it shall profit thee more than gold.
> Store up alms in thy treasure-chambers,
> And it shall deliver thee from all affliction.

All prosperity and affliction, according to an over-stressed emphasis of divine action among men, come from God; good works deliver from affliction; hence good works have a utilitarian purpose. Similarly in Tob. iv. 10: "Alms delivereth from death, and suffereth not to come into darkness" (so, too, xii. 9).

There was, thus, clearly a danger of attributing to works an erroneous efficacy (cp. Matth. vii. 21, 22). On the other hand, it is only right to point out that Ben-Sira does here and there recognize the action of divine grace (e.g. ii. 17; xxxix. 6). Something further will be said on the subject of works in Chap. VIII.

VII. MESSIANISM

The doctrine of the Messiah and of the Messianic Age, with one notable exception, plays but a small part in the books of the Apocrypha. That is not to be wondered at, for Messianic hopes and expectations, and all that is involved in these, came mainly within the prophetic sphere of teaching, and, in later days, in that of the Apocalyptists. Apart from *II Esdras*, therefore, Messianism is hardly to be looked for in our body of literature; but in *II Esdras* it is fully treated. Elsewhere only incidental references occur; the belief, in varying form, was of course held, but it lay in the background. It will be best to deal with the subject under the following heads:

I. *Incidental References to the Messianic Age.*

The thought of this Age was evidently in the mind of Ben-Sira in writing:

Give the reward unto them that wait for thee,
That thy prophets may be shown to be faithful.
Hear the prayer of thy servants,
According to thy favour towards thy people;
That the ends of the earth may know
That thou art the eternal God (Ecclus. xxxvi. 17 (22)).

It will be noticed that there is no mention of the Messiah here; but that need not occasion surprise, for the prophets themselves often speak of the Messianic Age without mentioning the Messiah. This is also the case in Tob. xiv. 7: "And all the nations shall bless the Lord, and his people shall give thanks unto God, and the Lord shall exalt his people; and all they that love the Lord God in truth and righteousness shall rejoice, showing mercy to our brethren." It is possible that in Tob. xiii. 16–18 (cp. Isa. liv. 11, 12) the thought of the Messianic Age may have been in the mind of the writer.

The Messianic hope seems to be implicit in several passages in *Ecclesiasticus*, *e.g.* in xlvii. 22:

He will not cut off the posterity of his chosen,
And the offspring of them that love him he will not destroy;
And he gave Jacob a remnant,
And to the House of David a root from him.

It is especially the last line that suggests the thought of the Messianic hope (see also xlvii. 11; xlv. 25). In xlviii. 24, 25, where the prophecies of Isaiah are spoken of, Messianic hopes must have been in the mind of Ben-Sira:

By a spirit of might he saw the last times (τὰ ἔσχατα),
And comforted the mourners of Zion.
Unto eternity he declared the things that shall be,
And hidden things before they came to pass (see also
    xlix. 12 and cp. Hag. ii. 7, 9);

and similarly in the Thanksgiving (which in the Hebrew comes after li. 12):

Give thanks unto him that causeth a horn to sprout for the
    house of David,
    For his mercy endureth for ever.

II. *The Signs of the Advent of the Messianic Age.*

As is to be expected, it is in *II Esdras* that we get the most elaborate account, common, in varied form, to all the apocalyptic writings, of the weird and supernatural signs which shall immediately precede the coming of the " times of the Messiah." We get the most detailed account of these in II Esdr. iv. 51–v. 13. This passage is too long to quote in full; the signs are, briefly: great panic among men; disappearance of faith and truth; increase of iniquity; the land laid waste; the sun shining by night, the moon by day; blood trickling from wood, stones speaking. General commotion among the peoples; an unexpected ruler shall wield sovereignty (the Antichrist); the birds will fly away, the fish will be cast forth from the sea; in places the earth will open and fire will burst forth; wild beasts will desert their haunts; women will bear monsters; and will bear before the time; infants will talk; the produce of the fields will cease; salt water will turn sweet; friends will attack one another; understanding will be lost; evil of every kind will flourish; righteousness will disappear. Some of these "Messianic Woes" are repeated in vi. 20-24, and a brief summary occurs again in ix. 3, with comments on them by the Seer in the verses which follow.

After these signs the inauguration of the Messianic Era is heralded by the destruction of the Gentiles (II Esdr. xiii. 5, 8-11, 49; see also Ecclus. xxxvi. 6-8); but in Tob. xiii. 11 they come rejoicing with gifts in their hands for the "King of Heaven," and in II Esdr. xiii. 12, 13, too, this seems to be implied; such inconsistencies, even in one and the same writing, are not infrequently met with. On the other hand, there is always agreement regarding the ingathering of Israel at this time (II Esdr. vi. 25, 26; Tob. xiii. 5).

III. *The Felicity of the Messianic Age.*[1]

In II Esdr. vi. 25-28, in reference to what shall be when the "Messianic Woes" are past, it is said:

And it shall be that whosoever remaineth after all these things that I have told thee of, he shall be saved, and shall see my salvation, and the end of my world. And they shall see the men that have been taken up, who have not tasted death from their birth [*i.e.* Enoch and Elijah, cp. Ecclus. xlviii. 9; Wisd. iv. 10, 11]; and the heart of the inhabitants of the world shall be changed and shall be turned unto a different mind. For evil shall be blotted out, and deceit shall be quenched; and faithfulness shall flourish, and corruption shall be overcome, and truth, which hath been so long without fruit, shall be made manifest."

In II Esdr. viii. 52-54 that bright future is expressed thus:

For unto you is Paradise opened, the tree of life is planted, the time to come is prepared, plenteousness is made ready, a city is builded, and rest is established,

[1] We use this word in its widest sense without restricting it to a purely Jewish national conception.

goodness is perfected, wisdom being made perfect afore-
hand [cp. 1 Cor. ii. 7]. The root of evil is sealed up from
you, weakness is done away from you, and death is
hidden; Hades is fled away, and corruption forgotten;
sorrows are passed away; and in the end is manifested
the treasure of immortality (see also ix. 7 ff.).

In this passage the Messianic Age is eternal in Paradise,
but elsewhere it is conceived of as established on the earth,
and will last for four hundred years (II Esdr. vii. 28, see
below), while in ix. 8 it is placed in Palestine, " in my land,
and within my border" (cp. xii. 13, 34, 48). The inconsistencies are due to the difference of authorship of the
component parts of the book (see below, pp. 146 ff.), and also
to the varieties of tradition which have been incorporated.

IV. *The Messiah.*

Here again, for the reasons just given, there are different
conceptions. In II Esdr. xiii. 3 it is the heavenly Messiah
that is thought of, ". . . who flew with the clouds of
heaven," who sends out of his mouth " a flood of fire, and
out of his lips a flaming breath, and out of his tongue he
cast forth a storm of sparks " (verse 10), wherewith his
enemies are consumed. His pre-existence is spoken of in
xiii. 32. But elsewhere the Messiah is presented as human
in so far as, like all men, he dies, but this is after a reign of
four hundred years: " For my son the Messiah shall be
revealed with those that be with him, and shall rejoice them
that remain, four hundred years. After these years shall
my son the Messiah die, and all that have the breath of
life " (vii. 28, 29). The earthly Messiah appears again in
the " Eagle Vision " (II Esdr. xi. xii.); here he is symbolized
as a lion, who destroys the eagle, symbolizing the Roman
empire, and brings peace and joy to his people; the passage
is worth quoting:

> And the lion, whom thou sawest rising up out of the
> wood, and roaring, and speaking to the eagle, and rebuking
> her for her unrighteousness . . . this is the anointed one,
> whom the Most High hath kept unto the end of days,

who shall spring up out of the seed of David, and he shall come and speak unto them and reprove them for their wickedness and their unrighteousness, and shall set in order before them their contemptuous dealings. For at the first he shall set them alive for his judgement, and when he hath reproved them, he shall destroy them. For the rest of my people shall he deliver with mercy, those that have been preserved throughout my borders, and he shall make them joyful until the coming of the end, even the day of judgement.

These inconsistent conceptions regarding the Messianic Age and the Messiah are due, as we have said, partly to difference of authorship and partly to the incorporation of varying traditional material; but that the final compiler of the book should have deliberately embodied writings containing this contradictory Messianic teaching may at first sight cause surprise; it is, however, in reality highly significant; it has been admirably pointed out by Volz [1] that the value of the " Ezra Apocalypse " lies in the fact that it contains a twofold eschatological tradition; there is the Jewish national eschatology, and there is the later world-embracing eschatology, and the compiler, in incorporating both, has to attempt the task, of which there are signs in the book, of combining the two. The compiler was living at a period during which the later, developed type of world-embracing eschatology was appropriate, nevertheless he utilizes the old traditional eschatology; this was because he was faced with the twofold problem of the dire distress of his own people, and the universal state of sin and confusion in the world in general; he finds the solution of the former in the hope of the Messiah and the ancient national expectation of the Messianic kingdom; that of the latter in the later doctrine of the coming of a second world-age. Hence the incorporation by the compiler of different documents representing this twofold problem; hence also, to a large extent, the incongruities and inconsistencies found in his book. But what demands special notice is that the compiler

[1] *Die Eschatologie der jüdischen Gemeinde im neutestamentlichen Zeitalter*, p. 30 (1934).

is more oppressed by the problem of the bigger issue, *i.e.*
the wickedness of the world, and its solution, than by that
of his people's distress and its remedy; for this reason it is
the coming of a new world-order which he places in the
forefront, whereas the Messianic kingdom is relegated to a
secondary position, a kind of interim kingdom; and he goes
so far as to contemplate the death of the Messiah, as we
have seen; indeed, in one passage (vi. 7–10) he eliminates
a Messianic kingdom altogether. All this shows that the
whole traditional Messianic conception has, for our compiler,
lost, to a great extent, its importance and significance.

VIII. The Hereafter

Inasmuch as the period covered by the books of the
Apocrypha is, roughly, B.C. 200–100 A.D., a period during
which developments regarding the conceptions about the
Hereafter took place, it is precisely what is to be expected
when we find a great variety of ideas on this subject.

I. *The Traditional Sheol-belief.*

This ancient, normal, belief of the Old Testament regarding the Hereafter meets us fairly frequently in this literature;
thus, in Tob. iii. 6, where Tobit expresses his desire to die,
he prays: " Command that I be now released from my
distress, and go to the everlasting place"; that by this
expression is meant Sheol (= Hades) is evident from iii. 10,
where it is said: ". . . and I shall bring down his old age
with sorrow to Hades " (cp. xiii. 2). Similarly Ben-Sira, in
a somewhat Epicuræan strain, says: " Give and take, and
indulge thy soul, for in Sheol there is no seeking of luxury "
(xiv. 16); and elsewhere in speaking of death which soon
overtakes sinners, he says:

The way of sinners is made smooth, without stones,
And the end thereof is the pit of Hades (xxi. 10,
Hades = Sheol; the Hebrew of the passage is not extant).

The forlorn condition of the spirit, or rather " shade," of

the departed in Sheol, quite in conformity with Old
Testament belief, is expressed in xvii. 28:

Thanksgiving perisheth from the dead as from one that
existeth not;

see also xxii. 11; and in xli. 4 Ben-Sira seems to take a
certain comfort in the thought of Sheol, for, as he says:

In Sheol there are no reproaches concerning life.

And yet, in entire contradiction with the ordinary Sheol
conception, he refers, thereby adopting the very ancient
pre-Sheol belief, to the consulting of the departed spirit of
Samuel:

And even after his death he was enquired of,
And he declared to the king his fate;
And he lifted his voice from the earth . . . (xlvi. 20).

But the normal Sheol conception occurs again in Bar. ii. 17:
". . . for the dead that are in Hades, whose breath is taken
from their bodies, will give unto the Lord neither glory nor
righteousness"; so, too, in the Prayer of Manasses, verse 13:
" Be not angry with me for ever, neither condemn me into
the lower parts of the earth."

II. *The Intermediate State.*

In a few passages in *II Esdras* and *II Maccabees* the old Sheol
conception undergoes a development in that it is described
as a place of temporary abode of both the righteous and the
wicked where they await the last Judgement; each, respectively, experience a foretaste of what their final destiny will
be. The main passage here is II Esdr. vii. 75–101, which
may be summarized thus: The seer says: " O Lord, shew
this also unto thy servant, whether after death, even now
when every one of us giveth up his soul, we shall be kept in
rest until those times come, in which thou shalt renew the
creation, or whether we shall be tormented forthwith";
the answer is that the wicked " shall wander and be in
torments forthwith, ever grieving and sad "; seven ways are
then described in which they shall suffer; among these is

that they shall see the reward laid up for the righteous, but shall also " consider the torment laid up for themselves in the last days." They will also see " the glory of the Most High before whom they have sinned whilst living, and before whom they shall be judged in the last times." The righteous, on the other hand, shall see with great joy " the glory of him who taketh them up "; they will " understand the rest which, being gathered in their chambers, they now enjoy with great quietness, guarded by angels, and the glory that awaiteth them in the last days." It is also shown unto them how " their face shall shine as the sun, and how they shall be made like unto the light of the stars, being henceforth incorruptible." In II Esdr. iv. 41, again, it is said that " the underworld (*infernum*) and the chambers of souls (cp. verse 35) are like the womb; for like as a woman that travaileth maketh haste to escape the anguish of the travail, even so do these places haste to deliver what hath been committed unto them from the beginning," *i.e.*, from all time these places have been prepared to receive the souls of the righteous pending their final destiny of bliss (see also xiv. 9). Once more, in II Macc. vi. 23 the martyr speaks of going to Hades; as he is one of the righteous, Hades (Sheol) must here denote an intermediate state before the time of resurrection spoken of elsewhere in this book (see below).

Here it must be added that the earthly Paradise, mentioned in the preceding section in connexion with the earthly Messiah, is also in some sense an intermediate state, though only for the righteous; the heavenly Paradise, on the other hand, is the place of eternal bliss, just as Gehenna is the place of eternal woe (Jud. xvi. 17; II Esdr. vii. 36; Wisd. iv. 19).

III. *The Judgement.*

A description of the Day of Judgement is thus given in II Esdr. vii. 39–44 :

This is a day that hath neither sun, nor moon, nor stars, neither cloud, nor thunder, nor lightning, neither wind, nor water, nor air, neither darkness, nor evening, nor morning, neither summer, nor spring, nor heat, nor winter, neither frost, nor cold, nor hail, nor rain, nor dew, neither moon, nor night, nor dawn, neither shining, nor brightness, nor light, save only the splendour of the glory of the Most High, whereby all shall see the things that are set before them; for it shall endure as it were a week of years. This is my judgement and its prescribed order (*constitutio ejus*).

This very extraordinary description of the Day of Judgement, which is to last for a week of years (cp. Dan. ix. 24, 25, where the seventy weeks = seventy weeks of years) is almost certainly derived from some traditional material, according to which the conditions at the end of the world will revert to what they were at the beginning : [1] " And the world shall be turned into the old silence seven days, like as in the first beginning; so that no man shall remain " (II Esdr. vii. 30; and cp. Gen. i. 2: "And the earth was waste and void "). Further, it may be conjectured that this traditional idea fell in with the writer's very pessimistic outlook; the world was evil, therefore before the new world can be created, the old corrupt one must be obliterated (cp. Rev. xxi. 1). Thus, in II Esdr. vii. 113, again, it is said: "But the day of judgement shall be the end of this age, and the beginning of the eternal age to come (*futuri immortalis temporis*, the reference is to unending time, not to the immortality of man, as suggested by the Revised Version): wherein corruption is passed away. . . ."

Another reference to the Judgement, explaining why it must be held, occurs in II Esdr. vii. 21-25, cp. verse 73. The central Person, the Judge, is spoken of in II Esdr. vii. 33, 34: "And the Most High shall be revealed upon the seat of judgement, and compassion shall pass away, and longsuffering shall be withdrawn; but judgement only shall remain . . ." According to Wisd. iii. 7 the righteous will be joyous even in the Day of Judgement:

---

[1] On the whole subject see Gunkel, *Schöpfung und Chaos in Urzeit und Endzeit* (1895).

H

And in the time of their visitation they shall shine forth,
And as sparks among stubble shall they run to and fro;

but the wicked shall have "no consolation in the day of decision," *i.e.* the Judgement (iii. 18).

IV. *The Resurrection.*

We may note first a few passages in which a general belief in immortality occurs; in Wisd. v. 15 it is said:

> But the righteous shall live for ever,
> And in the Lord is their reward,
> And the care of them is with the Most High (cp. viii. 13, 17).

Similarly, in II Macc. ii. 18: "In God have we hope, that he will quickly have mercy on us, and gather us together from under the heavens into the holy place."

A little doubtful, though worth quoting, is Tob. xiii. 1. 2:

> Blessed is God that liveth for ever,
> And blessed is his kingdom;
> For he scourgeth, and showeth mercy,
> He leadeth down to Hades, and bringeth up again . . .
>   (cp. verse 14).

The last line may merely mean that God brings men near to the grave, but saves them from actual death.

The *resurrection of the spirit* is directly mentioned, or indirectly implied, in a number of passages in *Wisdom*; the best-known instance is in iii. 1 ff.:

> But the souls ($\psi\upsilon\chi\alpha\iota$) of the righteous are in the hands of God,
> And there shall no torment touch them . . .

The Greek $\psi\upsilon\chi\acute{\eta}$ (*psyché*) is the equivalent of the Hebrew *nephesh* "soul," while the Greek $\pi\nu\epsilon\hat{\upsilon}\mu\alpha$ (*pneuma*, "spirit") is equivalent to the Hebrew *ruaḥ* ("spirit"); it is necessary that we should be clear in regard to the meaning of these words. The matter has been well set forth by Kautzsch in

Hastings' *Dict. of the Bible*, Vol. V. p. 666, and his words
are well worth quoting:

> The habit of putting upon the Old Testament a
> trichotomous view of human personality was due almost
> entirely to a false conception of the *nephesh* and its relation
> to the *ruaḥ*. This distinction between "soul" and
> "spirit" naturally caused the actually existing trichotomy
> of body (or flesh) and spirit of life, to be missed. The
> real state of things is as follows: As long as the divine
> breath of life is outside man, it can never be called
> *nephesh*, but only *ruaḥ* (more completely, *ruaḥ ḥayyim*, *i.e.*
> spirit, or breath, of life, in which sense we find also
> *nishmath ḥayyim* used, *e.g.* Gen. ii. 7). On the other
> hand, the breath of life which has entered man's body,
> and manifests its presence there may be called either
> *ruaḥ* or *nephesh*. The two alternate in poetical parallelism
> in such a way that the same functions are attributed at
> one time to the *nephesh* and at another to the *ruaḥ*.

When, therefore, in the passage before us the "souls" of
the righteous are spoken of, it is the spirit, as we understand
this, that is meant; and the same applies to other passages
in this book, in which the resurrection of the *body* is never
taught, see ii. 22–24; iv. 13, 14; vi. 17–20.

On the other hand, we meet with a number of passages
in *II Maccabees* and *II Esdras* in which the resurrection of
the body is clearly believed in. Thus, in the account of the
martyrdom of the mother's seven sons (chap. vii) one of
them says: ". . . but the King of the world shall raise up
us who have died for his laws, unto an eternal renewal of
life." That the body, in the most material sense, is meant
comes out in the words of the next martyr: "And when he
was required, he quickly put out his tongue and stretched
forth his hands courageously, and nobly said, From heaven
I possess these; and for his laws' sake I contemn these, and
from him I hope to receive these back again" (verses 10
11; see also verses 22, 23, 29, 36). Once more, in II Macc.
xii. 43, 44: ". . . he sent unto Jerusalem to offer a sacrifice

for sin, doing therein right well and honourably, in that he took thought for a resurrection. If he were not expecting that they that had fallen would rise again, it were superfluous and idle to pray for the dead." The same belief is expressed in II Esdr. vii. 32 : "And the earth shall restore those that are asleep in her, and so shall the dust those that dwell therein in silence, and the chambers shall restore those souls that were committed unto them "; again in verse 37 : "And then shall the Most High say to the nations that are raised from the dead . . ." In this passage the wicked, *i.e.* the nations, partake in the resurrection, but are immediately consigned to punishment; in II Macc. vii. 14, on the other hand, it is said : "It is good to die at the hands of men, and look for the hopes which are given by God, that we shall be raised up again by him; but as for thee (*i.e.* the king, Antiochus iv), thou shalt have no resurrection unto life." There is not always consistency in the apocalyptic literature regarding this subject.

IX. ANGELOLOGY

The frequent mention of angels in the books of the Apocrypha witnesses to a widespread belief in their activity. But the angelology which we meet with here is almost entirely of a popular character; the more sober official doctrine receiving only moderate notice.

The subject may be conveniently divided into : (i) angelic activity on this earth, and (ii) the functions of angels in the realms above; corresponding roughly to the popular and official views.

I. *Angelic Activities on Earth.*

Naturally enough, as we are dealing with Jewish beliefs, whatever it is that angels accomplish on earth, they are always the instruments of God, sent to carry out His will (Tob. iii. 17, xii. 18; Ep. of Jer. vi. 7; Bel and the Dragon, 34; II Macc. xi. 6; II Esdr. iv. 1).

The most elaborate picture of popular angelology occurs in the book of *Tobit*; here the angel is called Raphael : " I

am Raphael, one of the seven holy angels . . ." (xii. 15);
but he is not known to be an angel (v. 4), and gives himself
the name of Azarias (v. 12). He accompanies Tobias, the
son of Tobit, on his journey to Media, and helps him in a
variety of ways (v. 4, 16, 21; vi. 3 ff.; viii. 2, 3; ix. 1 ff.).
It must, of course, be remembered that *Tobit* is a folk-tale,
and the quaint things that are said about the angel (vi. 1–8,
10 ff., ix. 5) must be taken in this sense; in fact, the writer
himself makes the angel say, at the end of the story: "All
these days did I appear unto you; and I did neither eat
nor drink, but ye saw a vision" (xii. 19).

More fantastic is the story told about the angel in Bel and
the Dragon 33–39, who carries the prophet Habakkuk from
Palestine to Babylon, and back, by the hair in order that
he might give his dinner to Daniel in the lions' den.

In *Susanna*, again, 59 ff., an angel with a drawn sword
appears at the time when the two elders are pronounced
guilty, and casts fire upon them.

But it is in *II Maccabees* that we find the most elaborate
activity of angels in the affairs of men. Here we have, first,
the story of the attempt of Heliodorus, the chancellor of the
Syrian king, to plunder the Temple treasury; it is recounted
how, on entering the treasury,

> the Sovereign of spirits and of all authority caused a
> great apparition, so that all that had presumed to come in
> with him, stricken with dismay at the power of God,
> fainted and were sore afraid. For there was seen by them
> a horse with a terrible rider upon him, and adorned with
> beautiful trappings, and he rushed fiercely and smote at
> Heliodorus with his forefeet; and it seemed that he that
> sat upon the horse had complete armour of gold. Two
> others also appeared unto him, young men, notable in their
> strength, and beautiful in their glory, and splendid in their
> apparel, who stood by him on either side, and scourged
> him unceasingly, inflicting on him many sore stripes
> (iii. 22–26).

Heliodorus falls down in a faint, and all are filled with
terror; but Onias the High Priest brings a sacrifice for his

recovery, whereupon the apparition again appears before Heliodorus, bidding him give thanks to Onias who by his act had saved his life. Heliodorus then offers sacrifice to God, and, on his return home, proclaims what God had done for him (verses 27–36).

Another interesting illustration occurs in x. 29–31, during the battle between Judas Maccabæus and Timotheus the Syrian general:

> When the battle waxed strong, there appeared out of heaven unto their adversaries five men on horses with bridles of gold, in splendid array, leading on the Jews, and taking Maccabæus in the midst of them, and covering him with their own armour, guarded him from wounds, while on the adversaries they shot forth arrows and thunderbolts; by reason whereof they were blinded and thrown into confusion, and were cut to pieces, filled with bewilderment . . . (see also xv. 22–27).

In all these cases we have the idea of a national guardian angel, probably reflected already in Ecclus. xvii. 17:

> For every nation he appointed a ruler,
> But Israel is the Lord's portion.

In the Septuagint of Deut. xxxii. 8, 9 it is said: " When the Most High divided the nations, when he scattered the sons of Adam, he set bounds of the nations according to the number of the angels of God. And the Lord's portion was his people Jacob, the lot of his inheritance was Jacob." In the *Targum of pseudo-Jonathan* to Gen. xi. 7, 8 it is said that every nation has its own guardian angel who pleads the cause of the nation under his protection before God. In Dan. xii. 1 it is said: " And at that time shall Michael stand up, the great prince which standeth for the children of thy people "; similarly Michael is said to be Israel's guardian angel in the *Yalkut Shimeoni, Bereshith* 132.

A different function of angelic activity on earth meets us all through II Esdr. iii–x (The " Ezra Apocalypse "), where Uriel the archangel (iv. 36) instructs the seer regarding his visions.

II. *Angelic Activities in the Realms Above.*

This subject receives far less attention in our books. In II Esdr. vii. 85, 95 angels are said to guard the righteous in the intermediate state. Elsewhere it is in Heaven that their activities are referred to; in Tob. xii. 15 it is said that they " present the prayers of the saints, and go in before the glory of the Holy One " (cp. viii. 15). Ben-Sira, in praising the works of God, says:

The holy ones of God [*i.e.* the angels] have not the power
To recount the wondrous works of his might (xlii. 17).

See also II Esdr. viii. 21 and the Prayer of Manasses 15, where the presence of the angels in Heaven is spoken of.

X. DEMONOLOGY

It is somewhat remarkable that in view of the deep-seated belief in demons and their baneful activities among men, there should be such an extremely small notice of the subject in the books of the Apocrypha which otherwise so often reflect popular conceptions. But the fact is undeniable that demons are scarcely ever mentioned. The outstanding exception is the book of *Tobit*. Here Asmodæus,[1] the evil demon, plays a prominent and ominous part (iii. 8, 9), though an end is put to his evil doings by the angel (iii. 7, vi. 15), quaint as the means employed no doubt are (vi. 16, 17; viii. 2, 3). There is a passage in Ecclus. xxxix. 28 ff., which in all probability implies demonic activity (knowing as we do from other sources [2] the beliefs about demons), though they are not actually mentioned:

There are winds that are created for vengeance,
    And in their wrath lay on their scourges heavily;
And in the time of the end they pour out their strength,
    And appease the wrath of him that created them.

[1] See below, p. 166.   [2] *E.g.* often in the *Book of Enoch.*

Fire and hail, famine and pestilence,
  These also are created for judgement.
Beasts of prey, scorpions and vipers . . . [1]

It is exceedingly probable that we have here an echo of
earlier Babylonian beliefs regarding demons, of which there
are traces in the Old Testament.   Ashakku was the demon
who brought burning fever, there were special storm demons,
and the pest demons were Labartu and Namtaru; there was
also the demon of death, and many others.   In addition to
Babylonian influence there is every reason to believe that
both Persia and Egypt contributed their quota to belief in
demons among the Jews.   The mention of Satan, moreover
(Ecclus. xxi. 27), and the devil (Wisd. ii. 24) implies a belief
in demons as his army of subordinates.[2]   In Tob. iv. 7
sacrifices to demons are mentioned (cp. Deut. xxxii. 17),
and see also verse 35.

Thus, while it cannot be doubted that belief in the activity
of demons was widespread, the references to them in our
books are exceedingly scanty; in fact, in most of the books
they are not mentioned at all.

[1] Cp. *Test. xii Patr.* Levi. iii. 2: " . . . And it [*i.e.* the lowest heaven] has
fire, snow, and ice made ready for the day of judgement, in the righteous
judgement of God; for in it are all the spirits of the retributions for vengeance
on men."
[2] Cp. Enoch liv. 5, 6.

CHAPTER VIII

THE IMPORTANCE OF THE APOCRYPHA FOR THE STUDY OF THE NEW TESTAMENT

THE doctrinal teaching contained in the Apocrypha, dealt with in the preceding chapter, will have suggested a number of points of contact with important matters of Christian belief as set forth in the New Testament. The fact that we have in this body of literature what constitutes in many respects the background of the New Testament is sufficient to show its importance for the study of the latter. It is essential to recognize that the books of the Apocrypha are not isolated literary pieces thrown up at haphazard, but that they place before us the expression of the spirit of a people in a living development, and definitely related to that development, the continued process of which may be seen in the New Testament writings.

The books of the Apocrypha were written, some before, some during, and one at least (though embodying earlier thought and teaching) at the end of the first Christian century; the period, that is, during which the New Testament writings were composed. The writers of those books represent different types of Jews and different schools of thought. Ben-Sira was an orthodox Jew, more or less, with a leaning towards Sadduceeism, however, rather than Pharisaism. The writers of the books of *Tobit*, *Judith*, and others, were Jews of the more strictly Pharisaic type; the book of *Wisdom* represents the standpoint of the Hellenistic Jew; and the writings comprised in *II Esdras* are those of the Apocalyptic school of thinkers, orthodox in the main, but holding views which in some particulars were distasteful to official Pharisaism. Similarly in the New Testament, the Gospels contain much that deals with Sadduceeism, Pharisaism, and Apocalyptic; and in the Pauline epistles and other writings vital doctrinal questions receive much attention, a number of them being precisely the same as those which exercised the minds of the writers of the Apocrypha.

It is, thus, obvious that a body of literature which contains Jewish thought and teaching as these existed at the beginning of the Christian era, and with which, as the New Testament shows, the early Jewish Christians were familiar, must offer much that is of interest and importance for the study of the New Testament.

This is not the place to work out in detail the parallels, the developments, and the contrasts, between the Apocrypha and the New Testament; but it is worth while to indicate certain subjects which play an important part in the doctrinal teaching of each.

I. First, as to the *Law*. We have seen in the preceding chapter the supreme position assigned to the Law, and its literal observance, in the Apocrypha generally. This represents the Pharisaic belief and practice regarding the Law. It need hardly be pointed out that our Lord, in spiritualizing the Law, changed its whole nature; so that here we have a contrast between the Apocrypha and the New Testament which is fundamental; the former illustrates the general background of the Gospels in this particular. On the other hand, it must in fairness be recognized that a conception of the Law in a non-Pharisaic sense is observable here and there in the Apocrypha, see especially II Esdr. iii. 22, ix. 36, where the Law is represented as inadequate to save from sin; this approximates to St. Paul's teaching in Rom. viii. 3, 4: " For what the Law could not do, in that it was weak through the flesh, God sending His own Son in the likeness of sinful flesh, and as an offering for sin, condemned sin in the flesh; that the ordinance of the law might be fulfilled in us, who walk not after the flesh, but after the spirit " (cp. Gal. ii. 21).

For the higher conception of the Law as compared with that of the Apocrypha nothing could be more instructive than what is said in Rom. ii. 17–29, iii. 19. The value of the Apocrypha on this subject lies in the fact that we find there, especially in *Ecclesiasticus*, both the abstract ideas of

the Law, as well as the details of its observance, as these
existed during the New Testament period; it forms the
background, and enables us to understand the significance
of so much that is written in the New Testament about the
Law.

II. Closely connected with this is the subject of *Works*.
The fulfilment of the works of the Law, the merit acquired
thereby, and therefore justification, present us again with a
Pharisaic doctrine which is sharply combatted in the New
Testament. In Tob. iv. 7–11, for example, it is said:
" Give alms of thy substance . . . if thou have little, be not
afraid to give alms according to that little; for thou layest
up a good treasure for thyself against the day of necessity,
because alms delivereth from death, and suffereth not to
come into darkness. Alms is a good gift in the sight of the
Most High for all that give it " (see also, xiv. 11). This is
brought out more fully in a number of passages in *Ecclesiasticus*; we have seen that good works atone for sin (see above,
pp. 91 f.); he who accomplishes good works is "righteous"
(*tzaddik*), *i.e.* one who is justified in the sight of God (cp. xi.
17); his state of justification is due to his good works (cp.
iii. 31; xi. 27; xvii. 22; xxix. 9; xxxi. 9, 10, etc.; II Esdr.
viii. 33). With these widespread ideas among the Jews
contrast the words of St. Paul: " By the works of the Law
shall no flesh be justified in his sight " (Rom. iii. 20); " We
reckon therefore that a man is justified by faith apart from
the works of the law " (Rom. iii. 28); " This only would I
learn from you, Received ye the Spirit by the works of the
law, or by the hearing of faith? " (Gal. iii. 2). It is quite
exceptional, indeed, unique, in the Apocrypha, when we find
the thought expressed that divine mercy may be extended
to such as have no works to their credit: " For if thou hast
a desire to have mercy upon us, then shalt thou be called
merciful, to us, namely, that have no works of righteousness "
(II Esdr. viii. 32). This again approximates to the teaching
of St. Paul; but the passage is remarkable, and does not
reflect the normal teaching of the Apocrypha on the subject.
Many other quotations in the opposite sense from the Apocrypha could be given, illustrating the belief in the efficacy of

works, as well as from the New Testament, showing the error of this belief; but this is unnecessary. We see again, with the one exception mentioned, the religious environment of the early Jewish-Christians reflected in the books of the Apocrypha.

III. Of special importance is the doctrine of *Sin*, for in one direction, *i.e.* the doctrine of the Fall, there are points of attachment between St. Paul and *II Esdras*; most of the relevant passages from this book have been quoted above (pp. 86 ff.); here it may be pointed out that, according to the Seer, the entry of physical death into the world is directly connected with the Fall; after Adam sinned it is said: " Forthwith thou appointedst death for him and for his generation " (*i.e.* the human race descended from him, ii. 7, and cp. verse 21), while a spiritual death occurred through the grain of evil seed sown in his heart, the *yetzer ha-ra'* (" the evil tendency," see iv. 30–32). With this compare St. Paul's words in Rom. v. 12: " Through one man sin entered into the world, and death through sin; and so death passed unto all men." According to St. Paul it was through the deliberate act of the will that the Fall took place; this is not quite the same as the Seer's view, who traces the Fall to the evil inclination of man's heart; yet the difference is not fundamental:

There is no fundamental inconsistency between his (St. Paul's) views and those of his contemporaries. He does not indeed either affirm or deny the existence of the *cor malignum* before the Fall, nor does he use such explicit language as " but each one of us has been the Adam of his own soul "[1]; on the other hand, he does define more exactly than the Rabbis the nature of human responsibility both under the Law (Rom. vii. 7 ff.) and without it (Rom. ii. 12–15). But here, as elsewhere in dealing with this mysterious subject, he practically contents himself with leaving the two complementary truths side by side. Man inherits his nature; and yet he must not be allowed to shift responsibility from himself; there is that within him

[1] *Apoc. of Baruch* liv. 19.

by virtue of which he is free to choose; and on that freedom of choice he must stand or fall.[1]

A point of less importance, but not without interest, is the belief that the merits of the patriarchs can atone for sin: " Cause not thy mercy to depart·from us, for the sake of Abraham that is beloved of thee and for the sake of Isaac thy servant, and Israel thy holy one " (Prayer of Azarias 12) ; the overlooking of sin is implicit here. This doctrine of the merits of the fathers is fully recognized in Rabbinical literature. But in one passage (Manasses 8) there seems to be a tendency to modify this : " Thou therefore, O Lord, that art the God of the righteous, hast not appointed repentance unto the righteous, unto Abraham, and Isaac, and Jacob; but thou hast appointed repentance unto me that am a sinner " ; here one would naturally expect the merits of the patriarchs to be appealed to; that this is not done suggests that their merits were inefficacious. This recalls Luke iii. 8 to mind: " Bring forth therefore fruits worthy of repentance, and begin not to say within yourselves, We have Abraham to our father; for I say unto you that God is able of these stones to raise up children unto Abraham."

Once more, the traditional doctrine of the sins of the fathers being visited upon the children is often implied, e.g. Jud. v. 17 ff., Bar. i. 13, iii. 4, 7, 8, and elsewhere; in contrast to this we have such a passage as John ix. 2, 3: " . . . Rabbi, who did sin, this man, or his parents, that he should be born blind? Jesus answered, Neither did this man sin, nor his parents; but that the works of God should be made manifest in him."

IV. On the subject of *Wisdom* (= the *Logos* according to Wisd. iv. 1, and Philo) there is much in *Ecclesiasticus, Wisdom,* and *II Esdras,* which is important for the study of the background of John i. 1–14. A proper investigation of this would take us too far afield, especially as it would involve a discussion on the Philonian doctrine of the *Logos.* Our present purpose is merely to point to various ways in which the books of the Apocrypha are important for New Testament study.

[1] Sanday and Headlam, *The Epistle to the Romans,* p. 138 (1914).

On this particular subject it must, therefore, suffice merely to indicate certain passages in each body of literature; when these are read in conjunction with one another it will at once be seen wherein the importance of the Apocrypha passages lies. The following passages, which are not exhaustive, should be considered in studying John i. 1–14: " By the word of God (are) his works," *i.e.* were his works created (Ecclus. xlii. 15), the context shows that the works of the Creation are meant. " O God of our fathers, and Lord of mercy, who hast made all things by thy word, and by thy wisdom didst form man . . ." (Wisd. ix. 1, 2); " word " and " wisdom " must be regarded as synonymous.[1] In II Esdr. vi. 38 it is said: " O Lord, of a truth thou spakest at the beginning of the creation, upon the first day, and saidst thus: Let heaven and earth be made; and thy word perfected the earth."

Again, in several of the Pauline epistles where wisdom or its antithesis is spoken of there is sometimes identity or similarity of thought between what the Apostle writes and what is said in the book of *Wisdom*; whether St. Paul was influenced by the earlier writer, or not, is immaterial from our present point of view. Here, of course, Wisdom is presented from a different standpoint from that just considered. Thus, there is much similarity of language, and in some ways parallelism of thought between what is said about wisdom in Wisd. vii. 22–viii, ix. 6, 9–17, and what St. Paul says about the influence of the Spirit in I Cor. ii. 6–16. In spite of great difference in detail one cannot fail to see some community of thought between Wisd. xiii–xv and Rom. i. 18–32, where the antithesis of wisdom, namely sin, in forms which are more particularly illustrative of folly, are dealt with.[2]

[1] Goodrick, wrongly, denies this. As Gregg says: " The passage is Hebrew in tone, recalling Ps. xxxiii, 5, 6, and no contrast is intended between the two clauses. They are parallel, and ' wisdom ' is used in the second as a poetic variant for ' word ' in the first . . . There is no contrast suggested between the functions of Wisdom and the Logos, as if the former were the agent in the making of man, and the latter in the making of things; for Wisdom is the ' artificer of all things ' (vii. 22, cp. viii. 6)." Similarly Holmes: " Word and Wisdom are here synonymous."

[2] The whole subject is dealt with in detail by Grafe, *Das Verhältnis der paulinischen Schriften zur Sapientia Salomonis*, esp. pp. 251–286 (1892), and by

V. Next there are some matters connected with *Eschatology* regarding which the teaching in some of the books of the Apocrypha offers material of decided interest to the student of the New Testament.

In the Synoptic Gospels, as is well known, there are certain apocalyptic passages in which are described the " signs " of the last times; it is unnecessary to quote these; their purport is familiar (*e.g.* Mark xiii., Matth. xxiv. 29–31). In II Esdr. v. 1–12, vi. 21–24, vii. 39–42 descriptions of these " woes of the Messiah " are given; and we have here echoes of traditional beliefs which lie behind the eschatological picture contained in the Gospels.

In Wisd. ix. 15 it is said: " For a corruptible body weigheth down the soul; and the earthly tabernacle oppresseth the care-laden mind "; this is strongly reminiscent of II Cor. v. 1: " For we know that if the earthly house of our tabernacle (' earthly frame ') be dissolved, we have a building from God, a house not made with hands, eternal in the heavens " (cp. also the verses which follow, where the Apostle shows the fuller Christian belief). It is of profound interest to compared the teaching on immortality in Wisd. iii. 1–9; v. 15, 16 with such passages as, *e.g.* I Cor. xv.; II Cor. v. 1–10.

A further interesting point of comparison is the materialistic conception of the risen body in II Macc. vii. 10, 11, 22, 23; xiv. 46, and St. Paul's teaching on the risen spiritual body (I Cor. xv. 44).

VI. Finally, a few points of contact between the books of the Apocrypha and the New Testament, of a more general character, may be mentioned, as being not without interest.

In II Esdr. vi. 26 reference is made to " the men who had been taken up, and have not tasted death from their birth. . . . Then shall the heart of the inhabitants (of the world) be changed into a different mind " (or, spirit).[1] That Moses

---

Focke, *Die Enstehung der Weisheit Salomos*, pp. 113 ff. (1913). Each of these writers, as it seems to us, exaggerates his own standpoint in their opposing views, the former in favour, the latter against, affinities between St. Paul and *Wisdom*.

[1] This is doubtless what must be understood by: *et convertetur in sensum alium*.

and Elijah are meant here is obvious; this recalls what is said in the account of the Transfiguration of the appearance of Moses and Elijah (Mark ix. 4 ff., cp. Mal. iv. 4–6).

In Rom. ii. 4, the words: ". . . not knowing that the goodness of God leadeth thee to repentance," remind one forcibly of Pr. Man. 8: " Thou, O Lord, according to thy great goodness hast promised repentance and forgiveness to them that have sinned against thee." There is also a distinct community of thought between Hebr. i. 3 and Wisd. vii. 26; and Hebr. xi. 34, 35 seems to be based on I Macc. v. 1–7 and especially II Macc. vi. 18–31. The *Ep. of St. James* contains numerous points of contact with both Ecclus. and Wisd. (cp. also I Cor. ii. 10 with Jud. viii. 14).

It is quite possible that St. Paul was indebted to the writer of Wisd. xv. 7 for his metaphor of the potter in Rom. ix. 21: " Hath not the potter a right over the clay, from the same lump to make one part a vessel unto honour and another unto dishonour? " The *Wisdom* passage runs: " For the potter laboriously kneading the soft earth mouldeth each several thing for our service; but from the same clay doth he fashion both vessels which serve to clean uses, and those of a contrary sort, all in like manner; but what is to be the use of each of these the potter is judge "; see also Ecclus. xxxiii (xxxvi) 13. This is one of a number of other passages in the Pauline epistles (a few of which have been noted, see also Rom. i. 20–32 and Wisd. xii. 24) in which the Apostle seems to be influenced by the book of *Wisdom*; but so far as the *Ep. to the Romans* is concerned the remarks by Sanday and Headlam should be noted:

If St. Paul learnt from the Book of Wisdom some expressions illustrating the Divine power, and a general aspect of the question, he obtained nothing further. His broad views and deep insight are his own. And it is interesting to contrast a Jew who has learned many maxims which conflict with his nationalism but yet retains all his narrow sympathies, with the Christian Apostle full of broad sympathy and deep insight, who sees in human

affairs a purpose of God for the benefit of the whole world
being worked out.[1]

Again, the well-known passage in Eph. vi. 11–17 on " the
whole armour of God " has an interesting parallel in Wisd.
v. 17–20: " He shall take his jealousy as complete armour,
and make the creation his weapon for the repulse of his
enemies; he shall put on righteousness as a breastplate, and
array himself with judgement unfeigned as with a helmet;
he shall take holiness as an invincible shield, and shall
sharpen stern wrath as a sword." Doubtless both St. Paul
and the writer of *Wisdom* had Isa. lix. 17 in mind, but the
much closer parallel of the *Wisdom* passage with Eph. vi.
11–17 shows that, probably, St. Paul was indebted to *Wisdom*
here.

Once more; in II Esdr. vi. 58 the epithets " thy firstborn,"
" thy only begotten " are applied to the nation of Israel.
It is of interest to note that in Matth. ii. 15, " Out of Egypt
did I call my son," the Evangelist is applying to our Lord the
title " my son," in the sense of the Son of God, which in
Hos. xi. 1, from which the quotation is taken, is applied to
Israel; it hardly needs saying that " My son " in the
Christian sense, in reference to Christ, is equivalent to " the
first-born " (Rom. viii. 29) and " the only begotten " (John
i. 18). We have thus epithets originally applied to the
chosen nation transferred to Christ " the chosen of God "
(Lk. xiii. 35, cp. Isa. xlii. 1, " Behold, my servant whom I
have chosen ").

Two final small, but interesting, points; the idea of the
" regeneration " (Matth. xix. 28, cp. Rev. xxi. 1) of the world
occurs in II Esdr. vii. 75, " . . . those times in which thou
shalt renew the creation "; the thought is undoubtedly pre-
Christian.

Another old-world thought is that of the sounding of the
trumpet in heralding the advent of the last day and the
Judgement; this is referred to in II Esdr. vi. 23: " And the
trumpet shall sound aloud, at which all men when they
hear it shall be stricken with sudden fear "; similarly in

[1] *Op. cit.*, p. 269.

I

I Thess. iv. 16 " the trump of God" is to herald the resurrection, cp. I Cor. xv. 22.

The illustrations which have been given are far from exhaustive, but they will have shown in how many directions the books of the Apocrypha offer important material for the study of the New Testament.

CHAPTER IX

THE APOCRYPHA IN THE CHURCH

THE settlement of many Jews during the last three pre-Christian centuries in various parts of the Greek-speaking world, especially in Egypt, and the hellenization of Palestine itself, resulted in great numbers of Jews being unable to understand their Scriptures in their original language. Hence arose the need of translating the Hebrew Scriptures into Greek. The work of translation was begun about the latter half of the third century B.C. in Alexandria, when the Pentateuch was given to the Jews in a Greek form. In course of time the other books were translated, but it is not known at what dates. By the year B.C. 132, however, most of the Old Testament had been translated, since in this year the grandson of Ben-Sira translated his grandfather's book, *Ecclesiasticus*, and in the prologue of his translation mentions that " the Law, and the Prophets, and the rest of the books " were current in Greek at that time. But the Greek Bible consisted not only of the books of the Hebrew Bible as we now have it, but of a number of others which were added from time to time, and which were all regarded as belonging to the Scriptures. That Ben-Sira reckoned his book as Scripture is clear from his words: " And I, last of all, came as one that gleaneth after the grape-gatherers. By the blessing of the Lord I made progress, and, as a grape-gatherer, filled my winepress. Consider that I laboured not for myself alone, but for all who seek instruction. Hearken unto me, ye great ones of the people; and ye rulers of the congregation, give ear to me " (Ecclus. xxxiii. 16–18). Other books were added after his time, some translated from Hebrew, others written in Greek; these were also regarded as Scripture. While some of the books of this Greek Bible were held in greater veneration than others, all were included

under the category of the Scriptures; the idea of separating
off some as specially holy, and putting them into a class by
themselves, had not yet arisen. Thus, the books of our
Apocrypha, or most of them, ranked with the rest of the
books of the Old Testament as Scripture. This was the
Bible of the Jews of the Dispersion, and there is no reason to
doubt that it was also used by the Greek-speaking Jews of
Palestine. On the other hand, among the Aramaic-speaking
Jews the Scriptures, when read in the synagogue, were read
in Hebrew, and translated into Aramaic, verse by verse if
the passage was from the Pentateuch, three verses at a time if
from the Prophets. We are, however, concerned only with
the Bible in Greek, the work of the Alexandrian Jews;
and this was the Bible which was taken over by the Church.
In the words of Swete:

> As a whole, the work of translation was doubtless carried
> out in Alexandria, where it was begun; and the Greek
> Bible of the Hellenistic Jews and the Catholic Church
> may rightly be styled the Alexandrian Greek version of the
> Old Testament.[1]

In the early days of the Church the Septuagint was widely
used among the Jews; as a rule, though there are exceptions,
when the Old Testament is quoted in the New Testament it
is from the Greek, not the Hebrew, Bible that the quotation
is made. The early Jewish-Christians and the great majority
of the Jews had the same Bible, and Gentile converts,
obviously, could use no other Bible. It was not until after
the Fall of Jerusalem that the attitude of the Jewish religious
leaders towards the Greek Bible changed. There were
reasons for this; in the first place, the rift between the
Jewish and Christian communities had, even before this,
become pronounced; the Greek Bible, as the Bible of the
Christians, was a reason for it to be looked upon with disfavour by the Jewish Church; this was emphasized by the
fact that passages from the Greek Bible were used by Christians to demonstrate the falseness of Jewish views; the Jewish
religious leaders, having their Hebrew Scriptures, saw the

[1] *Introduction to the Old Testament in Greek*, p. 27 (1900).

numerous differences between these and their Greek form, some of which were used against the Jews by the Christians. Further, the movement, which had long been proceeding, towards the formation of a Canon, now became urgent, and for various reasons many books contained in the Septuagint were regarded as unworthy of being included in what was now becoming the Jewish Canon. This increased the antipathy felt towards the Septuagint.[1] The Greek and Hebrew Bibles thus became, respectively, those of the Christian and the Jewish Church.

Before we come to deal with the use of the books of the Apocrypha in the Christian Church, it may not be amiss if a few words be devoted to the question as to why these books were excluded from the Hebrew Canon when the reading of them had not been forbidden; doubtless they stood in a different category from the Pentateuch and the prophetical books; but there is no reason for doubting that, together with the " Writings," and probably many other books which have not come down to us, they were read as offering material for religious instruction and edification. Why, then, were they denied canonicity when others, unworthy of it, were included in the Canon?

The reasons varied for the different books. A few would not in any case come into consideration, as they were not written until after the Hebrew Canon had, in effect, been formed; this applies to *II Esdras* (the apocalyptic character of which would have been sufficient to condemn it), and probably also to *Baruch*, the *Epistle of Jeremiah*, and the *Prayer of Manasses*. The exclusion of *I Esdras* may have been due to the fact that the Hebrew form, for long familiar, was believed to be a purer form; perhaps also the extraneous elements met with disfavour. This last may possibly have been the reason why *Tobit* was excluded, assuming that it was known to the Jewish authorities that the extraneous elements were really such; otherwise it is not easy to under-

---

[1] The Jewish form of the Greek Bible translated by Aquila (*circa* 130 A.D.) was undertaken for polemical reasons. As it was translated from the Hebrew books after the fixing of their canonical character, this form of the Greek Old Testament does not contain the books of the Apocrypha.

stand why a book with a strong devotional element, an orthodox belief, and a frequent emphasis on the observances of the Law, should not have been put on a level with such a book as *Esther*. It is also to be noted that inasmuch as *Tobit* purported to have been written during the Exile, it complied with the condition of canonicity laid down by the Jewish authorities, viz.: that a book must have been written within what was called the "prophetical period," *i.e.* between the time of Moses and Artaxerxes.[1] As it was originally written either in Hebrew or Aramaic, there was no linguistic bar to its inclusion in the Canon. As to *Judith*, it is again difficult to account for its exclusion; it has a distinctly religious trend of the orthodox type, it is full of patriotic enthusiasm, it is extremely well composed, it purports to have been written in the time of Nebuchadrezzar, and it was certainly written originally in Hebrew, long before the Christian era. There is the possibility in the case of both *Tobit* and *Judith*, that they existed only in a Greek form at the time when the Hebrew Canon was fixed; if so, the reason for their exclusion is explained. The *Rest of Esther* is a Greek writing which naturally excluded it from the Canon, and the same applies to *Wisdom*. As to *Ecclesiasticus*, there are two things which can explain its exclusion: its Sadducæan tendency, observable here and there, and that it does not belong to the "prophetical period." The fixing of the Canon was in the hands of the Pharisees; that is a sufficient explanation of its exclusion. The *Additions to Daniel*, not being part of the original book, would, as one can understand, be excluded from the Canon. Of *I, II Maccabees* it is sufficient to say that inasmuch as their dates do not comply with the Rabbinical conditions of canonicity, they were *ipso facto* excluded.

What has been said does not profess to be more than the offering of suggestions to explain why the books of the Apocrypha were rejected by the Jewish Church; there were probably other reasons as well, unknown to us; but those given may certainly be regarded as having contributed to the Rabbinical decisions regarding our books.

[1] See, on this, Oesterley and Robinson, *An Introduction to the Books of the Old Testament*, p. 3 (1934).

In the Christian Church it was different. There can be no doubt that during the first two centuries all the books of the Greek Canon were regarded as Scripture. After this time the books of the Apocrypha came to be differently estimated according to the period and locality in which they circulated.

We have seen reason to believe that some of the New Testament books reflect the thought of much that occurs in the Apocrypha; this in itself is, of course, no proof that the New Testament writers regarded the books of the Apocrypha as Scripture; but the fact that the Septuagint was the Bible of the Church, and that most of the quotations from the Old Testament are from it, and not from the Hebrew, makes it certain these books were held to be Scripture by the New Testament writers.

In the earliest post-biblical Christian literature, some of the books are definitely quoted as Scripture; thus in the first *Epistle of Clement* xxvii. 5, Wisd. xii. 12 is quoted, being prefaced by the words: " By the word of his majesty did he establish all things, and by his word can he destroy them: 'Who shall say . . .'" In lv. 3–6 Judith and Esther are described as " women who received power through the grace of God . . ." Once more, in the *Epistle of Barnabas*, the writer, in discussing an Ezekiel passage (xlvii. 9) cites II Esdr. iv. 3, v. 5 with the words: " Similarly, again, he describes the Cross in another passage in another prophet." In the same epistle, vi. 7, Wisd. ii. 12 is quoted as though part of Isa. iii. 9, 10, an intermingling of texts which shows clearly that both books were regarded as of equal authority.

Nowhere in early Christian literature are the books of what we call the " Apocrypha " spoken of as " apocryphal books "; when the term " apocryphal " is applied to a book it refers to one belonging to some sect, and is used in an opprobrious sense.[1]

During the first two centuries, at least, the early Church both east and west, as represented by Clement of Rome, Irenæus, Tertullian, Cyprian, Clement of Alexandria, and

---

[1] *E.g.*, Irenæus, I. xx. i.

Origen, accepted all the books of the Apocrypha as inspired, *i.e.* as Scripture; the last two quote from almost every book.

Here it may also be mentioned, as illustrating the estimation in which the books of the Apocrypha were held in the early Church, that in the catacombs scenes depicting episodes described in the books of *Tobit, Judith,* and the *Maccabees* are frequently to be met with.

By the fourth century a change is to be observed; the eastern Church, as represented by Athanasius, Cyril of Jerusalem, Epiphanius, Eusebius of Cæsarea, and Gregory of Nazianzus,[1] did not recognize the books of the Apocrypha as canonical; nevertheless, in citing them they use the same formulas as when citing from canonical books. In the western Church, on the other hand, which was farther from the home of the Hebrew Canon, and which knew the Old Testament chiefly through the Latin Version of the Septuagint, there was no scruple about mingling together the books of the Greek and Hebrew canons; thus, the western Church, as represented by the Synods of Hippo (393 A.D.) and Carthage (397 A.D. and 419 A.D.), and by Augustine, Innocent I, and Gelasius, held the books of the Apocrypha to be canonical. But the western Church was not unanimous on this matter; Jerome formed a notable exception, due, in part at any rate, to his sojourn in Palestine, where he learned Hebrew, and, in general, to his intercourse with the east. By his time the Greek Church, as we have seen, had ceased to regard the books of the Apocrypha as canonical Scripture, and following this example, he came to look upon all books not included in the Hebrew Canon, and therefore all those books of the Septuagint which were not represented in the Hebrew Bible, as what he called " apocryphal "; by this term he meant " libri ecclesiastici," as distinguished from " libri canonici." Jerome's use of the word " apocryphal " was new, and was not intended to be an opprobrious term; but, unlike the great majority of the Fathers of the western Church, he did not recognise these books as canonical.

[1] See also the synodical lists of canonical books of the Eastern Church, Swete, *op. cit.*, pp. 203 ff.

Jerome was not, it is true, the only notable figure in the western Church to take this line; Hilary of Poictiers and Rufinus also rejected the books of the Apocrypha as inspired writings, owing doubtless to their contact with the east; but they formed a very small minority in face of the otherwise unanimous attitude of the western Church.

This unanimity is further illustrated, in addition to what is said in the writings of the Latin Church Fathers, by what is found in the great Biblical manuscripts; thus, in the Vatican Codex (B) all the books of the Apocrypha are included, with the exception of the two books of the *Maccabees*; it is the same in the Alexandrian Codex (A) and Cod. Venetus (V); but in these the books of the *Maccabees* are also included; the Sinaitic Codex (‎א‎) is incomplete, but in its original form it doubtless contained all the books of the Apocrypha, for a number of those of unquestioned canonicity—*Amos, Hosea, Micah*, and others, are also missing; *I, II Maccabees* are included. In all these manuscripts the books of the Hebrew Canon and of our Apocrypha are interspersed; no differentiation is made between them.

Since the three great Codices B ‎א‎ A were almost certainly copied in the Egyptian–Palestinian area, they testify to the fact that in the fourth century there was no universal rejection of the books of the Apocrypha even in the eastern Church. In this connexion there is another significant fact, viz. that while the original Peshitta Old Testament, translated from the Hebrew in the second century, did not contain the books of the Apocrypha, the Syriac Apocrypha was added in the fourth century.[1]

In any case, as Swete has said:

From the end of the fourth century the inclusion of the non-canonical books in Western lists is a matter of course. Even Augustine has no scruples on the subject; he makes the books of the Old Testament forty-four (*de doctr. Chr.* ii. 13: *his xliv libris Testamenti Veteris terminatur auctoritas*), and among them Tobit, Judith, and the two books of

[1] On this point see Dennefeld, *Introduction à l'Ancien Testament*, p. 212 (1934).

Maccabees take rank with the histories; and the two Wisdoms, although he confesses that they were not the work of Solomon, are classed with the Prophets. His judgement was that of his Church (Conc. Carth. iii. can. xlvii: *sunt canonicæ scripturæ Salomonis libri quinque . . . Tobias, Judith . . . Machabæorum libri duo*). The African Church had probably never known any other canon, and its belief prevailed wherever the Latin Bible was read.[1]

In somewhat later days the Greek Church reverted to the attitude of the earliest Church in accepting all the books of the Apocrypha; for at the council *in Trullo* (692 A.D.) the decision of the council of Carthage was adopted; similarly Photius in the ninth century. Finally, at the council of Jerusalem in 1672, most of the books not included in the Hebrew Canon were rejected, but *Tobit, Judith, Ecclesiasticus,* and *Wisdom* were accepted as canonical.

While in the Western Church the Greek Canon continued to be accepted, there were not wanting some notable leaders who rejected certain books; thus, Gregory the Great held that the two books of the *Maccabees* were not canonical, but should be read for edification; Alcuin rejected *Ecclesiasticus,* and Walafrid Strabon, *Baruch*; these two lived during the ninth century. During the following centuries different opinions were held by foremost Churchmen, some regarding all the books as canonical, others rejecting them.[2]

At the Council of Trent, in 1546, all the books of the Apocrypha, with two exceptions, were pronounced canonical; the exceptions were *II Esdras* and the *Prayer of Manasses*; these were placed in an Appendix at the end of the New Testament, showing that they were intended to be read for edification. In some of the ancient manuscripts the *Prayer of Manasses* is found among the Canticles added to the Psalter. The Roman Church thus adhered to the Greek Canon, in conformity with the early Church. It was when the Reformers rejected the Apocrypha, that the Council of Trent re-affirmed the canonicity of the books, and added the

---

[1] *Op. cit.*, pp. 223 f.
[2] They are mentioned by Dennefeld, *op. cit.*, p. 214.

anathema clause to their decree. But even after this there have not been wanting prominent Roman Catholics who challenged the canonicity of the Apocrypha, for example, Sixtus of Sienna, Lamy, and J. John (1802). Hence the Vatican Council of 1870 officially confirmed the decree of the Council of Trent.

The Protestant Churches, on the other hand, followed the Hebrew Canon; but their attitude towards the Apocrypha varied. In Luther's translation of the Bible (1534) it is said in the Preface: " The books of the Apocrypha are not to be regarded as Holy Scripture, yet they are useful and good to be read "; appended to his translation are all the books of the Apocrypha with the exception of the two books of *Esdras*. Other reformed Churches on the Continent at first followed this usage, but later the entire Apocrypha was omitted from the printed Bible.

The sixth article of the Church of England declares that " the other books (*i.e.* those of the Apocrypha) the Church doth read for example of life and instruction of manners." Against this declaration of the Church, in the Westminster Confession it is decreed that these books are not " to be otherwise approved or made use of than other human writings."

In the Preface prefixed to the books of the Apocrypha in the Genevan Bible, it is said:

As books proceeding from godly men they are received to be read for the advancement and furtherance of the knowledge of history and for the instruction of godly manners; which books declare that at all times God had especial care of His Church, and left them not utterly destitute of teachers and means to confirm them in the hope of the promised Messiah.

Summing up, then, it is of importance to recognize that while, on the whole, the Apocrypha has been in the Bible of the Church from the earliest times, with the exception of the Protestant Church, it has never, since the end of the second century, been unchallenged—first in the east, and then by a long line of westerns, and then again in the east. On the other hand, the Protestant rejection has only been absolute in certain sections of the Protestant community; other sections, including Luther and the Anglican Church, having allowed it edifying value. The more rigid canonization in the Tridentine decree was doubtless due to reaction against the Protestant seizing on that strain in Catholic tradition which doubted the canonicity of the Apocrypha, while the fact of the Tridentine decree tended to make more absolute the rejection of the Apocrypha in Protestant circles.

It is a welcome fact that in modern times the value of the Apocrypha is being increasingly recognized as a source for the understanding of the background of the New Testament in all circles, and that the modern view of inspiration, which does not hold that inspiration guarantees the historic and scientific accuracy of every statement, but that inspiration lay in the spiritual principles and message set forth, and that it worked through the personality of the writer, which could therefore dim the message—that this modern view of inspiration can find much in the Apocrypha which is as truly inspired as much that is in the Old Testament.

PART II

THE BOOKS OF THE APOCRYPHA

I ESDRAS (THE "GREEK EZRA")

I. TITLE

THE titles of the various books connected with the name of Ezra are somewhat confusing owing partly to the fact that the canonical books of *Ezra* and *Nehemiah* are sometimes regarded as one book, at other times as two; and also to the fact that in the Vulgate the different parts of the " Ezra Apocalypse " are differently designated.

As to the book with which we are now concerned, this is known by three different titles:

> *I Esdras ; i.e.* Esdras α' of the most important Greek MSS., and this is followed by the pre-Hieronymian and the Syriac Versions.
>
> *II Esdras ;* in the Lucianic recension;[1] but this must not be confused with Esdras β' of the Septuagint, of which chaps. i–x = the canonical *Ezra*, and chaps. xi–xxiii = the canonical *Nehemiah*. In the Lucianic recension *I Esdras = Ezra–Nehemiah*, regarded as one book.
>
> *III Esdras ;* this is the title in the Latin Bibles since the time of Jerome.[2]

On the other hand, the common arrangement, following the later Latin MSS., gives these titles to the different Ezra books:

> *I Esdras*; this is the canonical *Ezra–Nehemiah* regarded as one book.
>
> *II Esdras*; this comprises chaps. i. ii of II Esdras in the Apocrypha.
>
> *III Esdras*; as mentioned above, this is the Vulgate

---

[1] Published by Lagarde, *Librorum Vet. Test. canonicorum Pars prior græce* (1883).
[2] In the Vulgate it is placed in an Appendix, together with the *Prayer of Manasses* and *IV Esdras*, after the New Testament.

title of I Esdras of the Apocrypha; the book under
consideration.

IV Esdras; this includes chaps. iii–xiv of *II Esdras* in
the Apocrypha.

V Esdras; this is the title of chaps. xv. xvi of *II Esdras*
in the Apocrypha.

The title by which our book is now generally known is
the "Greek Ezra," to distinguish it from the more literal
translation of the canonical *Ezra–Nehemiah* (Esdras β').

II. Contents of the Book

With the exception of the section iii. 1–v. 6, it will be
seen that our book is more or less identical with parts of
the canonical books of *II Chronicles, Ezra,* and *Nehemiah*:

i. 1–24: The celebration of the Passover in the eighteenth year of Josiah.

ii. 25–33: The death of Josiah at the battle of Megiddo
(B.C. 608).

ii. 34–38: Jehoahaz is made king, but is deposed three
months after by the Egyptian king, who puts
Jehoiakim in his place.

ii. 39–58: Nebuchadrezzar carries Jehoiakim captive
to Babylon (but see II Kgs. xxiv. 1–6).
Jehoiachin reigns for three months and ten
days; he is carried captive to Babylon, and
Zedekiah is set on the throne of Judah by
Nebuchadrezzar. The siege and fall of Jerusalem. The Exile.

This section is more or less identical with II Chron.
xxxv. 1–xxxvi. 21.

ii. 1–7: The decree of Cyrus permitting the rebuilding
of the Temple and the return of the exiles,
i.e. in B.C. 538/7 (= II Chron. xxxvi. 22, 23,
Ezra i. 1–4).

ii. 8–15: Gifts are given to those who are returning to
their own land by their fellow-exiles. Cyrus

delivers up the holy vessels carried off by Nebuchadrezzar. Sanabassar (Sheshbazzar) governor of Judaea (= Ezra i. 5–11).

ii. 16–30: In response to the Samaritan leaders who protest against the rebuilding of the walls of the city and of the Temple, Artaxerxes I (B.C. 465–425) forbids the work to proceed; it ceases until the second year of Darius (B.C. 520). This corresponds, with certain variations (*e.g.* there is no mention of the rebuilding of the Temple) with Ezra iv. 7–24.

iii. i.–v. 6: The great feast given by Darius I: three young Jews of the king's bodyguard undertake a contest in the utterance of wise sayings; Zerubbabel, the winner, is rewarded by the king in being permitted to make a request; he asks that the exiled Jews be allowed to return to their own land and that the city and Temple may be rebuilt. The request is granted. Zerubbabel's thanksgiving to God. A list, incomplete, of those who went up to Jerusalem. The first return thus takes place under Darius I.

This section is peculiar to our book, though it occurs, with some variations, in Josephus, *Antiq.* xi. 33–63.

v. 7–46: A list of the exiles who returned with Zerubbabel (= Ezra ii. 1–70).

v. 47–55: Sacrifices are offered on the return, and the feast of Tabernacles is celebrated (= Ezra iii. 1–7).

v. 56–65: The foundation of the Temple is laid (=Ezra iii. 8–13).

v. 66–73: The rebuilding of the Temple is hindered by the Samaritans; the work ceases " all the time that king Cyrus lived; so they were hindered from building for the space of two years until the reign of Darius," *i.e.* in his second year, B.C. 520 (= Ezra iv. 1–5, 24).

K

vi–vii: The rebuilding of the Temple is completed, *i.e.* in B.C. 516 (= Ezra v–vi).

viii. 1–7: The arrival of Ezra in Jerusalem in " the seventh year of Artaxerxes " (= Ezra vii. 1–10).

viii. 8–24: The decree of Artaxerxes, *i.e.* in his seventh year, B.C. 458, permitting the return to Jerusalem of Ezra and those who wish to accompany him (= Ezra vii. 11–26).[1]

viii. 25–26: Ezra's thanksgiving (= Ezra vii. 27–28).

viii. 27–67: The list of the returned exiles; their arrival in Jerusalem (= Ezra viii. 1–36).

viii. 68–ix. 15: The prohibition of mixed marriages (= Ezra ix. 1–x. 17).

ix. 16–36: The list of priests who had married foreign wives (= Ezra x. 18–44).

ix. 37–55: The reading of the Law by Ezra (= Neh. vii. 73–viii. 12).

Arising out of this brief survey of the contents of our book there are some points which demand notice:

(*a*) Both the beginning and conclusion are abrupt, so that the impression is gained that we have not before us the book in its original complete form.

(*b*) According to iii. 1–v. 6 the first return of the exiles (under Zerubbabel) took place in the reign of Darius I (see especially iv. 43 ff.); but, according to ii. 1–14, this takes place under Cyrus.

(*c*) In ii. 16–30 the decree of Artaxerxes (presumably the first of the name, B.C. 465–425), forbidding the rebuilding of the Temple, is placed before the reign of Darius (see especially verse 30).

(*d*) The section iii. 1–v. 6, recording the intellectual competition between the three young men belonging to Darius' bodyguard, is peculiar to this book.

(*e*) According to vi. 18, Zerubbabel and Sheshbazzar are

[1] From this it would appear that Ezra's mission was in B.C. 458, but there are substantial grounds for thinking that it was actually in B.C. 397. The text does not indicate which Artaxerxes, of three, is meant. See, on the whole problem, Oesterley and Robinson, *A History of Israel*, ii. 114 ff. (1933).

distinct personalities, and contemporaries; and Sheshbazzar lays the foundation of the Temple (vi. 20). But according to vi. 27, 29, it is Zerubbabel who lays the foundation of the Temple; this would seem to imply that, in spite of vi. 18, the two were regarded as one and the same; and this is further borne out by ii. 1-15, where Sheshbazzar alone is mentioned (verse 12). All these passages refer to the reign of Cyrus.

(f) Between the end of the canonical *Ezra* and the beginning of *Nehemiah* there is a gap in the history of twelve years, according to the chronology of *Ezra–Nehemiah*; but our book ignores Neh. i–vii. 72, so that it makes Neh. viii follow immediately after the end of *Ezra*, thus continuing the Ezra-narrative without the break occasioned by the insertion of Neh. i–vii. 72ª, an obviously more logical sequence.

(g) In the section on the reading of the Law (ix. 37-55) there is no mention of Nehemiah taking part in this, as in Neh. viii. 9.

A word or two may be added regarding these points:

(a) The abrupt beginning and ending of the book would suggest that it is an incomplete extract from a larger work; or it may conceivably be due to the original MS. having been damaged.

(b) This extraordinary contradiction may be accounted for on the supposition that iii. 1–v. 6 (the competition between the three members of the royal bodyguard) was not an original part of the book, but was taken from some source by the compiler and inserted in order to explain how it came about that Zerubbabel obtained permission to go to Jerusalem and undertake the rebuilding of the Temple. The compiler added the name of Zerubbabel in iv. 13 (cp. v. 6), but omitted to alter the name of Darius wherever it occurred.

(c) This section (ii. 16–30) was taken from Ezr. iv. 7–24 (the form of which differed in many respects from that with which we are familiar); the compiler, therefore, did not trouble about the historical blunder; how *that* arose is not our present concern; for this the commentaries on *Ezra–Nehemiah* must be consulted.

(*d*) See under (*b*).

(*e*) As to the identity or otherwise of Sheshbazzar and Zerubbabel, if our compiler did identify the two—what he says is ambiguous—it was another of his not infrequent mistakes; that they were different personalities is well shown by Kittel.[1]

(*f*) The fact that our book has nothing to correspond to Neh. i–vii. 73ª, thereby making the historical sequence more logical, shows that, in some respects, it represents a more reliable record than the canonical *Ezra–Nehemiah*. It is also an indication that *I Esdras* is independent of the Septuagint of *Ezra–Nehemiah*. For the question as to how and when the insertion of Neh. i–vii. 73ª came to be made, recourse to the commentaries is necessary.

(*g*) The non-mention of the name of Nehemiah in the section on the reading of the Law is one of the arguments against Nehemiah and Ezra being contemporaries; it, therefore, probably witnesses to more reliable history.[2]

It will thus be seen that there are various errors and inconsistencies in *I Esdras*; and there are many others of less importance which the study of the book reveals.

III. The Historicity of the Book

The chaotic condition of the historical material presented in the book is seen most clearly by noting the following points:

The first return of the exiles takes place under Cyrus, their leader is Sheshbazzar (ii. 1–15); the narrative then goes on to deal with the rebuilding of the city walls and the laying of the foundation of the Temple, which occurred during the reign of Artaxerxes (ii. 16 ff.); the first return of the exiles is then recorded as having taken place in the reign of Darius, their leader being Zerubbabel (iii–v. 6);

---

[1] *Geschichte des Volkes Israel*, iii. 348 ff. (1929).
[2] On this see further, Oesterley and Robinson, *op. cit.*, ii. 114 ff. (1933).

the narrative immediately tells of the first return of the exiles under Cyrus, the moving spirits being Zerubbabel, Jeshua, and Nehemiah (v. 7 ff.).

It is clear that the compiler of our book was not concerned about historical sequence; his object was to record how it came about that the Temple was rebuilt and its services re-inaugurated.

Nevertheless, many attempts have been made to account for the disorder of the material; the solutions offered all have their difficulties, but the least difficult is Torrey's theory: he holds that the compiler " introduced between ii. 15 (14) and iii. 1, the incident of the interruption of the building of the Temple (the wall) under Artaxerxes in order to supply a motive for Zerubbabel's petition to Darius; and the story of iii f. having once broken the true historical connexion, it became necessary to transfer to Darius' time events which in the document before the compiler were brought into the reign of Cyrus (v. 7–73)." [1]

Another intricate problem is presented by the relationship of our book to the Masoretic text on the one hand, and to the Septuagint of the relevant sections of *Ezra–Nehemiah* and *II Chronicles* on the other. Nestle [2] has shown that these latter were not taken over by the compiler of our book, but that his work is based directly on a Hebrew-Aramaic text, which often offered more reliable details than the Masoretic text. Interesting is the fact that Josephus (*Antiq.* xi. 1–5) follows, in general, *I Esdras*, not the canonical *Ezra*, which means that in his time our book was regarded as quite as authoritative as the latter, and it must be granted that, as already remarked, here and there it strikes one as more reliable than the canonical *Ezra*, *e.g.* in making Neh. v. 73[b] follow immediately upon Ezr. x. 44, and by the omission of the name of Nehemiah in the account of the reading of the Law (see Neh. viii. 9), suggesting that he and Ezra were not contemporaries.

---

[1] *Encycl. Bibl.* ii. 1492; see also his *Ezra Studies* (1910); on the other hand, see Bayer, *Das dritte Buch Esdras und sein Verhältnis zu den Büchern Esra–Nehemia* (1911), and Walde, *Die Esdrasbücher der Septuaginta, ihr gegenseitiges Verhältnis untersucht* (1913).

[2] *Marginalien und Materialien*, pp. 23–29 (1893).

I Esdras is thus not dependent on the canonical books, but is probably an older translation of a Hebrew-Aramaic original.[1]

The historical *data*, therefore, of both the apocryphal and canonical books leave much to be desired; the chaos in each is due in part to ignorance of the facts; but probably still more to preconceived notions on the part of the compilers. In the case of *I Esdras* there is also the possibility that its chaotic state may have been aggravated by dislocation of the sheets of a MS. in course of transmission, as has been the case with *Ecclesiasticus*. On the other hand, there are, as we have seen, a certain number of passages suggesting more reliable *data* than the canonical *Ezra*.

IV. TEXT AND VERSIONS

The text of our book is contained in the great Septuagint MSS. BA, etc.; it is wanting in א, though as this MS. has Esdras β', *I Esdras* evidently figured in it originally.[2] It is also found in a number of Lucianic MSS., but these have been worked over in order to make the text conform to that of the Masoretes.[3]

There are two Old Latin versions, one of which appears in the Vulgate.[4]

The only Syriac version is the Syro-Hexapla [5] of Paul of Tella; *I Esdras* does not appear in the Peshitta. The other versions, Ethiopic, Arabic, and Armenian, are not of importance for the Greek Text, though with regard to the first Torrey says that it is "a valuable witness to the Hexaplar text." [6]

---

[1] This does not, however, apply to the narrative of the competition between the pages of the king's body-guard, which was Greek in its origin; but this is not the opinion of some scholars, see, *e.g.*, Eissfeldt, *Einleitung in das Alte Testament*, p. 633 (1934).

[2] It may be mentioned that some scholars hold the view, for which much is to be said, that just as the true Septuagint of *Daniel* was replaced by Theodotion's Version, so *I Esdras* is the original Septuagint, while *II Esdras* of the Greek MSS. is the Version of Theodotion, which secured a place beside the former (instead of displacing it as in *Daniel*), save in the Syro-Hexapla.

[3] See, for details, Moulton in *ZATW* xix. 211 ff. (1899), xx. 1 ff. (1900).

[4] Sabatier, *Bibl. Sacr. Lat.*, iii. 1041 ff. (1751).

[5] See Walton, *Biblia Sacra Polyglotta* (1657, etc.), and Lagarde, *Libr. Vet. Test. Apocryph. Syr.* (1861).

[6] *Ezra Studies*, p. 101 (1910).

V. Date

The canonical books *Chron.–Ezra–Nehemiah* belong, at the earliest, to the middle of the fourth century B.C.; Josephus used our book about 100 A.D.; these are the outside dates; a more precise date is difficult to determine; " the affinities between I Esdr. iii. 1 ff. and Esther i. 1–3, as also between *I Esdras* and *Daniel* (Septuagint), give our nearest indications for any approximate determination of date."[1] We shall not be far wrong in assigning as the date of our book some time during the second century B.C.; and near the beginning of this century, rather than later, is the more probable date.

For Egypt as the place of origin of the " Greek Ezra " see S. A. Cook in Charles, *Apocr. and Pseudepigr. of the O.T.* i. 5 (1913).

VI. Literature

Fritzsche, in *Kurzgefasstes exegetisches Handbuch zu den Apokryphen des alten Testaments*, i. 3 ff. (1851).

Volkmar, *Handbuch der Einleitung in die Apokryphen* (1860).

Lupton, in Wace, *The Holy Bible according to the Authorized Version with an Explanatory and Critical Commentary . . . Apocrypha* ii. 373 ff. (1888).

Ball, *The Variorum Apocrypha* (1892).

Guthe, in Kautzsch, *Die Apokryphen und Pseudepigraphen des Alten Testaments*, i. 1 ff. (1900).

Howorth, Articles in *Proceedings of the Soc. of Biblical Archaeology* (1901–1910).

André, *Les Apocryphes de l'ancien testament*, pp. 132 ff. (1903).

Torrey, *Ezra Studies* (1910).

Bayer, *Das dritte Buch Esdras und sein Verhältnis zu den Büchern Ezra–Nehemia* (1911).

Walde, *Die Esdrasbücher der Septuaginta, ihr gegenseitiges Verhältnis untersucht* (1913).

S. A. Cook, in Charles, *The Apocrypha and Pseudepigrapha of the Old Testament*, i. 1 ff. (1913).

Tedesche, *A Critical Edition of I Esdras*, Diss. phil. Yale Univ. (1928).

---

[1] Volz, in *Encycl. Bibl.* ii. 1493.

II ESDRAS (THE "EZRA APOCALYPSE")

I. Title

THIS book does not appear in any Septuagint MS. hitherto come to light; therefore it is not known what the Greek title was; nor, in consequence (for the Greek was translated from a Hebrew original, see below), is it known what the Hebrew title was.

The title "II Esdras" of the Authorized and Revised Versions was taken from the Genevan Bible, and is found in some Latin MSS. In the Vulgate the title is: *Liber quartus Esdrae*, although it opens with the words: *Liber Esdrae prophetae secundus*. The Vulgate places this book, together with the *Prayer of Manasses* and *III Esdras* (the "Greek Ezra"), in an Appendix at the end of the whole Bible. Owing to the different designations between the Latin and the English Versions the title now usually given to the book is "II (IV) Ezra"; but inasmuch as the original book consisted of only chaps. iii–xiv., which are purely apocalyptic, the more appropriate title given to it now-a-days is the "Ezra Apocalypse." Chaps. i. ii. and xv. xvi, not being part of the Apocalypse, were originally independent of it; this is recognized by some of the Latin MSS. in which chaps. i. ii are entitled "II Esdras," while chaps. xv. xvi. are given the title "V Esdras."

II. Contents of the Book

The book is divided into three unequal portions, viz. chaps. i. ii; iii–xiv; and xv. xvi; but taking it as we now have it, the contents are as follows:—

i. 1–3 : The genealogy of Ezra.
i. 4–12 : Israel's ingratitude to their God, shown forth by wickedness and idolatry, in spite of divine

mercies in the past. Ezra is bidden to indicate
by symbolic action that the recreant nation is
cast off.

i. 13–27: God's mercies in the past are recorded; yet
in spite of this the people proved themselves
unfaithful; consequently God will turn to
other nations, and give them His name that
they may render Him obedience. In for-
saking their God Israel's punishment is self-
inflicted.

i. 28–32: Israel is cast out from God's presence.

i. 33–40: In place of Israel another nation, "from the
east," will be chosen; this nation shall have
as its leaders the patriarchs and the prophets
of old.

ii. 1–9: Israel shall be scattered among the nations,
and its name shall be blotted out. "Assur"
shall, however, be punished because it shel-
tered the unrighteous.

ii. 10–14: The "kingdom of Jerusalem," which was to
have been given to Israel shall be given to
another nation.

ii. 15–32: The Church, personified like Jerusalem, is
bidden to be of good cheer. God's promises
to the Church. It seems probable that the
whole of this section is of Christian origin.

ii. 33–41: Ezra's message to Israel is rejected; he turns
to the Gentiles, to whom everlasting life is
promised if they will hearken and understand.
The Church, spoken of as Sion, is told that the
number of her children is fulfilled. Another
Christian section.

ii. 42–48: Ezra's vision of the Son of God; also of
Christian origin. The "Apocalypse of Ezra,"
which begins with chap. iii, consists of five
visions, to which are added two other independent ones.

iii. 1–v. 19: The *First Vision*. The main purport of
this vision is the problem of the desolation of

Sion and the prosperity of Babylon. How can God permit this? The Seer's argument with the archangel Uriel; in reply to the questions put by the former, the archangel gives an explanation consisting of three theses: man cannot apprehend the ways of God; the age to come will see all the incongruities of the present world-order set right; a condition of the dawning of the age to come is that the predestined number of the righteous shall be fulfilled. The vision ends with a description of the signs which will herald the end of the present world-order, and the approach of the new age.

v. 20–vi. 34: The *Second Vision*. The problem of the oppression of God's chosen people, together with the archangel's reply that man cannot understand the ways of God, is repeated in this vision. A further question is raised regarding the lot of those who die before the present world-order has passed away; in reply, the archangel says that their lot will be similar to that of those who are still living,—a reply which is no answer to the question. This vision closes, like the previous one, with a description of the signs of the end.

vi. 35–ix. 25: The *Third Vision*. The two main theses of this long drawn-out section are, the question of the small number of those who will be finally saved, and a description of the Judgement, and the fate of the righteous and the wicked, respectively.

ix. 26–x. 59: The *Fourth Vision*. Preceding the Vision itself is the Seer's lament over his people (ix. 26–37). The Vision then follows: a woman appears in deep mourning for the loss of her son who died on entering the marriage-chamber. The Seer tells her that she has lost but one son, whereas Sion has lost a great

number; but the woman refuses to be comforted. As the Seer is thus speaking with her
she becomes transfigured, and he sees that in
place of the woman there is " a city builded."
Thereupon the vision is explained: the woman
is the heavenly Sion (x. 25): her son is the
earthly Jerusalem, and his death is the destruction of the city.

xi. 1–xii. 39: The *Fifth Vision*. The Seer sees an eagle
rising from the sea; it has three heads, twelve
wings, and eight other smaller wings. A roar-
ing lion comes from a wood, and denounces
the eagle; by degrees all the wings and heads
disappear; the body of the eagle is then
burned. In the explanation which follows it
is said that the eagle is the fourth kingdom
which Daniel saw, and that the lion is the
Messiah.

xii. 40–51: Following the vision, it is said that the
people, who had been awaiting Ezra's return,
come to him and beg him not to leave them;
he promises that he will in due time return to
them. Here the " Ezra Apocalypse " proper
ends; the last two visions are separate pieces
(see further the next section).

xiii. 1–58: The *Sixth Vision*. A man arises from the
sea; his enemies come against him, but they
are all destroyed; then a peaceful multitude
comes to him at his bidding. In the explanation of the vision it is said that the man from
the sea is the pre-existent Messiah; those who
came to fight against him are the Gentiles,
the peaceful multitude are the ten tribes.

xiv. 1–48: The *Seventh Vision*. Ezra hears a voice from
a bush which tells him that he is to write down
all the dreams and their interpretations. He
obeys, and receives inspiration to write by
drinking a cup of water which has the colour
of fire. He writes ninety-four books. He is

then commanded to publish twenty-four of the books which he has written (*i.e.* the books of the Old Testament) ; but the seventy others are to be kept secret, being reserved for the wise among his people; these probably refer to apocalyptic writings.

xv. 1–4 : Ezra is commanded to write down what the Lord will tell him.

xv. 5–27 : Punishment on all men because of their wickedness.

xv. 28–33 : A vision describing wars in Syria.

xv. 34–63 : Various historical accounts of wars among the peoples.

xvi. 1–17 : Denunciations against Babylon, Asia, Egypt, and Syria.

xvi. 18–78 ; A continuation of historical references with denunciations against evil-doers; but the elect shall be saved.

III. The Component Parts of the Book, and their Dates

It has already been mentioned, in passing, that chaps. i. ii and chaps. xv. xvi are not parts of the central portion, chaps. iii–xiv, but form two independent pieces; each of these three component parts must, therefore, be dealt with separately.

(1) *Chapters i. ii.*

The striking feature about this literary piece is that it contains both Jewish and Christian elements. Belonging obviously to the former is the genealogy of Ezra, put in the forefront in order to show Ezra's priestly descent. The denunciation of the people, quite in the prophetic style, together with the historical retrospect (i. 13 ff.), is also characteristically Jewish. On the other hand, the passage which follows (i. 24–40) can hardly have been written by a Jew. There are here various verses reminiscent of the New Testament; *e.g.* verse 30 is a quotation from Matth.

xxiii. 37; verse 32 is based on Matth. xxiii. 34, 35, cp. Luke xi. 49, 51; further, with i. 35 cp. Rom. x. 14 ff., and with i. 39 cp. Matth. viii. 11. Again, ii. 7–9 exhibits a somewhat bitter anti-Jewish feeling, witnessing to a definite rift between Jews and Christians; the following passages should also be compared: ii. 10, 11 with Matth. xxi. 5, Luke xvi. 9; ii. 13 with Matth. vii. 7, 8, Luke xi. 9, 10; ii. 16 with Matth. xxvii. 53; ii. 26 with John xvii. 11; ii. 41 with Rom. viii. 29, 30; and ii. 42–48 are strongly reminiscent of various passages in the New Testament *Apocalypse.* These do not exhaust the Christian elements; in fact, it almost looks as though the Jewish element formed only a small portion of the whole.

As to date, while the definitely Jewish portions are earlier, in their present form these chapters may be, approximately, assigned to the second century A.D. Thus, the references to the Gospels would make the very end of the first century A.D. the earliest possible date; but the writer shows some knowledge of the Greek *Apocalypse of Baruch* (*e.g.* i. 40), which would bring the date down to the early part of the second century A.D.; James has, however, shown conclusively that the writer was acquainted with the *Apocalypse of Zephaniah*,[1] which would bring the date down to a still later time, viz. after the middle of the second century A.D.; so that in its present form this section of our book must be dated after 150 A.D., but there is no sufficient reason for dating it long after this date.

(2) *Chapters iii–xiv.*

There is much diversity of opinion on the question as to whether these chapters are all from the same writer. Perhaps the most persuasive advocate of unity of authorship is Violet; he says:

The Ezra Apocalypse is a beautiful little work from one mould (*aus einem Guss*). . . . The whole book shows the use of the same artistic forms; characteristic of the

[1] See his Introduction (pp. lxxix f.) to Bensly's *The Fourth Book of Ezra* (1895); the *Apocalypse of Zephaniah* (fragments of a Coptic version) was published by Steindorff in Gebhard and Harnack's *Texte und Untersuchungen* (1899).

entire book is the thoroughly Rabbinic use of the number seven, also of the double seven, the *Tessaradeka*, and the careful avoidance of the divine name; throughout the book one discerns the same pious, struggling soul of one to whom the essence of the matter means everything, the form being of little account.[1]

On the other hand, Kabisch, for example, holds that there was originally a book written under the pseudonym Salathiel, consisting of the main part of our present book; into this a redactor worked three smaller apocalypses, together with an historical fragment, under the pseudonym of Ezra; the whole thus became an Ezra-book; but the four added pieces are each to be regarded as independent.[2] With this Box agrees, in the main:

The Salathiel-Apocalypse is contained within chaps. iii–x of our book; while outside of, and independent of, this at least three other independent sources have been used, viz. the Eagle-Vision (xi. xii), the Son of Man Vision (xiii), and an Ezra-piece (xiv).[3]

All authorities are agreed that redactional elements of a *minor* character are abundant; others, however, assign a great deal more to redactors (see below § iv). As the views just stated represent the different standpoints of one or other of the great majority of scholars who have written on the book—so far as this particular subject is concerned—it will not be necessary to cite other authors.

The view here to be presented on this question agrees on the main point with Kabisch and Box; it will, therefore, be well to state the reasons in favour of diversity of authorship.

That the *Eagle-Vision* (xi. xii), which is a self-contained piece, can have come from the same hand that wrote the Ezra-Apocalypse (iii–x) is, to begin with, improbable on account of the difference of religious outlook; the problem of the triumph of wickedness, the soul-struggle, seeking to fathom the ways of God, the despair at the doom of

---

[1] *Die Apokalypsen des Esra und des Baruch . . .*, p. xliii (1924).
[2] *Das Vierte Buch Esra auf seine Quellen untersucht*, p. 3, 93 ff. (1889).
[3] *The Ezra-Apocalypse*, pp. xxiv f. (1912).

mankind in general—in a word, the yearning to be faithful
to God in spite of overwhelming difficulties, which pulsates
through the Ezra-Apocalypse, finds no place in the Eagle-
Vision; and yet the whole purport of that vision, until the
end is reached, would seem to call for some consideration
of the problem of the protracted prosperity and cruelty of
the wicked Roman empire. The mention of the Roman
empire—for all authorities are agreed that the Eagle is a
symbol of this—points to a second reason against unity of
authorship. The writer of the Ezra-Apocalypse is, beyond
a doubt, permeated with a religious spirit; how could such
an one have penned a vision of such an entirely political
character as the Eagle-Vision? One whose whole outlook
was dominated by God-ward thoughts would inevitably
have given some signs of his irrepressible bent had this
vision been written by him.

Further, the writer of the Ezra-Apocalypse is almost
wholly concerned with thoughts regarding the world to
come; the present world is transitory, the Seer's gaze is
concentrated on the future; this is his attitude throughout.
But in the Eagle-Vision the writer is wholly concerned with
the present world; the destruction of the eagle, symbolizing
Rome, the enemy of God, is not represented as the prelude
to the advent of the world to come (contrast, *e.g.*, ix. 1–16),
but as the condition of a more prosperous time on the earth:
" And therefore appear no more, thou eagle, nor thy horrible
wings, nor thy evil little wings, nor thy cruel heads, nor
thy hurtful talons, nor all thy vain body; that all the
earth may be refreshed, and be eased, being delivered
from thy violence . . ." (xi. 45 f.). Moreover, in the
Eagle-Vision it is the Roman power with its ruthless cruelty
and oppression which is the cause of all the misery and un-
happiness of men; quite different in this respect, too, is
the outlook of the writer of the Ezra-Apocalypse; according
to him all the evils and the sorrows of this world are due to
the wickedness of the human race in general (cp., *e.g.*, vii.
[46–48]); only the abolition of sin can bring happiness.
This difference of outlook is very significant. Another
point of contrast between the two is that the writer of the

Ezra-Apocalypse has constantly in mind the individual sinners or righteous, whereas in the Eagle-Vision the Seer thinks always in terms of his nation. Finally, the *rôle* of the Messiah is entirely different as between the two visions; in the Ezra-Apocalypse there is to be the rule of the Messiah of four hundred years' duration, *i.e.* he is an earthly Messiah; but in the Eagle-Vision the Messiah, symbolized by a lion, will destroy the Roman power, it is true; he is, nevertheless, a transcendental Messiah, " the anointed one, whom the Most High hath kept unto the end " (xii. 32).

When all these points are taken into consideration, it must be allowed that it is difficult to believe that these two visions can have come from the same writer.[1]

Coming next to the *Vision of the Man from the Sea* (xiii), it will be seen that here, too, there are reasons for regarding it as an independent piece.   In this vision there is a curious mixture of *traits* indicating adaptations from Babylonian myth and Iranian eschatology; to deal with these in detail here would take us too far afield;[2] but it is evident from the explanation of the vision given in verses 21–52 that the writer did not understand various points in the vision, showing that he utilized traditional extraneous material, the origin and meaning of which were not within his ken. This would not of itself necessarily mean that the writer of the Ezra-Apocalypse was not the author; for in that vision, too, use is made of extraneous material (ix. 38–x. 4), where again the explanation of the vision (x. 40–49) does not tally with all the details of the vision itself. But the kind of extraneous material used in this Man from the Sea vision is so different from anything occurring in the Ezra-Apocalypse that it strikes one as very improbable for both visions to have come from the same writer. A quite convincing argument, however, for difference of authorship is the presentation of the Messiah in the Man from the Sea vision; he is a pre-existent, heavenly Messiah, not the Davidic Messiah, born into the world; he appears suddenly, rising out of the sea, a supernatural being, not the Messiah of the

---

[1] For various views regarding the interpretation of the Eagle-Vision, see the present writer's *II Esdras* (*The Ezra-Apocalypse*), pp. 144 ff. (1933).

[2] See the book just referred to, pp. 158–164.

Ezra-Apocalypse, who, in due course, dies (vii. 27-29). The way in which the Messiah destroys His enemies is quite different from anything in any other part of the book; this is so striking that the passage may well be quoted:

> And, lo, as he saw the assault of the multitude that came, he neither lifted up his head, nor held spear, nor any instrument of war; but only I saw how that he sent out of his mouth as it had been a flood of fire, and out of his lips a flaming breath, and out of his tongue he cast forth sparks of the storm . . . and fell upon the assault of the multitude which was prepared to fight, and burned them up everyone, so that, upon a sudden, of an immeasurable multitude nothing was to be perceived, but only dust of ashes and smell of smoke (xiii. 9-11).

It is difficult to believe that the writer of the Ezra-Apocalypse, with his utterly•different conception of the Messiah, could have been the author of this very un-Jewish Messianic presentation.

As to the section about Ezra and the holy writings (xiv), there are certain features which are reminiscent of the Ezra-Apocalypse; such as the pessimistic attitude adopted (verses 10, 20, 21), and reverence for the Law (verses 22, 30, 31); but other elements point to difference of authorship. In the Ezra-Apocalypse the Seer reckons himself among the sinners (*e.g.* viii. 31, 32, 49), but in this section he is represented as different from ordinary men: " . . . renounce the life that is corruptible, and let go from these mortal thoughts, cast away from thee the burdens of man, put off now thy weak nature, and lay aside the thoughts that are most grievous unto thee, and haste thee to remove from these times " (verses 13-15). Further, in the Ezra-Apocalypse Ezra's future is veiled in darkness (iv. 41-52, in this last verse it is said: " as touching thy life I am not sent to show thee, for I do not know it "); but in this section it is said of him: " thou shalt be taken away from men, and from henceforth thou shalt remain with my Son, and with such as be like thee " (verse 9). Such divergent views are unlikely to have been set forth by the same writer.

L

It is also worth noting that in spite of the writer's reverence for the Law, he regards it as worthy of less honour than the apocalypse (verse 46); this is very unlike anything found in the Ezra-Apocalypse. And, finally, the Messianic conception in the two writings is different; we have seen how the Messiah is conceived of in the Ezra-Apocalypse, but here he only appears at the end of the times (verse 9).

As these four literary pieces are, according to the view here held, of different authorship, their respective dates must be considered separately.

The date of the Ezra-Apocalypse (iii–x) is given at the opening (iii. 1): " the thirtieth year after the ruin of the city " (cp. iii. 29); the mention of Salathiel (= Ezra) and Babylon shows that this purports to be the thirtieth year after the fall of Jerusalem in B.C. 586, i.e. B.C. 556. Almost all modern commentators, however, are convinced that this apocalypse was written centuries later; Box well expresses this consensus of opinion in saying that there is every reason to suppose that this apocalypse

> was intended by its author to bear a typical and allegorical significance. Salathiel, living in captivity thirty years after the first destruction of Jerusalem (in B.C. 586) speaks to a later generation that finds itself in similar circumstances. We are, therefore, justified in concluding that the date, like other features in S (= Salathiel Apocalypse [1]) was intended to bear a typical significance, and that it typifies the thirtieth year after the destruction of Jerusalem by Titus, i.e. the year 100 A.D. Consequently S may be regarded as having been originally written and put forth in 100 A.D.[2]

With this we are in entire agreement. But inasmuch as, in the most recent discussion of the date of this apocalypse, the writer argues in favour of a B.C. 556 date, it will be well to consider first the arguments for such an early date.

Kaminka [3] contends for this early date for the following reasons: He begins by stating that the grounds for the

---

[1] On this, see below, pp. 156 ff.   [2] Op. cit., p. xxix.
[3] Beiträge zur Erklärung der Esra-Apocalypse . . . (1934).

generally accepted late date are, first, the complicated interpretation of the Eagle-Vision; and, secondly, the supposition that the deep grief over the destruction of the Temple is in reference to the second Temple, so that by " Babylon " (iii. 1, 2) Rome is to be understood. But Kaminka makes no mention of the two most convincing arguments for the late date, namely the doctrinal standpoint and the eschatology of the book, both of which would be quite unthinkable in the sixth century B.C. To go into details would be impossible here, for that would take us too far afield;[1] but the words of another Jewish scholar are worth quoting:

> Not only did the writer belong to the scribal party in Jabne, but he also stood in close personal touch with it. Indeed, we must look upon him as a pupil of one of the most outstanding teachers of that circle, namely Rabbi Eliezer ben Hyrkanos, the influence of whose spirit and teaching is to be discerned in so many passages of our book.[2]

As Violet rightly points out, the problem which occupies the Seer throughout, and which finds expression at the outset (iii. 3 ff.), was just the problem with which the Rabbis of the first century A.D. were occupied.[3]

Kaminka's contention that the great grief expressed over the fall of the Temple cannot apply to the second Temple because there was no general or overwhelming grief over the fall of the second Temple, is far from convincing; he quotes Jochanan ben Zakkai and one of his pupils to show that the destruction of the Temple and the cessation of the sacrifices were not regarded as a great calamity; but against this we may quote a prayer of Akiba, in which the yearning for the rebuilding of the city and for the restoration of the sacrifices, certainly points to anything but indifference :.

Grant, O Yahweh, our God and Lord of our fathers,

---

[1] See, e.g., Box, op. cit., pp. xxxiv ff.
[2] F. Rosenthal, *Vier Apocryphische Bücher aus der Zeit und Schule Akibas*, pp. 70 f. (1885).
[3] *Op. cit.*, p. xl.

that we may rejoice again at the festivals, and delight in the building of Thy city, and be full of joy at Thy sacrifices. Then shall we eat of the Passover lambs and of the burnt offerings, whose blood sprinkled the side of Thine Altar. We will thank Thee for our redemption with a new song. Praised art Thou, Yahweh, who redeemest Israel.[1]

Kaminka argues, further, that the way in which Babylon's living in prosperity and Jerusalem's lying waste (iii. 2) are expressed would be too weak and inadequate if the mighty Roman empire were meant; also, that one writing during the Roman period could not have written about Babylon and Sion as he does in iii. 30, 31,[2] when it was well known that Babylon *had* been punished, and that there could be no mourning over the loss of the ark (x. 22) in Roman times. And, once more, the primitive conception of the writer concerning the earth's surface, to which he assigns one-seventh to water (vi. 42, 47) points to a time before Herodotus (B.C. 484–425). Finally, Kaminka urges that the usual expression for God in the book, *Altissimus*, the Most High (= ὕψιστος, עֶלְיוֹן), is used only in the ancient poetical writings, especially the Psalms; and that the classical Hebrew style in which the book was originally written is comprehensible only of a writer who knew the historical and poetical books of pre-exilic times [3] (on this see further below, § v).

We have given Kaminka's arguments for an early date in some detail because it is the only attempt in modern times which has been made. They strike us as entirely

[1] In the Midrash *Pesikta*, x. 6. With this may be compared, too, the seventeenth Benediction of the ancient synagogal prayer, *Shemoneh 'Esreh*: "Accept, O Lord our God, Thy people Israel and their prayer; restore the service to the oracle of Thy house; receive in love and favour both the fire-offerings of Israel and their prayer; and may the service of Thy people be ever acceptable unto Thee."

[2] "For I have seen how Thou sufferest them sinning, and hast spared the ungodly doers, and hast destroyed thy people, and hast preserved thine enemies . . . are the deeds of Babylon better than those of Sion?" One would have thought that the deduction drawn from this would be precisely the opposite to that drawn by Kaminka!

[3] *Op. cit.*, pp. 47–59.

unconvincing; but to refute them would take up too much space here. We regret that Kaminka does not explain why an authentic book belonging to the sixth century B.C., and written in classical Hebrew, was not received into the Canon.

The date of the *Eagle Vision* (xi. xii) is not difficult to indicate within certain limits; but an exact date is more problematical as it depends upon the interpretation of some of the details in the vision. The eagle obviously symbolizes the Roman empire, and indications in the vision point to some time during the reign of Domitian, *i.e.* before 96 A.D.; some would date it 90 A.D., and others slightly earlier, during the reign of Vespasian (69–79 A.D.).[1]

The Vision of the *Man from the Sea* (xiii) is, in all probability, slightly earlier. As in verses 38–40 it is said that the nations shall be destroyed, but that the ten tribes shall be gathered together to their own land, the two tribes are in Palestine. This, as Box, following Kabisch, points out, " implies a historical situation for the interpretation of the vision before 70 A.D., when the nation (= the two tribes) is in peaceful possession of Palestine. After 70 A.D. the situation of the two tribes is always represented as that of the exile (a Babylonian exile)."[2] How long before this year the Seer wrote his vision cannot be said with certainty; possibly towards the end of 66 A.D., when, after the outbreak of the War, the Jews had gained some initial successes, the writer may have written this vision in the belief of coming victory through divine help.

The content of Chap. xiv suggests its date; as it deals with the inspiration both of the Canonical Scriptures and of the Apocalypses, it is likely to have been written during the period when the question of the Canon was being discussed; this would be some time between about 100 A.D. and 120 A.D.

(3) *Chapters xv. xvi.*

These chapters may, with some confidence, be assigned

---

[1] For details, see Box, *op. cit.*, pp. 247 ff., and the present writer, *op. cit.*, pp. 144 ff.
[2] *Op. cit.*, p. 286.

to a time between 240 A.D. and 270 A.D. The subject-matter of these chapters is not of sufficient importance to require a detailed examination of the reasons for assuming this date.[1]

IV. REDACTIONAL ELEMENTS

The question of redactional elements in the book is of some importance, and there are considerable differences of opinion on the subject; it merits, therefore, some little discussion.

At the beginning of the apocalypse we are confronted with a somewhat curious phrase which is the first point demanding attention. In iii. 1 the writer speaks of himself as: " I Salathiel who am also Ezra " (*Ego Salathiel qui et Ezras*);[2] these words have naturally occasioned a good deal of discussion. It is held by some that " who am also Ezra " is a redactor's addition; the name of Ezra occurs in other parts of the book (i. 1, ii. 10, 42, xiv. 1), so that the compiler who gathered together the component parts may have added these words, or possibly a later redactor, reading the book in its present form (though probably without chaps. xv, xvi), put them in; in either case the object would have been to indicate that the whole was the work of Ezra. According to this view, the words should be deleted, and instead of speaking of an " Ezra-Apocalypse," this should be called the " Salathiel-Apocalypse." James, however, accounts for what may appear to be an addition in a different way: " I believe I have found evidence," he writes, " to show that there was a Jewish tradition which identified Esdras with Salathiel inde-pendently of this book. Epiphanius (*On the Twelve Gems*) speaks of an ' Esdras the priest—not that Esdras who was called Salathiel, whose father was Zorobabel, which Zorobabel was son to Jechonias.' Epiphanius—who is wrong, by the way—in his genealogy, nowhere shows any know-

---

[1] See the present writer's *op. cit.*, pp. 179 ff.
[2] It may be noted, however, that one of the Arabic Versions reads: " I Ezra, called Shealtiel " (Violet, *op. cit.*, p. 3). See further, James, *op. cit.*, p. xxv.

ledge of *IV Esdras*. It is evident from what he says, and from other sources, that the name Esdras was supposed to have been that of several persons; authority definitely states that Esdras the prophet, the author of *IV Esdras*, and Esdras the scribe, the author of the canonical *Ezra*, lived about 100 years apart; also *IV Esdras* is dated, in its opening words, in the thirtieth year after the ruin of the city, whereas Ezra the scribe belongs to the middle of the next century.[1] The equation of Salathiel with Esdras is based, I believe, upon 1 Chron. iii. 17, where we read, *and the son of Jeconiah, Assir, Salathiel, his son ;* [2] and Assir, in despite of phonetic laws, was thought to be, or was forcibly assimilated to, Ezra; Assir and Salathiel being taken as two names for one man." [3] Rosenthal refers to *Sanhedrin* 37[b] (Bab. Talmud), where Assir (= " prisoner ") is identified with Shealtiel on account of his having been born in captivity.[4]

James' explanation would, at any rate, dispose of the theory of a " Salathiel-Apocalypse," for the existence of which there is otherwise no evidence. Thus, the words, " who am also Ezra " are not necessarily due to a redactor.

We come next to consider four eschatological passages (iv. 52–v. 13[a]; vi. 11–29; vii. 26–44; viii. 63–ix. 12), which are held by some scholars to be a redactor's additions. With the exception of the first, these passages read perfectly smoothly in their contexts, and do not give the impression of being insertions; iv. 52–v. 13[a] does, it is true, come in somewhat awkwardly, but apocalyptic writers are frequently loose and unconventional in their style, according to modern ideas. Kabisch, followed by Box, regards all these passages as not belonging to the original book, but as having been added later by a redactor; the reasons given

---

[1] His date is now held by many modern scholars to be about half a century later.

[2] The text of this verse is uncertain; the Masoretic text has: " And the sons of Jeconiah, Assir, Shealtiel his son "; but another reading is: " And the son of Jeconiah, Assir, Shealtiel ": the Septuagint reads: " And the sons of Jeconiah, Assir, Salathiel his son."

[3] *Op. cit.*, pp. 79 ff.; see also his articles in the *Journal of Theological Studies* for 1917, pp. 167 ff., and for 1918, pp. 347 ff.

[4] *Op. cit.*, p. 57 n. 1.

by Box for this contention are elaborately set forth,[1] but they do not carry conviction. The signs of the end described in these passages are just what one would expect from an apocalyptic writer; if they contain inconsistencies, or if they are inconsistent with other parts of the same writing that is only what is found again and again in the apocalyptic literature. To assign these passages to a redactor is, therefore, we hold, unjustified.

A number of other passages are undoubtedly to be assigned to the hand of a redactor; but, as in the case of the canonical books, there is always some compelling reason for regarding them as redactional elements.

V. The Original Language of the Book

As early as the beginning of the last century, Bretschneider contended for a Hebrew original of our book;[2] half a century later, Ewald likewise expressed his belief in this;[3] but the idea was considered to be out of the question by Volkmar[4]—though he allowed that the writer thought in Hebrew—and by Hilgenfeld,[5] both maintaining that Greek was the original language. Later, however, both Wellhausen[6] and Gunkel[7] made it quite evident that Hebrew was the language in which it was originally written; this was further developed by Violet,[8] and Box[9] has given a number of illustrations to prove this. More recently still, Kaminka has given many examples to prove a Hebrew original, and has shown how difficult passages owe their obscurity to an initial misunderstanding of the Hebrew text.[10] He maintains, moreover, that the original was written in classical Hebrew in the style and language of the great prophets of the eighth century B.C.; he is, however, careful to add that it is doubtful whether this applies to the whole

---

[1] See op. cit., pp. xxv. f., 108 ff., 199 ff.   [2] Das Messiasreich (1806).
[3] Geschichte des Volkes Israel, vii (1859).
[4] Das vierte Buch Esra, p. 328 (1863).   [5] Messias Judæorum, p. xliii (1869).
[6] Skizzen und Vorarbeiten, vi. 234 ff. (1899).
[7] In Kautzsch's Die Apokryphen und Pseudepigraphen des Alten Testaments, ii. p. 333 (1900).
[8] Op. cit., ii. xxxi. ff.   [9] Op. cit., pp. xiii. ff.
[10] Op. cit., passim, but especially pp. 7–23.

of chaps. iii–xiv; in attempting to translate the whole of these chapters back into Hebrew he finds that there are some parts which do not lend themselves to this; especially in chaps. xi–xiii he notices many passages which strike him as un-Hebraic, and he gives examples to show this.[1]

Thus there can be no shadow of doubt as to the original language of the bulk of the book, though chaps. xi–xiii, and probably certain passages in other parts of the book, may have been originally written in Greek.

VI. The Versions

The widespread popularity which our book must at one time have enjoyed is shown by the large number of versions in which it has come down to us. Of the original Hebrew text nothing has survived, unless some of the quotations in Rabbinical literature cited by Rosenthal contain traces of this.[2] Similarly with regard to the Greek version; three direct quotations occur in early Church writings, and also some reminiscences which are not actual quotations;[3] but otherwise no traces of this version have been preserved.[4]

All the other versions are derived from the Greek. The most important of these is the Latin; of this there are four main MSS., the oldest of which is *Codex Sangermanensis*[5] (in the Bibliothèque Nationale of Paris), and this is "the parent of the vast majority of extant copies,"[6] which follow it in omitting the long passage vii. 36–140 (placed in square brackets in the Revised Version). This "Missing Fragment" was discovered by Bensly in a MS. in the communal library at Amiens.[7] It is generally recognized that the various Latin MSS. represent two types of text, the French and the Spanish, of which the former is the better.

The other Versions are the Syriac, Ethiopic, Arabic (of

[1] *Op. cit.*, pp. 5 f. Violet also points to a few verses which may be of Greek origin, ii. p. xxxix.
[2] *Op. cit.*, pp. 23–47.
[3] James, in Bensly, *op. cit.*, pp. xxvii. ff.; Violet, *op. cit.*, i. xiv.
[4] A fragment of another part of our book (xv. 57–59) in Greek was discovered by Hunt.
[5] Published in Sabatier's *Bibliorum sacrorum latinæ versiones antiquæ*, iii (1749).
[6] James, *op. cit.*, p. xiii.
[7] *The Missing Fragment of the Fourth Book of Ezra* (1875).

which there are two), Armenian, and fragments of a Sahidic;
and traces of an old-Georgian Version also exist.[1]

VII. LITERATURE

Bretschneider, *Das Messiasreich* (1806).

Volkmar, " Das vierte Buch Esra," in *Handbuch der Einleitung
in die Apokryphen*, i. 3 ff. (1863).

Ewald, *Geschichte des Volkes Israel*, vii (1868).

Hilgenfeld, *Messias Judaeorum* (1869).

Rosenthal, *Vier Apocryphische Bücher aus der Zeit und Schule
Akibas* (1885).

Lupton, in Wace, *op. cit.*, i. 71 ff. (1888).

Kabisch, *Das Vierte Buch Esra auf seine Quellen untersucht*
(1889).

Bensly, *The Fourth Book of Ezra* (1895).

Gunkel, in Kautzsch, *op. cit.*, ii. 331–401 (1900).

Schürer, *Geschichte des Volkes Israel* . . . iii. 315–335 (1909).

Violet, *Die Esra-Apokalypse :* Erster Teil, Die Ueberlieferung
(1910).

Violet, *Die Apokalypsen des Esra und des Baruch* (1924).

Box, *The Ezra-Apocalypse* (1912); and in Charles, *op. cit.*,
ii. 542 ff. (1913).

Oesterley, *II Esdras : The Ezra Apocalypse* (1933).

Kaminka, *Beiträge zur Erklärung der Esra-Apokalypse und zur
Rekonstruktion ihres hebräischen Urtextes* (1934).

[1] For details regarding all these Versions see Violet, *op. cit.*, I. xiii–xliv; II.
xiii–xxxi; in the first volume all the Versions are printed in parallel columns,
the Latin text itself, and German translations of the rest, excepting the
Armenian which is given in Latin. See also Box, *op. cit.*, pp. iv–xiii.

THE BOOK OF TOBIT

I. TITLE

THE original Greek title of the book, according to Codd. אBA, was: Βιβλος λογων Τωβειθ (B—ιτ, A—ειτ), which suggests the Hebrew title: ספר דברי טובי ; that the book was originally written in Hebrew is extremely probable. Some scholars are inclined to regard Aramaic as the original language; but as the Greek title seems to represent Hebrew, it is more likely that this was the original language, apart from other indications.[1]

II. CONTENTS OF THE BOOK

Tobit, a devout Jew, was carried away captive from his native home in Naphtali, in Galilee, to Nineveh, in the reign of Shalmaneser (cp. II Kgs. xviii. 9–11), *i.e.* in B.C. 721. Unlike so many of his race, Tobit had from early youth always been loyal to the Law. His father Tobiel died while Tobit was still young. On reaching manhood he married Anna, and begat a son whom he named Tobias. In the land of his captivity he continued his good deeds among those of his own race; and was especially zealous in honouring the dead by burying those of his kindred who had been the victims of the cruelty of Sennacherib, who was now king. This was brought to the ears of the king, and Tobit had to flee from Nineveh.

But after the death of Sennacherib, his successor, Esarhaddon, appointed Ahikar, Tobit's nephew, his chief minister; through his uncle's influence Tobit was permitted to return to Nineveh (i. 1–22).

Tobit's first care on returning was to continue his good works as heretofore; he sent out his son to bring in the

[1] See further, Simpson, in Charles, *op. cit.*, i. 180 ff.

poor to be fed; while carrying out his father's behest
Tobias came across the dead body of one of his race which
lay unburied; immediately on being informed of this Tobit
went out and buried it.

That night, owing to the heat, Tobit slept out of doors
in the courtyard; but as he slept the droppings of a sparrow
fell and settled on his eyes and blinded him; for four years
he was "impotent in his eyes" [1] (ii. 1–iii. 6).

Now there dwelt at this time, in Ecbatana, a widowed
virgin, Sarah by name, the daughter of Raguel; she had
had seven husbands, but every one had died on entering
the bridal chamber, having been slain by the evil demon
Asmodæus (iii. 7–15).[2] A parenthetical passage is then
added, saying that both Sarah's prayer for a husband (iii.
15) and Tobit's prayer for sight—which is not recorded—
were "heard before the glory of God," and the angel
Raphael was sent to help both of them (iii. 16, 17).

In the meantime, Tobit, who believes that the hour of
death is at hand, sends his son Tobias to Gabael, who lived
in Rages, in Media, to receive from him a sum of money
which had been left in his care. Before Tobias starts on
his journey, his father admonishes him to do what is right
in all things (iv. 1–21).

Tobias obeys his father, and sets out under the guidance
of Raphael, whom he does not, however, know to be "an
angel of God" [3] (v. 1–22).

While on the journey Tobias bathes in the Tigris, and
suddenly a great fish leaps out of the water; he is bidden
by Raphael to cut open the fish and to take out its gall,
heart, and liver, and to preserve them.

On arriving in Ecbatana, Tobias and his guide take up
their abode with Raguel, who recognizes Tobias as his
kinsman, and at his request gives him his daughter Sarah
to wife, though warning him of the untoward fate of her
former husbands. On entering the bridal chamber, Tobias,
following Raphael's directions, places the heart and liver of
the fish on the ashes of incense; the smoke of this drives
away the demon Asmodæus who had purposed to kill

[1] So Cod. ℵ.   [2] Cp. II Esdras x. 1, 2.   [3] So Cod. ℵ.

Tobias as he had killed the other seven husbands of Sarah.

The wedding festivities are then celebrated, and they are continued for fourteen days. While this is going on Raphael, at the request of Tobias, goes to Rages, and receives from Gabael the money which Tobit had left in his care (vi–ix).

In the meantime, Tobit and his wife are anxiously awaiting the return of their son. On the arrival of Tobias with his wife, Sarah, they are received by his parents with great joy. Thereupon Tobias, at Raphael's directions, places the fish's gall on his father's eyes, who forthwith receives his sight again (x. xi).

In token of his gratitude Tobit offers Raphael half the money which had been brought from Gabael; but Raphael tells him who he really is, and bids him thank God for His mercies (xii).

Tobit thereupon offers a prayer of rejoicing and praise (xiii).

The book closes with Tobit's last words to his son, after which he dies at the age, it is said, of 158 years. Finally, Tobias too, after a long life, dies at the age of 127 (xiv).

III. The Main Themes of the Book

There are certain subjects in our book which receive special emphasis; these must be briefly examined.

First and foremost there is the strict observance of the Law, which is often mentioned, and this includes the constant practice of charitable deeds. At the opening of the book there is pointed reference to Tobit's many alms-deeds, to his punctual keeping of the feasts prescribed in the Law, to his giving of first-fruits and tithes, and to his rendering of the priestly dues; he is forward in the support of widows, orphans, and proselytes (i. 3–8, 16, 17; ii. 2). Similarly, when giving what he believes to be his final words of advice to his son, Tobit urges him to do acts of righteousness, to give alms, to keep himself pure, and to love his brethren (iv. 5–19; see also xii. 8).

Other points of legal observance mentioned are: refraining from partaking of Gentile food (i. 10–12); purification after touching a corpse (ii. 6); washing before eating (vii. 9, ℵ); and the need of marrying within the kin (iv. 12; vi. 10; vii. 13); special mention is made of the law of Moses in vi. 13, vii. 13 and 14, ℵ, cp. xiv. 9.

Not less marked is the stress laid on piety: honouring God (xii. 7, 8, 17, 18, 22), the recognition of divine mercies (viii. 5–9, 16, 17; xi. 14–17, and elsewhere), and the frequent prayers which are offered up (iii. 1–6, 11–15; ix. 15–17; xiii. 1–18).

These all illustrate the strongly Jewish colouring of the book; to them must be added the solidarity of the family and the strength of kinship which are noticeable all through the book (i.e. i. 9, 21, 22; ii. 10; v. 13, etc.), as well as the need of racial purity (vi. 15 and elsewhere).

But interspersed with these pronounced Jewish elements, which are the main characteristics of the book, there are some others; and these, as we shall see in the next section, have quite evidently been borrowed from extraneous sources. They consist of three themes: the faithful travelling companion who, in our book, is represented as an angel (v. 3 ff., etc.); the honouring of the dead by burial of corpses lying untended (i. 17, 18; ii. 3, 4; xii. 12–14); and the overcoming of the evil demon Asmodæus (iii. 8, 17; vi. 7, 14, 17; viii. 3). To these must be added the mention of Aḥiḳar (Achiacharus, i. 21, 22; ii. 10; xi. 17; xiv. 10); while this cannot exactly be called one of the themes borrowed from extraneous sources, the writer of our book was certainly acquainted with the popular narrative of the *Story and Wisdom of Aḥiḳar*, and made some use of it (on this see the next section). Various theories have been put forward as to the place of origin of our book, but none of these is really convincing [1] with the exception of that which assigns Egypt as its home. Among those who hold this view Robertson Smith, Löhr, André, Simpson, and others, none has put forth the arguments in its favour so cogently

[1] Schürer feels uncertain as to whether the eastern Diaspora or Palestine should be regarded as its home; he is followed by Eissfeldt; but neither gives adequate grounds for the contention.

as Simpson; in showing the weakness of other theories and
the strength of his own, he has finally decided the question.[1]

IV. SOURCES OF THE BOOK

It is generally recognized that our book contains material
borrowed from non-Jewish sources. Authorities may differ
as to the extent of this borrowing; but that parallels to the
three themes mentioned occur in other popular literature
does not admit of doubt. The various steps in the transmission of this popular literature which has been handed
down from ancient times are now lost, though traces of the
subject-matter under consideration are distinctly discernible
in, at any rate, one ancient Egyptian document.[2]

The three themes mentioned are found combined in a
folk-tale which must at one time have enjoyed world-wide
popularity since it exists in many countries in varied forms;
the best known is that which appears in the German folk-
tale called: *Der gute Gerhard und die dankbaren Toten;*[3] but
the form which approximates most closely to the three
themes in *Tobit* is the Armenian. This runs briefly as
follows: Once upon a time a wealthy merchant purchased
the mutilated corpse of one who during his lifetime had
been a debtor; the price was paid to one of his creditors,
and having obtained possession of the dead body the
merchant accorded it a decent burial. Now in course of
time it happened that this wealthy merchant lost all his
possessions and was reduced to poverty and dire need.
One day a stranger came to him and advised him to marry
the only daughter of a rich man who lived in the same
city; she had already, it is true, had five husbands, each
of whom died on the wedding-night; but this does not
deter the merchant from following the stranger's counsel;
so he married her. On the night of the wedding, as he
entered the bridal chamber a serpent issued from the mouth

[1] In Charles, *op. cit.*, i. 185 ff.
[2] *The Tractate of Khons*, see Wiedemann in Hastings' *D.B.*, extra vol., p. 185;
Simpson in Charles, *op. cit.* i., 187 f.
[3] Simrock (1856), who has collected a number of variant forms of the
story.

of the bride, intending to kill him; but suddenly the stranger appeared again and destroyed the serpent. Then he made himself known as the dead man whose corpse the merchant had with such good intent buried. Thus was he rewarded for his pious deed.

In spite of marked differences between this and the *Tobit* story, there is no mistaking the essential identity between the main themes. Whether during a journey or at any other time, there is the good companion; between an angel and the appearance of a dead man there would not have been any real difference to the ancient Jewish mind (cp. Acts xii. 15); the reward for burying the derelict corpse is much the same in each story; so, too, the death of the many husbands on the wedding-night; and the difference between Asmodæus the evil demon and the serpent is only apparent, for all serpents were looked upon as demons in those days.

The mention of the name of the evil demon Asmodæus, however, does suggest indebtedness to another source; and here, too, the prominence given to the angel Raphael brings us to the question of Persian influence.

That Persian angelology and demonology, especially the latter, exercised a powerful influence on the popular beliefs of the Jews does not admit of doubt.[1] It is usually held that Asmodæus is the counterpart of the Persian *Aeshma daeva*,[2] one of the six arch-fiends in the service of *Angra Mainyu*, the " Prince of Evil "; he is, after *Angra Mainyu*, the most dangerous of all the demons, and has under him seven especially powerful demons. In all probability the method of driving away the evil demon, as described in Tob. viii. 3,[3] is due to Persian influence. Other signs of this influence are mentioned by Moulton, who points out

---

[1] See the relevant sections in Stave, *Ueber den Einfluss des Parsismus auf das Judentum* (1898); Böklen, *Die Verwandtschaft der jüdisch-christlichen mit der Parsischen Eschatologie* (1902); Scheftelowitz, *Die altpersische Religion und das Judentum* (1920); Bousset, *Die Religion des Judentums im späthellenistischen Zeitalter*, pp. 478 ff. (1926).

[2] Scheftelowitz maintains, however, that Asmodæus is not equivalent to *Aeshma daeva*, but that the name is derived from the root *shamad*, " to destroy," in later Hebrew " to force to apostasy " (*op. cit.*, p. 61), cp. Bousset, *op. cit.*, p. 488, who leaves the question open.

[3] Scheftelowitz, *op. cit.*, p. 66.

that it was to late Persian religion, *i.ę.* Magianism, not Zoroastrianism, that the writer of *Tobit* was indebted.[1]

The *rôle* of the angel Raphael as the protector of Tobias during his journey has also its parallel in Persian angelology, according to which every good man is accompanied by an angel in his walk through life.[2]

The last extraneous source is the *Story and Wisdom of Ahikar*.[3] · A certain number of passages in *Tobit* show the writer's acquaintance with this story; thus i. 21, 22, where the official position of Achiacharus in Nineveh is spoken of, is apparently based on Ahikar iii. 9–11. In Tob. ii. 10, xiv. 10 there are evident references to episodes in the story of Ahikar (see iv. 12, viii. 2, 37, 41, of this latter). Parallels between wise sayings such as in Tob. iv. 10, 15, 18, cp. Ahikar ii. 19, 43, 12 and 72, do not necessarily point to indebtedness; they are merely items belonging to the Wisdom literature in general. But one instance there is which the writer of *Tobit* imitated from Ahikar, viz. the precept: " Pour out thy bread and thy wine on the tomb of the just, and give not to sinners " (iv. 17 Cod. א); in *Ahikar* ii. 10 it is said: " My son, pour out thy wine on the graves of the righteous, rather than drink it with evil men."

There are also some " literary and structural models," and " a not inconsiderable amount of Ahikar's parenetic sections," to which Simpson points as having been adopted by the writer of *Tobit*.[4] There can, therefore, be no doubt about the use of this source.

V. INTEGRITY OF THE BOOK

Various attempts—more or less ingenious, but sometimes far-fetched, and based in part on the different forms of text appearing in the MSS. and Versions—have been made to

---

[1] *Hibbert Lectures*, " The Magian Material of Tobit." Appendix to Lecture vii. (1912).
[2] Scheftelowitz, *op. cit.*, p. 153.
[3] See especially Harris, Lewis, and Conybeare, in Charles, *op. cit.*, ii. pp. 715 ff.; Nau, *Histoire et Sagesse d'Ahikar l'Assyrien* (1909).
[4] In Charles, *op. cit.*, i. 191.

M

prove that the book contains interpolations, inconsistencies, and redactional manipulations; its integrity has thus been called in question, and it is contended that the book is not a unity. Erbt, *e.g.*, in his searching inquiry,[1] points to the fact that the first person is used in i. 1–iii. 6, the third person in the remainder of the book, to a number of contradictions, to the Aḥikar references, to the wisdom passages, especially in chaps. iv and xii, and to one or two other matters, as proof that the book has gone through successive stages of growth, that " copyists and translators have treated their text with a good deal of arbitrariness," and that its original form was very different from that which we now have. Very thorough and discerning as Erbt's investigations are, it may be doubted whether modern standards of what constitutes a logical, orderly, and consistent narrative are really applicable to an ancient oriental writing such as this. It cannot be denied that inconsistencies occur, and that the narrative does not always run smoothly and in a straight-forward manner; but when a writer is confessedly making use of extraneous material for the purpose of enhancing the interest of his book, and, like many another ancient oriental writer, is less concerned with the niceties of com-position than with telling his story graphically, one must not look for rigid literary propriety. Simpson's view strikes us as being decidedly more in accordance with facts, and therefore the more acceptable; he holds that the book is " characterized throughout by a unity of purpose well con-ceived in its plan, and natural and simple in its develop-ment, the work, in short, of a single author of more than average taste and ability."[2]

VI. DATE

The book purports to have been written early in the seventh century B.C., but this is merely a literary device (cp. *Judith*); there is ample evidence to show that it belongs to a much later period. To begin with, the writer, as we have seen, was familiar with the *Story and Wisdom of Aḥikar*,

[1] In *Encycl. Bibl.* iv. 5110 ff.   [2] See Charles, *op. cit.*, i. 194.

a work which belongs to a period, at the very latest, about the middle of the fifth century B.C.[1]

Further, the writer's knowledge of the latest portions of the Pentateuch [2] shows that he must have lived during the Greek period. This will bring the date of the book down to a time later than 300 B.C.

But the most convincing indication as to the date is afforded by the writer's religious standpoint. That there is no mention of the resurrection, especially in such passages as iii. 6, 10, 13, where this would reasonably be looked for, shows that belief in the resurrection of the body had not yet become a dogma of Judaism, whatever individuals may have believed; this would point to a time, approximately, towards the end of the third century B.C. A similar date is suggested by some of his utterances in regard to the Law, especially the stress laid on prayer, fasting, and alms (xii. 8), and the efficacy of almsgiving (xii. 9). On the other hand, the book must have been written before the building of Herod's Temple, begun in 20 B.C., for it is evident from xiv. 5 that it is the second temple with which he was familiar (" and they shall build the house, but not like the former "; he purports to be writing during the Exile), not that of Herod. There is nothing in the book which suggests that it was written during the Maccabæan era (*i.e.* approximately 175 B.C.–125 B.C.); it must therefore have been written either before or after this epoch-making struggle; but it can hardly have been written after this period, because the writer does not represent the specifically Pharisaic religious standpoint, which would be looked for in one who had such an ardent respect for the Law; it will, therefore, have been written before this era. Thus, we are forced to assume a date before 175 B.C., and it may, therefore, be assigned, approximately, to 200 B.C.

---

[1] Sachau, *Aramäische Papyrus und Ostraka aus Elephantiné*, p. xxii (1911), places it between 550 and 450 B.C. Cowley favours a date *circa* 550 B.C. (*Aramaic Papyri of the fifth century B.C.*, p. 208 [1923]).

[2] For details, see Simpson in Charles, *op. cit.*, i. 192, note 6.

VII. Manuscripts and Versions

The Greek MSS. of *Tobit* fall into three classes representing three recensions of the text: (i) Codd. BA, followed by the bulk of the MSS. both uncial and cursive, as well as by one of the Syriac Versions up to vii. 9; (ii) Cod. ℵ, followed by the Old Latin Version, more or less; (iii) three cursives numbered 44, 106, 107; the text of these shows affinities with Cod. ℵ so far as vi. 9–xiii. 8 are concerned, the remainder representing the recension of Codd. B, etc.; one of the Syriac Versions follows the text of these three cursives from vii. 9 onwards.[1]

Which of these three recensions represents the earliest Greek form of the book offers an intricate problem, and is still a subject of controversy; but the arguments in favour of the priority of that represented by Cod. ℵ put forth by Schürer and Simpson are very convincing.

The Versions include the Old Latin, of which there are three types of text, the Vulgate, two Syriac Versions, the Aramaic, which follows, in the main, the Cod. ℵ recension, two late Hebrew Versions, and the Ethiopic. For the relative importance of these see Simpson,[2] who remarks that they " are indispensable for a critical investigation of the text (*a*) as showing the form in which the book was read in various quarters of the world in several different languages; (*b*) as being by no means insignificant aids to the recovery of the true text of the various chief recensions to which they belong; (*c*) as conceivably containing among their unique readings a few potentially original ones."

VIII. Literature

Fritzsche, *op. cit.*, ii. 3 ff. (1853).
Scholz, *Commentar zum Buche Tobias* (1889).
Ball, *Variorum Apocrypha* (1892).
Löhr, in Kautzsch, *op. cit.*, i. 135 ff. (1900).

[1] Schürer, *Gesch. des jüd. Volkes* . . . iii. 242 (1909); Simpson, *op. cit.*, pp. 174 f.
[2] *Op. cit.*, pp. 176 ff.

Plath, "Zum Buche Tobit," in *Theologische Studien und Kritiken* (1901), pp. 377 ff.

Marshall, in Hastings' *Dict. of the Bible*, iv. 788 ff. (1902).

André, *op. cit.*, pp. 170 ff. (1903).

Erbt, in *Encycl. Bibl.*, iv. 5110 ff. (1903).

Müller, J., *Beiträge zur Erklärung und Kritik der Buches Tobit* (1908).

Schürer, *op. cit.*, iii. 237 ff. (1909).

Moulton, "The Iranian Background of Tobit" in *The Expository Times*, xi. 257 ff. (1899–1900).

Moulton, *Hibbert Lectures*, "The Magian Material of Tobit," Appendix to Lecture vii, and see the whole of the Lecture itself (1912).

Simpson, in Charles, *op cit.*, i. 174 ff. (1913).

For the older literature see Schürer, *op. cit.*, iii. 246 f.

THE BOOK OF JUDITH

I. TITLE

As in the case of Tobit, the spelling of the name varies in the MSS.: Ἰουδείθ, —διθ, —δηθ [1]; the name stands alone in the title; it is found elsewhere only in Gen. xxvi. 34 as that of a woman of Hittite extraction.

II. CONTENTS OF THE BOOK

i. 1–6: War breaks out between Nebuchadrezzar, who is spoken of as the king of Assyria, and Arphaxad, king of the Medes, supported by many other nations.

i. 7–16: Nebuchadrezzar calls the Western nations to his assistance, but they refuse to join him; he thereupon swears to take vengeance on them. The battle between Nebuchadrezzar and Arphaxad takes place; the latter is defeated, and Nebuchadrezzar returns to Nineveh.

ii. 1–13: Nebuchadrezzar determines to punish the Western nations for having refused to support him. He commands Holofernes, the chief captain of the host, to go with a great army against them.

ii. 14–38: Holofernes sets out, and ravages all the lands in his progress westwards.

iii. 1–10: The lands on the western sea-coast send messengers to Holofernes offering submission; on his arrival in their midst he is received with much rejoicing.

iv. 1–15: The Israelites, hearing of the approach of Holofernes, are filled with fear, but prepare to resist him. Supplication is made to God for His protection and help.

[1] Swete, *op. cit.*, pp. 201 ff.

x. 1–xi. 4 : Judith decks herself in gay apparel, and, taking her maid with her, goes out of the city at night to the camp of the enemy. She is brought to the tent of Holofernes, by whom she is welcomed.

xi. 5–23 : Judith beguiles Holofernes with persuasive, but deceptive, words.

xii. 1–xiii. 10 : For three days Judith remains in the enemy's camp; on the fourth day Holofernes invites her to a feast. After the feast Judith is left alone with Holofernes, who, being overcome with wine, lies prone upon his bed. Judith then takes his sword and severs his head from his body; the head she gives to her maid to place in a bag brought for the purpose; both flee from the camp and arrive safely before the gates of Bethulia.

xiii. 11–20 : Judith is received with great joy by the people to whom she shows the head of Holofernes. Ozias calls down a blessing upon her.

xiv 1–xv. 7 : At Judith's direction the head of Holofernes is hung out from the battlement of the city wall. The next morning the Israelites sally forth armed as though for battle; seeing this, Bagoas hurries to the tent of Holofernes to bid him lead out his army to victory; on hearing no sound from within he enters and sees what has happened. The Assyrians are seized with panic and flee; they are pursued by the Israelites and wholly overcome.

xv. 8–13 : The high-priest Joakim comes from Jerusalem to honour Judith; in this he is joined by all the people.

xvi. 1–17 : The song of praise and thanksgiving of Judith and all the people.

xvi. 18–25 : Rejoicing and feasting are continued for three months in Jerusalem. Thereafter Judith returns to Bethulia, where she abides in honourable widowhood for the rest of her days. She dies at the age of 105, having beforehand distributed all her wealth to the nearest kindred of her long-departed husband, and to her own kindred. " And there was none that made the children of Israel any more afraid in the days of Judith, nor a long time after her death."

III. Character and Purpose of the Book

As a literary product the qualities of the book of *Judith* are incontestable. The story is graphically told; the scenes depicted are realistic and follow one another in logical sequence; unnecessary details are avoided; and the characters of the *dramatis personæ* are skilfully set forth. In reference to Judith's thanksgiving (xvi. 1–17) it is no exaggeration when Fritzsche says: " I put it unhesitatingly by the side of the best poetical products of the Hebrew genius "; and one must endorse André's words: " As to the ' Canticle of Judith ' (xvi. 1–17), it is a model of its kind, written by a master hand and worthy to be placed side by side with the Song of Deborah " (Judg. v. 1 ff.).

The standpoint of the book is Pharisaic; thus, the care for and veneration of the Temple find frequent expression (iv. 2, 3, 11–15; viii. 21; ix. 1, 8, 13; xvi. 18–20, and elsewhere); such a passage, *e.g.*, as xi. 3, which tells of how the people of Bethulia were castigated for thinking of encroaching on the tithes reserved for the Temple, even when they were besieged and desperate, shows, in fact, that what we have here is not the kind of veneration that was found in earlier days, but the exaggerated veneration of the Pharisees; fasting and prayer are insisted upon (viii. 6; the prayer of Judith in ix; xi. 17; xii. 8; xiii. 4, 5); the dietary laws are mentioned or implied (x. 5; xi. 12–15; xii. 1–9, 19); ritual purifications are referred to (xii. 7, 9); proselytism also finds expression (xiv. 10); the denunciation against idolatry in viii. 18–20 is what we should expect, together with the glorification of the God of Israel (ix. 11;

xvi. 6, 7, 11, 12). A pronounced mark of the Pharisaic standpoint is the balance held between the doctrines of determinism and free-will, compare *e.g.* viii. 11–27; ix. 5–14; xvi. 13–17, where God's over-ruling power is insisted upon, with viii. 32–34; x. 9; xv. 9, 10, where human free-will has full play. On the other hand, it cannot fail to be noticed that the miraculous element is wholly lacking; there is no mention of angels; no reference to a future life, and no word about the Messianic hope; probably this is to be explained by the nature of the story (see below).

There are, further, some elements in the book which are far from attractive; candour demands that these should not be ignored. Thus, the glorification of war, though from the spirit of the times one can understand this, is an un-beautiful *trait*; and the way in which the Almighty is called upon to take part in it does not betray a high ideal; in ix. 8 it is said: "Dash thou down their strength in thy power, and bring down their force in thy wrath"; and in various other passages a religious sanction is given to fighting (*e.g.* ix. 8, 13; xiii. 14; xv. 10). Then, again, although this is quite comprehensible, a bitter hatred against the heathen is evinced (*e.g.* iii. 2–4, 8, 10; xiii. 5; xiv. 4; xv. 5 ff.; xvi. 17).

Another thing which points to a lack in the writer's ethical standard is the way in which he, in effect, contends that the end justifies the means; and worse still, that the Almighty condones this and furthers it; thus in ix. 13 Judith prays: ". . . and make my speech and deceit to be their wound and stripe, who have purposed hard things against thy Covenant . . ." Again, lying, ruse, and assassination, as a means to a good end, are praised, for they are of profit to God's people, and forward the religious ideals of Israel (see xi. 5–19; xii. 14; 18; xiii. 17 ff.; xiv. 7, 9; xv. 9 ff., and elsewhere).

And lastly, there are some distinctly revolting passages, bringing out what André rightly calls *la sensualité raffinée*, which do not heighten one's ideas of the writer's good taste (x. 3, 4; xii. 14, 15, 18; xiii. 16; xvi. 22 and some others); and André says: "le romancier seul, qui connaissait la fin de l'histoire, pouvait ne pas être choqué."

The purpose of the story is to show how God protects His own people against their most inveterate and mighty foes; the instrument whereby His will is wrought may be ever so weak provided there is genuine trust in Him, and provided that His law is observed; hence the choice of a woman as the central figure; and Judith is represented as one who is never lacking in religious duties (see viii. 11–27; ix. 2–14; xi. 9–16, etc.); and in such passages, moreover, the writer exhibits his legal and theocratic ideas.

IV. HISTORICITY AND DATE

The prominence given to some well-known historical names would at first sight lead one to suppose that the book of *Judith* contained history. Thus, *Nebuchadrezzar* reigned over the Neo-Babylonian empire B.C. 605–562. *Holofernes* (or Orophernes) was the name of the brother of the Cappadocian king Ariarathes, the vassal of Artaxerxes Ochus (B.C. 359–338); he fought successfully under the Persian king in one of his Egyptian campaigns; [1] Holofernes was also the name of a Cappadocian king who lived in the middle of the second century B.C. [2] Bagoas is mentioned as one of the generals of Artaxerxes Ochus during his campaign against the Phoenicians and Egyptians in B.C. 351, [3] the Jews joined in this revolt and suffered severely in consequence; [4] Diodorus speaks of this Bagoas as a eunuch [5] (cp. Jud. xii. 11); presumably this is the same Bagoas as the one just mentioned. At any rate, both Holofernes and Bagoas lived during the reign of Artaxerxes Ochus, and both are mentioned together in our book (xii. 10 ff.); it is for this reason that Robertson Smith and others regard it as "probable that the wars under Ochus form the historical background of the Book of Judith." [6] Once more, the name of *Arphaxad* occurs in i. 1, 2 as the king of Media, who fortified Ecbatana;

[1] *Diodor.* xxxi. 19, 2–3. [2] *Diodor.* xxxi. 32. [3] *Diodor.* xvi. 47, 4.
[4] Hecataeus of Abdera, in reference to this, says: " The Persians formerly carried away many ten thousands of our people to Babylonia " (Josephus, *Contra Ap.* i. 194), cp. Eusebius, *Chronicon*, ed. Schoene, ii. 112, 113 (1866).
[5] *Diodor.* xvii. 5, 3.
[6] *The Old Testament in the Jewish Church*, p. 439 (1895); Sulpicius Severus identifies the Nebuchadrezzar of this book with Artaxerxes Ochus.

no Median king of this name is known; it is probably a place-name and not a personal name at all [1]; in any case, according to Herodotus i. 98, it was Deioces, the son of Phraortes, who fortified Ecbatana about the year B.C. 700. In spite of these historical *data* it is clear enough that the book of *Judith* does not contain history. But further, it is said in i. 1 that Nebuchadrezzar was king of the Assyrians, and lived in Nineveh; he was, however, king of the Neo-Babylonian empire, and the Assyrian empire had ceased to exist before he came to the throne, and Nineveh was destroyed in B.C. 612.

And once more, while the events recorded in the book are represented as having taken place during the reign of Nebuchradrezzar, *i.e.* before the Exile, it is stated in iv. 3 that the Jews "were newly come up from captivity, and all the people of Judæa were lately gathered together." More-over, a High-priest is head of the community (iv. 6, xv. 8), and the Temple, which Nebuchadrezzar destroyed, is standing (iv. 2, 11, etc.).[2]

It is, thus, impossible to reconcile the historical setting of the book with actual history. If the author had claimed to write history, or had even intended to make some historical event the basis of his story he would assuredly have avoided committing the extraordinary historical blunders which figure so prominently.

The idea that the book contains either recent or contemporary history disguised under significant names is difficult to accept.[3] The book is in reality a novel, like that of *Tobit*; historical names are used for convenience; but it does not contain, nor is it intended to contain, history.

On the other hand, the *historical conditions* which are discernible in the book enable us to date the time of its composition with tolerable certainty.

[1] See Cheyne in *Encycl. Bibl.* i. 318.

[2] For further errors in the book, historical, chronological, and geographical, see André, *op. cit.*, pp. 152 ff.; his conclusion is thus expressed: " Le livre de Judith n'est qu'un roman national dont le cadre, artificiellement historique, est composé de notices éparses et de noms pêchés au petit bonheur, sans liens les uns avec les autres, et sans le moindre souci de la vraisemblance le plus élémentaire."

[3] See C. J. Ball's clever, but unconvincing and not always consistent, arguments, in Wace, *op. cit.*, pp. 248 ff. (1888).

It is a time at which the people are clearly in fear of losing their independence owing to the advent of a foreign foe: "And they were exceedingly afraid before him, and were troubled for Jerusalem, and for the temple of the Lord their God " (iv. 2); and again in viii. 21: ". . . for if we be taken so, all Judæa shall sit upon the ground, and our sanctuary shall be spoiled." The intention of the enemy is to root out the Jewish faith: ". . . and it had been given unto him to destroy all the gods of the land, that all the nations should worship Nebuchadrezzar only, and that all their tongues and all their tribes should call upon him as a god " (iii. 8).

These conditions point to the Maccabæan period and to some time during the years of Jonathan's leadership (B.C. 160/159–142/1), for by this time the Temple had been regained by the orthodox Jewish party, and the Jews were enjoying virtual independence; at the same time, the Syrian menace was by no means yet overcome.

Then, again, the fierce hatred and desire for vengeance on the Gentiles exhibited (e.g. in ix. 2–4), and the general war-like spirit throughout our book is precisely that which existed during the Maccabæan wars (cp., e.g., 1 Macc. ii. 40; iii. 18–22; iv. 7–14, 30–33).

Once more, in our book there is the frequent expression of a firmly grounded faith that God will help His people (see, e.g., iv. 9–13; vi. 18–19; vii. 29–31, etc.); similarly in *I Maccabees* trust in God upholds the people (e.g., iii. 18–22; iv. 8–11).

Significant, too, is the fact that it is the High-priest who takes the lead in war-like preparations, and his directions are followed (iv. 6–8); in I Macc. x. 21 we read of how Jonathan " put on the holy garments," i.e. became High-priest. It may also be mentioned that the book of *Judith* was read at the feast of *Ḥanukkah*, which was initiated in Maccabæan times; this, at any rate, strengthens the belief in the connexion of our book with the Maccabæan age.

Finally, throughout our book there is a strongly marked orthodoxy, reminding us of the time, during Jonathan's leadership, when the hellenistic Jews had been entirely overcome by the orthodox party; during the earlier years of the Maccabæan period the enmity between the Jewish parties is emphasized in I Macc. (*e.g.*, i. 11–15, 34–40, 42; ii. 46, 47, etc.); but in our book there is no hint of this.

Thus, both from the political and religious points of view, the conditions presented in our book are parallel with those of the Maccabæan era, and more especially with the period of Jonathan's leadership. It should also be added that in ii. 28 of our book Azotus (Ashdod) is mentioned as being inhabited; as this city was destroyed by Jonathan in 147 B.C. (see I Macc. x. 34; xi. 4, cp. xiv. 34), our book must have been written before that year. As against the view, held by some, that our book belongs to the Roman period, it may be remarked that it is quite evident from the book that Galilee had not yet been incorporated with Judæa; this took place during the High-priesthood of Aristobulus I. (B.C. 103/2).

V. The Original Language of the Book

That our book was originally written in Hebrew admits of no doubt as soon as the attempt is made to re-translate the Greek into Hebrew. There are many curious mistakes in the Greek which are at once explained in the light of what the corresponding Hebrew must have read. As Cowley has remarked: "The translation is so literal that it can be put back into Hebrew with ease, and in some cases becomes fully intelligible only when it is so re-translated." Many illustrations of this could be given, but this is not the place for these. It is generally recognized that Hebrew, not Aramaic, was the original language. Jerome says he translated the book from the Chaldee; but it is probable, as Porter points out, that "an interpreter rendered the Chaldee into Hebrew, and Jerome dictated a Latin Version of the Hebrew to a scribe." Evidently, however, Jerome knew of the existence of the original Hebrew, as he says that the book was read "apud Hebræos"; but he was unable to procure a copy himself. Of this original Hebrew no fragment has come down to us.

VI. THE VERSIONS

The Greek Version, having been made directly from the original Hebrew, is by far the most important of these. It exists in three recensions, of which that represented by BℵA and most of the cursives is the best. A second recension, much worked over, is preserved in the cursive 58; with the text of this MS. the Old Latin and Syriac Versions show close affinity. The third is represented in the cursives 19 and 108; but these agree largely with Cod. 58.

The Old Latin Version, made from the Greek, is " often merely latinized hebraistic Greek, and sometimes misunderstands the Greek which it translates " (Cowley). Five MSS. of this Version are collated by Sabatier [1]; since his day Berger [2] has discovered some others; altogether eleven MSS. of *Judith* have been found; they vary considerably from one another.

The Vulgate, having been made by Jerome, as we have seen, from a Chaldee Version, of which nothing is otherwise known, differs in many particulars from the Septuagint; it omits various incidents, and numerous geographical details; Judith's apparently sensuous behaviour is toned down, and frequent homiletic remarks are inserted, so that it partakes of the character of a paraphrastic recension; according to Cowley, it omits, about one-fifth of the book.

The Syriac Version, of which there are two recensions, [3] is closely allied with the Old Latin.

The Syro-Hexaplar and the Ethiopic Versions are unimportant.

There are various late Hebrew forms of our book which differ in length, character, and content. [4] None of them are translations, but merely mediæval " free sketches of a well-known story, set down from memory in more or less detail according to the taste of the writer " (Cowley).

---

[1] *Bibliorum sacrorum Latinæ versiones antiquæ*, i. 744 ff. (1743).
[2] *Histoire de la Vulgate* . . ., pp. 19 ff. (1893).
[3] Schürer, *op. cit.*, iii. 198.
[4] For the oldest of these see Gaster: " An unknown Hebrew Version of the History of Judith," in the *Proceedings of the Soc. Bibl. Arch.* for 1894, pp. 156 ff., and by the same author, *The Chronicles of Jerahmeel* (1899).

VII. Literature

Fritzsche, *op. cit.*, ii. 113 ff. (1853).
Volkmar, *op. cit.*, i. 3 ff. (1860).
Ball, in Wace, *op. cit.*, i. 241 ff. (1888).
Weissmann, *Das Buch Judith, historisch-kritisch beleuchtet* (1891).
Scholz, *Kommentar über das Buch Judith* . . . (1896).
Löhr, in Kautzsch, *op. cit.*, i. 147 ff. (1900).
André, *op. cit.*, pp. 147 ff. (1903).
Cowley, in Charles, *op. cit.*, i. 242 ff. (1913).

THE REST OF THE CHAPTERS OF THE BOOK OF ESTHER

I. Purpose and Contents of the Additions

These Additions, which are six in number, and comprise 107 verses not occurring in the Hebrew text,[1] were inserted in the Greek Version of *Esther* with the twofold purpose of giving expression to the religious element so gravely wanting in the canonical *Esther*, and of providing some further details of events which were considered to be insufficiently treated there.

In the Vulgate these additions are placed at the end of the canonical *Esther*, which " has had the effect of making them unintelligible ";[2] in the Revised Version of the Apocrypha they are gathered together under the title: " The Rest of the Chapters of the Book of Esther, which are found neither in the Hebrew, nor in the Chaldee "; but their respective positions in the text of the Septuagint Version of the canonical *Esther* are indicated in the margin.

Our first task must be to consider each addition in relation to the context in which it stands in the Septuagint. We follow the Cambridge Septuagint in designating the additions by the letters A–F respectively.

The First Addition (A = xi. 2-xii. 6 in the Vulgate). This stands at the beginning of the book, and is intended to be an introduction summarizing what follows in the first three chapters. Religious notes are struck in A 9 (= xi. 10): " They then cried unto God . . .," and in A 11 (= xi. 12), where what is about to happen is ascribed to the will of God. The addition consists of two sections: Mordecai's dream (A 1-10 = xi. 2-11), and the events which followed

[1] Swete, *The Old Testament in Greek*, p. 257 (1900).
[2] *Ibid.*

183

(A 11–17 = xi. 12–xii. 6). In his dream Mordecai per-
ceived a great uproar on the earth, in the midst of which
two dragons appeared ready to fight each other; at the
noise of their strife all nations prepared to fight against
"the righteous nation"; but the people of the latter cried
to God; in answer to their cry there came a great river
"from a little fountain"; whereupon "the light of the
sun rose up, and the lowly were exalted, and devoured the
glorious." The two dragons are, of course, Haman and
Mordecai, the little fountain is Esther (see Addition F).
In the second section it is told how Mordecai, on awaking,
overheard two eunuchs who were hatching a plot against
the king. Mordecai reports this to the king, and is rewarded
for his loyalty. Upon this Haman, who was presumably in
league with the conspirators, determines to avenge himself
upon Mordecai.

Some inconsistencies between this Addition and the book
itself may be noted: According to the Addition, Mordecai
was a "servitor in the king's court" in the second year of
Artaxerxes (= Xerxes), whereas in ii. 16 of the canonical
book it is said that this was in his seventh year. In the
Addition, Mordecai notifies the king of the plot against his
life, but in ii. 22 of the book itself Esther does this. In the
Addition, again, Mordecai is immediately rewarded for his
fidelity; in the canonical *Esther* he is at first altogether
forgotten, and only after a lapse of time does he receive his
reward. And, once more, in the Addition, Haman's
animosity against Mordecai is due to the latter having discovered the plot against the king, in consequence of which
(according to the best reading) the eunuchs were put to
death; but in the canonical *Esther* Haman's bitterness against
Mordecai is occasioned by the latter refusing to show due
honour to Haman (iii. 1 ff.).

These differences show that the Addition cannot originally
have formed part of the book.

The Second Addition (B = xiii. 1–7 in the Vulgate). This
is inserted after iii. 13 of the canonical *Esther*, and purports
to be a copy of the decree of Xerxes mentioned, but not
quoted, in Esth. iii. 13–15. The decree is sent, according to

the tradition, to the princes of the one hundred and twenty-seven provinces of the kingdom; in it the king declares it to be his purpose to rule his people peaceably, showing "equity and mildness" in his dealings with them. He had, therefore, summoned his counsellors to give him advice. At this conclave Haman, "who excelled in wisdom," and occupied the second place in the kingdom, warned the king that there was "a certain malignant people," who, having their own laws, set at defiance the royal commands. Thereupon the king, following Haman's advice, had put forth his decree, according to which this people (*i.e.* the Jews) should be utterly destroyed by the sword, with their wives and children "without all mercy and pity, the *fourteenth* day of the twelfth month of Adar of this present year."

The only point in this Addition at variance with the Septuagint, as well as the Hebrew, of the canonical *Esther*, is that in these the massacre is to take place on the *thirteenth* day of the twelfth month (iii. 13; viii. 12; ix. 1, though in iii. 13 of the Septuagint the day is not indicated). In this Addition no religious note is sounded, which is hardly to be expected, the content being what it is.

The Third Addition (C = xiii. 8–18 and xiv. 1–19 in the Vulgate). This Addition consists of two distinct parts which follow immediately after iv. 17 of the canonical *Esther*. First, there is the prayer of Mordecai, in which he prays that the mourning and fasting of the Jews, mentioned in the immediately preceding verse of the canonical *Esther*, may be turned into feasting. The passage is a beautiful one and breathes the deepest piety. Beginning with an ascription of might to the Almighty, and emphasizing His creative work, the prayer continues: "Thou knowest all things, and thou knowest, Lord, that it was neither in contempt nor pride, nor for any desire of glory, that I did not bow down to proud Aman" (cp. iii. 2, 3 of the canonical *Esther*). It was Mordecai's refusal to bow down to Haman which was the cause of the latter's determination to destroy all the Jews (see Esth. iii. 5, 6).

The second part of this Addition is the prayer of Esther.

She takes off her glorious apparel, putting on instead " the garments of anguish and mourning." The prayer, which is somewhat drawn out, begins by recalling how in the past God had ever performed what He promised; then it tells of how the enemy threatens to destroy God's inheritance; there follows the most impressive part of the prayer: " Remember, O Lord, make thyself known in the time of our affliction, and give me boldness, O King of the gods, and holder of all dominion. Give me eloquent speech in my mouth before the lion (*i.e.* the king); and turn his heart to hate him that fighteth against us, that there may be an end of him (*i.e.* Haman), and of them that are like-minded with him; but deliver us with thine hand, and help me that am desolate and have no other helper but thee, O Lord."

The Fourth Addition (D = xv. 4–19 in the Vulgate). This Addition, which follows immediately after the preceding, gives in fuller detail the narrative in v. 1, 2 (Septuagint and Hebrew). It tells of how Esther, having ended her prayer, put on fitting apparel, and, attended by her two maids, appeared before the king. He receives her in anger, whereupon Esther falls down in a faint. It then continues to say that God changed the spirit of the king into mildness, " who in an agony leaped from his throne, and took her in his arms, till she came to herself again, and comforted her with soothing words." Esther responds with adulatory words; but she is overcome by the king's graciousness and again swoons away. The Addition ends with the words: " Then the king was troubled, and all his servants comforted her," after which the canonical text continues at v. 3: " Then said the king unto her . . ."

A few variations from what is said in the canonical *Esther* occur, but they are unimportant.

The Fifth Addition (E = xvi. 1–24 in the Vulgate). In the Septuagint this Addition follows after viii. 12. This purports to be the copy of an edict of Xerxes, mentioned, but not quoted, in viii. 13 of the canonical *Esther*. It revokes the earlier edict, given in the second Addition. After a somewhat diffuse passage showing the wickedness of Haman, who is called a Macedonian, he is accused of seeking the king's life in order to seize the throne, and also of seeking the death of Mordecai, " who saved our life," and of Esther, " the blameless partaker of our kingdom, together with their whole nation." The Jews are then praised as being the " children of the most high and most mighty living God." It is then commanded that " ye shall aid them, that even the same day (*i.e.* that on which the massacre of the Jews had been ordered by Haman), being the thirteenth day of the twelfth month Adar, they may defend themselves against those who set upon them in the time of their affliction." Those who fail to obey the royal command " shall be utterly destroyed with spear and fire."

Three special points are to be noted here: (1) the prominence of the religious element; not only does the king recognize " the most high, and the most mighty living God," but he adds that He " hath ordered the kingdom both unto us and to our progenitors in the most excellent manner "; further, it is said that Haman's punishment was the divine vengeance rendered according to his deserts; and, finally, the edict runs: " For Almighty God hath made this day to be a joy unto them, instead of the destruction of the chosen people." (2) Haman is represented as a Macedonian, and therefore described as a foreigner. (3) In verse 22 of this Addition it is said: " And ye shall therefore among your commemorative feasts keep it a high day with all feasting "; the reference here is to the feast of *Purim*, so that the Persians are also required to keep this feast;—this, by the way, is contrary to what is said in the canonical *Esther* (ix. 20–28), where it is ordained to be observed among the Jews only in every city.

The Sixth Addition (F = x. 4–xi. 1). This Addition comes after x. 3 of the canonical *Esther*, i.e. it forms the conclusion of the book. It is an interpretation of Mordecai's dream recorded in Addition A: " As for the little fountain that became a river . . . it is Esther . . . and the two dragons are I and Amon." All that happened, as described in the book, was by the will of God, it is said; the Addition concludes with the words: " So God remembered his people, and justified his inheritance. Therefore these days shall be unto them in the month Adar, the fourteenth and fifteenth day of the month, with an assembly, and joy, and with gladness before God, throughout the generations for ever among his people Israel." There follows then this subscription: " In the fourth year of the reign of Ptolemy and Cleopatra, Dositheus, who said he was a priest and Levite, and Ptolemy his son, brought the foregoing epistle concerning Phrurai (i.e. *Purim*), which they said was (genuine), and that Lysimachus, son of Ptolemy, one of those (dwelling) in Jerusalem, had translated it." This subscription is clearly intended to apply to the whole of the book of *Esther* (cp. ix. 29); we shall refer to it again.

II. ESTHER LEGENDS

The Additions to the *Book of Esther*, which appear for the first time in the Septuagint, probably represent current material, *i.e.* they were not, in the first instance, written in literary form, but enlargements of the original story handed down orally.[1] These Greek Additions, however, formed the basis for an extraordinary growth of Esther legends, which show what an immense popularity the book enjoyed (doubtless the feast of *Purim* was in part responsible for this) in later times. The various forms of the Esther legend, which appeared during the earlier part of the Middle Ages, though in substance they are, of course, much older, are as follows:[2] We have, first, the two Targums, *i.e.* translations or rather explanatory paraphrases in Aramaic, of the Hebrew *Book of Esther*. It would seem that in both cases current material was utilized, and not merely the Septuagint additions; Esther legends, it is likely enough, were known quite apart from these latter. Of these two Targums, called respectively *Targum Rishon* (" first ") and *Targum Sheni* (" second "), the former restricts itself to matter directly concerned with the Esther story; but the latter contains material " not germane to the Esther story," and may be characterized

---

[1] For the haggadic material found in Josephus (*Antiq.* xi. 184 ff.), see Jacob, in the *Zeitschrift für die A.T. Wissenschaft*, for 1890, pp. 262 f.

[2] See Ryssel, in Kautzsch, *op. cit.*, i. 195 f.; Prince, in the *Jewish Encycl.* v. 234a; see also Erbt, *Die Purimsage in der Bibel* . . . (1900).

as " a genuine and exuberant midrash." ¹ In their present form these belong, respectively, to about 700 A.D. and 800 A.D. Extracts from them are given by Fuller in Wace, *op. cit.* i. 370 ff., see also Paton, *A Critical and Exegetical Commentary on the Book of Esther*, pp. 22 f. (1908).

A Midrash on the whole of the canonical *Esther* (Hebrew) is contained in the Babylonian Talmud, tractate *Megillah* 10b–14a, dating from the sixth century A.D. Another Esther legend is contained in *Pirke de Rabbi Eliezer*, belonging to the eighth century A.D.² Again, in the *Sepher Josippon* written by Joseph ben Gorion (early tenth century A.D.), an Esther legend appears among a number of other legendary stories.³ Other mediæval writings in which Esther legends occur are: *Midrash Megillath Esther*, called also *Haggadath Megilla* (circa eighth century A.D.); ⁴ *Midrash Lekah Tob*, about the eleventh century A.D. ; ⁵ *Midrash Tehillim*, on Ps. xxii (known also, from its opening words, as *Shoher Tob*, " He that diligently seeketh good," Prov. xi. 27), not later than the eleventh century A.D.; ⁶ and in the *Yalkut* (" collection ") *Shimeoni*, a great collection of Midrashic material ranging over the entire Old Testament.⁷

The difference in content between these various forms of Esther legends and the Additions in the Septuagint lies in the exaggerative and often fantastic character of the former. With the exception of what is said in the fifth Addition, that all the Persians are to keep the feast *Purim*, and that those who fail to do so are to be " utterly destroyed without mercy with spear and fire," the Additions are sober and often edifying, and there is but little to which exception can be taken. It is very different with the later legends which abound in exaggerations and absurdities.

¹ They are both published by Lagarde in *Hagiographa Chaldaice* (1873); for the former see also Posner, *Das Targum Rishon* (1896), for the latter, Cassel, *Das Buch Esther* (1891).
² An English translation is given in Gerald Friedlander's *Pirke de Rabbi Eliezer*, pp. 396–409 (1916).
³ No modern edition of this work has been published, but Gaster gives some extracts in *The Chronicles of Jerahmeel* (1899).
⁴ German translation in Horwitz's *Sammlung Kleiner Midrashim* (1881).
⁵ Published by Buber, *Sifre di-Agadta* (1880).
⁶ The Hebrew text is published by Buber, *Midrash Tehillim* (1891).
⁷ No modern edition has been published.

A few examples may be given:

Esther is described as one of the four most beautiful women ever created, and she never grew old. Her name Hadassah (" myrtle ") is said to indicate that she was seventy-four years old when she married Ahasuerus; this is deduced from the fact that the numerical value of the letters of this name in Hebrew make up seventy-four. In arraying herself for the feast she was assisted by the Holy Spirit, and was accompanied into the royal presence by three angels. Mordecai is said to have known seventy languages, and it is explained that the words of Ps. xxxvii. 37 (" Mark the perfect man, and behold the upright, for the latter end of that man is peace ") were written in reference to him. In one of the stories Elijah is introduced; he disguises himself as one of the royal chamberlains and counsels the king to have Haman hanged on a tree fifty cubits high which had been taken from the Holy of Holies!

These few examples will suffice to show the difference in character between the Septuagint Additions and the later legends. One can, however, well understand the purpose for which these wonder-tales were written; the story of Esther tells of a wonderful deliverance of the Jewish people from an impending terrible persecution; it was calculated, therefore, to be of great comfort and encouragement to them when, as so often happened in later days, repeated persecutions were their lot; but the simple story, as originally told, was not thought to be sufficiently realistic; people in dire distress will often be heartened and cheered by having their thoughts directed away from the cruel present; and if the story-teller's imagination runs riot in exalting national heroes and degrading the persecutors, the effect on the hearers, downtrodden and despised, is very comforting. This will account for the large number of Esther legends put forth in later days.

III. The Original Language of the Book

It has been maintained that the Additions were originally written in Hebrew or Aramaic, the present Greek form being a translation;[1] that they formed part of the original Hebrew or Aramaic text; and that, therefore, the present Hebrew book of *Esther* is an abbreviated form, while the Septuagint with its Additions represents the full form, the whole having been translated from a Hebrew or Aramaic original which contained the Additions. One reason for this contention is that the later Esther legends, being written either in Hebrew or Aramaic, are based on early Semitic material which lay behind the whole body of the Esther stories, in both the Hebrew and the Septuagint forms. Against this it must be urged that there is not the slightest evidence of the existence of Semitic originals of the Additions or other early material outside the canonical *Esther*; moreover, the Hebrew and Aramaic Esther legends referred to are all, as we have seen, of much later date than the Additions; besides which they are, in large measure, themselves based upon the Additions. Finally, the Greek Additions do not bear any marks of translation; there are always indications which intrude themselves in a Greek writing translated from a Semitic original; but nothing of the kind is to be discerned in the present instance. The Hebraisms which occur are characteristic of all Jewish hellenistic writers; they simply show that the writer was a Jew. Both Fritzsche[2] and Fuller[3] have shown that in the case of many passages of the Additions it is a difficult task to translate the Greek into Hebrew, which would not be so if Hebrew were the original language. It may, therefore, be regarded as certain that the Greek form of these Additions is the original one.

IV. Date

The subscription which comes at the end of the Sixth Addition after the conclusion of the book (see above, p. 188), tells us that the Greek translation was brought

---

[1] *E.g.* Scholz, *Kommentar über das Buch Esther mit seinen Zusätzen*, pp. xxi ff. (1892); Kaulen, *Einleitung in das Alte Testament*, pp. 271 f. (1890); see also Willrich, in *Judaica* for 1900, p. 15.

[2] *Kurzgefasstes exegetisches Handbuch zu den Apokryphen des A.T.*, i. 71 (1851–1860).

[3] In Wace, *op. cit.*, i. 365 (1888).

from Jerusalem to Egypt in the fourth year of king Ptolemy whose wife was Cleopatra. It does not say, however, which of the fourteen kings of this name is meant. As Ptolemy VI Philometor (B.C. 181/0–145) was very friendly disposed towards the Jews, and permitted them to build their temple at Leontopolis,[1] it has been supposed that this is the king in question, in which case the date would be B.C. 178. But, as Jacob has pointed out,[2] the only Ptolemy who married a Cleopatra in the fourth year of his reign was Ptolemy VIII Lathyrus (B.C. 117/6–108/7), which would make the date B.C. 114/113,[3] if we are to be guided by this subscription. There are, however, some reasons for doubting the reliability of what is said in the subscription.[4] To begin with, the vagueness of the reference to a Ptolemy and a Cleopatra, when a single word would have given the needed definiteness, excites suspicion. Then, the "he said," "they said," is also somewhat vague; and the roundabout way in which occurences are described does not give the impression that the writer was certain about his facts. But a more serious objection is the writer's assertion that the book was translated into Greek in Jerusalem and then brought to Egypt. "We know," says Jacob, "how scanty and meagre the knowledge of the Greek language in Palestine was from the time of Eupolemos, a contemporary of the Maccabæans, to that of Josephus and the New Testament writers. Josephus, especially, by his own confession, proves how extremely difficult it was for a native Palestinian to attain to a mastery of the Greek language. But we have seen how that the translation of our book exhibits undeniably a knowledge and command of Greek." Nöldeke answers this objection by saying that "the name of the translator Lysimachus, the son of Ptolemy, at once suggests an Egyptian Jew,"[5] implying, presumably, that Lysimachus had been residing in Jerusalem and had learned Hebrew, thereby

[1] Ptolemy VI married a Cleopatra, but not in the fourth year of his reign, see Bevan, *The Ptolemaic Dynasty*, p. 283 (1927).

[2] *Op. cit.*, pp. 278 f.

[3] He married a second time in the fourth year of his reign, but the name of his second wife was also Cleopatra (Selene).

[4] See Jacob, *op. cit.*, pp. 279 ff., who is followed by Ryssel, *op. cit.*, i. 196 f.

[5] In the *Encycl. Bibl.* ii. 1405.

being in a position to make the translation; but this, after all, is only an assumption. Jacob, moreover, shows by a careful examination of the language and thought that the Greek translation of the whole book of *Esther*, as well as of the Additions, can have been written nowhere but in Egypt.[1] A further objection is that the subscription comes at the end of the book, and applies, therefore, to the whole book, not merely to the Additions; but these are later than the original book of *Esther*, which belongs, in all probability, to the earlier stages of the Maccabæan struggle.[2] The translation of such a favourite book is likely to have taken place not long after; and the Additions may well have been inserted during the later stages of the Maccabæan period, approximately B.C. 130–125, possibly a little earlier. Whether the Additions all come from a single hand is difficult to decide, but there does not seem to be any compelling need for postulating more than one hand.

V. Manuscripts and Versions

" The Greek Book of Esther has come down to us in five main recensions and only through a comparison of these can one hope to restore the primitive form of the text," [3] and the same applies, of course, to the Additions which form an integral part of the Greek text. The first and most important recension is represented by the great uncials BℵA, and the eighth or ninth century uncial N (*Codex Basiliano-Vaticanus*); to these must be added the cursives 19, 55, 93, 108 (the last two contain also the Lucianic recension) and 249. This, according to Paton, is the unrevised Greek text, and represents, upon the whole, the current form of this text in the Christian Church before later revisions were made.

The first of these revisions was made by Origen during the first half of the third century, and is represented by the cursive 93 (which contains, however, also the recension of Lucian, see below).

[1] *Op. cit.*, pp. 274 ff.
[2] See Oesterley and Robinson, *An Introduction to the Books of the Old Testament*, p. 137 (1934).
[3] Paton, *A Critical and Exegetical Commentary on the Book of Esther*, p. 31 (1908).

Next, there is the revision of Hesychius (second half of the fourth century); it is represented by a number of cursives which differ in many instances from Cod. B; they are, according to Jacob, divided into sub-groups; 74, 76, and 68, 120, while 236 stands by itself.

The revision, or rather recension, of Lucian belongs to the beginning of the fourth century; it is represented in the cursives 19, 93, 108 (containing also the Hesychian recension); the Lucianic text varies very greatly from other texts, so that it is more than a revision, rather a new edition.

The only version of any importance is the Old Latin;[1] as this was made in the middle of the second century, before the revisions just mentioned had been taken in hand, its witness to the earlier form of the Greek is of great value, especially as it follows the Greek closely; it has, besides the Additions, many further insertions, evidently also translated from a Greek original; but, according to Jacob, certain errors occur which point to an ultimate Hebrew or Aramaic source. Paton notes instances in which the Old Latin has readings nearer to the Hebrew than those of any of the Greek recensions; "these cannot be due," he says, "to re-editing of the Latin from the Hebrew, but must be survivals of better Greek readings than any found in our present codices."

The Vulgate is of very little use, being often a paraphrase rather than a translation of the Greek.[2]

VI. LITERATURE

Fritzsche, *op. cit.*, i. 69 ff. (1851).

Fuller, in Wace, *op. cit.*, i. 361 ff. (1888).

Jacob, " Das Buch Esther bei den LXX," in *Zeitschrift für die A. T. Wissenschaft*, 1910, pp. 241 ff.

Scholz, *Commentar über das Buch Esther mit seinen Zusätzen und über Susanna* (1892).

---

[1] Publ. by Sabatier, *Bibliorum sacrorum Latinæ versiones antiquæ, seu Vetus Italica*, i. 796–825 (1751).

[2] For full discussions on the MSS. and Versions, see Jacob, *op. cit.*, pp. 242–262, and Paton, *op. cit.*, pp. 31–38.

Ryssel, in Kautzsch, *op. cit.*, i. 193 ff. (1900).

André, *op. cit.*, pp. 195 ff. (1903).

Streane, *The Book of Esther* (1907).

Paton, *A Critical and Exegetical Commentary on the Book of Esther* (1908).

Gregg, in Charles, *op. cit.*, i. 665 ff. (1913).

THE WISDOM OF SOLOMON

I. TITLE

THE great Greek uncial manuscripts have the title " Wisdom
of Solomon." The Old Latin Version, which is contained
in the Vulgate, has " Liber Sapientiæ "; but since this
Version is translated from the Greek, it is highly probable
that originally the name of Solomon appeared in the title,
and that this was omitted by Jerome, for in his preface to
the books of Solomon he regards it as pseudepigraphic.
The Peshitta has an extended superscription rather than a
title in the ordinary sense: " The book of the Great Wisdom
of Solomon, the son of David; of which there is a doubt,
whether another Wise man of the Hebrews wrote it in a
prophetic spirit, putting it in the name of Solomon, and it
was (so) received." The titles occurring in the writings of
the Fathers are of interest only in that the earliest of them,
Clement of Alexandria, Tertullian, Origen,[1] and Cyprian
ascribe it to Solomon, while Jerome [2] and Augustine [3]
clearly do not believe in Solomonic authorship. Interesting
is the reference to our book in the " Muratorian Fragment ":
" Wisdom, written by the friends of Solomon in his honour "
(*Sapientia ab amicis in honorem ipsius scripta*). Zahn,[4] following
Tregelles, explains " ab amicis " as a misunderstanding of
ὑπὸ Φίλωνος, in the Greek, this having been read as ὑπὸ φίλων;
in this case Philo would have been regarded as the author;
others both in early and later days held the same view; but
on this see § III. The book was certainly regarded in the
early Church as one of the most important, probably *the*
most important of all the books comprised in the Apocrypha.

[1] Origen, however, is often sceptical about Solomonic authorship, see
Schürer, *op. cit.*, iii. 509.
[2] Jerome held that it was written by Philo.
[3] Augustine ascribes the book to Ben-Sira.
[4] *Geschichte des Neutestamentlichen Kanons*, ii. 95 ff. (1888–1890).

II. Contents of the Book

An exhortation to seek the Lord and His righteousness without which Wisdom is unattainable. This is followed by a warning against the wicked. God created men for righteousness; Hades has no power over the godly, but the wicked have made a covenant with Hades (Death); thus, immortality is the possession of the righteous, but the portion of the wicked is death (i. 1-16).

The point of view of the ungodly: Life is short and sorrowful, and there is no hope of a hereafter; the body at death turns to ashes, the spirit into thin air. Therefore men should make the most of life and enjoy everything they can; let no consideration for others stand in the way of this; might is right. Since this conception of life is opposed by the righteous man, let him be persecuted (ii. 1-20).

They who argue thus are blinded, and contradict God's purpose in creating man (ii. 21-24).

The lot of the righteous hereafter: though they seem to die and their death looks like destruction, they are in peace and reign with God for ever (iii. 1-9).

The punishment of the ungodly, together with their kith and kin, contrasted with the reward of immortality for the righteous (iii. 10-iv. 6).

The righteous man is blessed, even though he die prematurely; for old age is not reckoned by years, but by the measure of a man's faithfulness to God; to die young is to be saved from a possible falling away from the right path (iv. 7-14^{b}).

Retribution will surely come upon the ungodly; they do not understand the ways of the Lord; therefore terrible punishment is reserved for them in the end (iv. 14^{c}-20).

The remorse of the ungodly when the Judgement comes; they will then compare themselves with the righteous, and will be brought to recognize their own wickedness, and will see that there is no hope for them (v. 1-14).

Eternal life, a glorious kingdom, and a diadem of beauty from the hand of the Lord, will be the reward of the righteous hereafter; but as for the ungodly, they will be annihilated by the divine wrath (v. 15–23).

An exhortation and a warning to rulers; it is from the Lord that they receive their power; if, therefore, they do not rule according to His will, stern judgement will be meted out to them; they must strive for wisdom and the words of the Lord, for " they that holily observe holy things shall be made holy " (vi. 1–11).

The desire for wisdom results in the acquisition of power,— thus does the Sage sum up the reward of him who searches after wisdom.   To the man who desires wisdom there is the certainty that she will be ever ready to respond.   The love for wisdom is shown by observing her laws; this is a guarantee of incorruption; and incorruption is the means of coming near to God; and he who is near to God is mighty in power (vi. 12–20).

Rulers who honour wisdom may look forward to unceasing rule; the Sage promises to instruct suchlike regarding the nature and origin of wisdom (vi. 21–25).

The Sage, in personating Solomon, declares that he is only an ordinary mortal, but that he prayed for wisdom which was to him a priceless gem worth more than sceptres or thrones or wealth; since he prayed for wisdom he received wisdom, and made full use of it (vii. 1–14).

God alone is the giver of wisdom; He guides men into all the knowledge of the mysteries of Nature (vii. 15–22^a).

A description of the nature and essence of wisdom (vii. 22^b–viii. 1).

The Sage, in the name of Solomon, tells of how he sought wisdom; he describes, in praise of wisdom, how she teaches men all the virtues, and instructs them in all knowledge; he declares how, through his possession of wisdom, he was held in honour of all men; finally he ascribes honour to God through whom alone he received the gift of wisdom (viii. 2–21).

A prayer, uttered in the name of Solomon, in which acknowledgement is made of the gift of wisdom having been received from God (ix. 1–11).

As a result of the gift of wisdom, Solomon is made to say

that he was able to rule righteously. A meditation on the excellence of wisdom (ix. 12–18).

A continuation of the meditation in which mention is made of wisdom's activity among Israel's forefathers. In this long section references are made to the past history of the nation; and it is shown how through wisdom enemies were overcome (x. 1–21).

The historical retrospect is continued (xi. 1–20).

A hymn of praise to God for His manifold mercies accorded to men (xi. 21–xii. 2).

Not only towards Israel has God been merciful in the past, but even towards the Canaanites, the ancient inhabitants of His holy land, did He show His long-suffering (xii. 3–11).

A further outpouring in praise to God for His righteousness and forbearance (xii. 12–18).

In continuation of the recognition of the forbearance which God has manifested, it is said that this was vouchsafed in order that men should follow the divine example (xii. 19–22).

The unrighteous (the Egyptians of old are here meant) who did not recognize and acknowledge God, received judgement (xii. 23–27).

A denunciation against those who worship false gods, whether conceived of as fire, wind, or water, or the luminaries of heaven (xiii. 1–3).

Nevertheless, if these are recognized as the works of the Creator of all things, they may be the means of bringing idolators to worship the One and only God (xiii. 4–9).

Utter folly, however, is the worship of objects of man's handiwork, gold, silver, wood, and stone. A scathing rebuke is directed against those who make gods of such things (xiii. 10–19).

A further denunciation of idolatry, the evil effects of which are described in detail (xiv. 1–31).

Contrasted with this idolatry is Israel's faithfulness to God; as His people they know Him, His longsuffering and mercy, and therefore they are not led astray by the evil devices of men's art (xv. 1–6).

o

The Sage then reverts once more to the subject of the
folly of idolatry, and denounces the senseless stupidity of
those who worship idols (xv. 7–17).

The same subject is continued, the worship of the Egyptians
being especially condemned. A contrast is drawn between
the punishments meted out, respectively, to the Egyptians
and to the erring Israelites; the latter suffered indeed for
their idolatry, nevertheless, they were healed by the word of
the Lord (xv. 18–xvi. 14).

Continuing the subject of the punishment of the Egyptians,
the first great enemies of Israel, it is stated, in somewhat
exaggerated style, that the very elements were inimical to
them, but showed themselves friendly to the Israelites
(xvi. 15–29).

The punishment of the Egyptians is further described; it
is said that " lawless men "—the whole context shows that
the Egyptians are meant—" thinking to lord it over the holy
nation, were prisoners of darkness, and fettered captives of a
long night." Many details of a fantastic nature, very
possibly echoes of Jewish legend, are then given, describing
the terrors of the darkness to which the Egyptians were consigned. In contrast to this it is said that " for thy holy ones
there was a very great light "; instead of darkness there
appeared before them "a burning pillar of fire," as a guide
for them in their unknown journey, i.e. during the wander-
ings in the wilderness. It was fitting that the Egyptians
should be deprived of light, and be imprisoned by darkness,
it is said; but the Israelites, on the other hand, who had
enjoyed the light, gave to the world " the incorruptible light
of the Law " (xvii. 1–xviii. 4).

A description of how the Egyptians were punished in yet
another way, viz. by the death of their first-born children;
while the Israelites were offering sacrifice to their God and
praising Him, it is said, " there sounded back in discord the
cry of the enemies, and a piteous voice was borne abroad by
a lamentation for the children " (xviii. 5–19).

But though the hand of death was rampant among
Israel's enemies, the people of God themselves were not
exempt from its ravages; yet, through the mediation of a

blameless man, *i.e.*, Aaron, the relentless hand was stayed (xviii. 20–25).

A description of the crossing of the Red Sea; here again there are imaginative details, possibly the product of the author's brain (xix. 1–12).

There follows then a description of the punishment of the Egyptians, who were "encompassed with yawning darkness" (xix. 13–17).

The miraculous transmutation of the elements (xix. 18–22).

Here the book ends, very abruptly it must be confessed. Among the various explanations put forth to account for this, much sympathy must be felt for that expressed by Goodrick, who puts it down to the "absolute weariness of the author with his subject." We heartily endorse what he says in continuation: "Anyone who reads carefully the last chapter or two, with their tautologies in language and their repetitions of matter, will agree that they are the work of a man whose enthusiastic rhetoric had found its limit. He has no more to say, and it is a pity that he did not recognize this before. His vocabulary and his imagination are alike exhausted." [1]

III. AUTHORSHIP

From chapter ix it is clear that the book purports to have been written by Solomon, who addresses himself to the rulers and kings of the earth (cp. i. 1, vi. 1), adjuring them to love righteousness and to seek God in singleness of heart. But this purported authorship of Solomon is merely a literary device; the most cursory reading of the book shows the utter impossibility of its having been written by Solomon; to labour the point would be waste of time.

At a very early period Philo, as we have seen, was thought to have been the author, and in later days, too, this theory has been held; but against this authorship there are strong objections; the more important of these may be summarized thus:

The Logos, according to the teaching of Philo, is the Wisdom of God, His creative word, the "idea of ideas," the archangel of many names, the high-priest for the world,

---

[1] *The Book of Wisdom*, p. 376 (1913).

the mediator between God and the world, the intercessor
for men, and their saviour. Philo thus personifies the *Logos*.
In the book of *Wisdom*, on the other hand, *Logos* is used in a
purely abstract sense as the will of God; its mention occurs
three times; " O God of our fathers, and Lord of mercy,
who madest all things by thy word " (ix. 1). " For,
indeed, it was neither herb nor unguent that healed them,
but thy word, O Lord, that healeth all things " (xvi. 12).
" Thine all-powerful word from heaven out of the royal
throne leapt, a stern warrior, in the midst of the doomed
land, bearing as a sharp sword Thine unalterable commandment; and standing, it filled all things with death;
and it touched the heaven, yet trod upon the earth "
(xviii. 15, 16). At first sight this last passage might suggest personality being attributed to the *Logos*, but as
Gregg remarks, " although in Wisd. xviii. 15 the *Logos*
is the agent in the destruction of the firstborn, and
although in the *Jerusalem Targum* it is the " Word of the
Lord " that slew all the firstborn in the land of Egypt,
yet in the source-passages, Exod. xi. 4 and xii. 29 (LXX),
God Himself is spoken of as the agent. Hence it seems
plain that the writer had no intention of hypostatising
the *Logos*, but had in mind only the customary Jewish
periphasis for the Lord, *i.e.* the ' Memra of Jehovah.'.
This expression means ' the divine Being in self-mani-
festation.' " [1]

There is thus a far-reaching difference between Philo and
the writer of this book on a fundamental matter of doctrine.

Another difference between the two is that while Philo
appears not to hold a dualistic view in any form, and to
regard evil as but the negation of good, Wisd. ii. 24 refers
to the devil as the source of evil: " But by the envy of the
devil death entered into the world, and they that belong to
him experience it " (*i.e.* death, contrasted with the life of
the righteous hereafter, as described in iii. 2 ff.).

Again, Philo was an ardent student of Greek philosophy;
one of the most striking illustrations of this is his doctrine
of the nature of man; in discussing this Moore says:

[1] See Etheridge, *The Targums on the Pentateuch*, pp. 14 ff. (1862, etc.).

" . . . so we may properly say that man is intermediate
between the mortal and immortal nature, sharing in each
so far as needs be, and that he is at once mortal and immortal—mortal as to his body, immortal as to his intellect.
Greek philosophy, however, here contributed everything
but the text (Gen. ii. 7). The ' breath of life ' (πνοὴ ζωῆς)
which God breathed into Adam's nostrils, thus making him
a ' living soul ' (person), turns into a πνεῦμα-soul of obvious
Stoic extraction, for which, as the immortal in man, Philo
in the end substitutes ' intellect ' (διάνοια), like a true
Platonist." [1] How could it have been possible for one who
taught this to write Wisd. ix. 15:

For a corruptible body weigheth down the soul,
And the earthly tabernacle oppresseth the care-laden
    mind,

thus making " soul " and " mind " synonymous? It is
true, the writer may have been indebted to Greek philosophy
for the idea of the body as an " earthly tabernacle "; " the
metaphor of a tent for the body was widespread among
Greek philosophers (Pythagoreans and Platonists), and the
view that the body is a burden or prison to the soul (σῶμα
σῆμα) was a common one with Platonists and Stoics, and was
a fundamental idea of the Alexandrian philosophy "; [2] but
in our book knowledge of Greek philosophy is quite super-
ficial; for a philosopher like Philo to have written it is
unthinkable.

Once more, there is a striking difference in the allegorizing
of our book and Philo; very pointedly Farrar writes:

Philo allegorizes rather than exaggerates; Pseudo-
Solomon exaggerates rather than allegorizes. It seems
strange that any commentator who is at all familiar with
Philo's habitual method of dealing with Scripture should
suppose that he could possibly have written a book of
which the method is so un-Philonian as that of the Book
of Wisdom. [3]

[1] *Judaism*, i. 452 (1927).
[2] Thackeray, *The Relation of St. Paul to contemporary Jewish Thought*, p. 132
(1900).   [3] *Wisdom*, p. 412b.

More could be said to show that the book could not have
been written by Philo; but further arguments are unnecessary. Other theories as to the identity of the author
are not sufficiently important to merit mention; it must be
recognized that there are no means of ascertaining who the
author was.

We have spoken of "the author" hitherto, but whether
unity of authorship can be claimed for the book is by no
means certain; indeed, there are some weighty reasons for
questioning whether the whole book can have come from the
same writer, and there are not wanting some outstanding
scholars who insist on the composite authorship of the book.

The problem centres on the manifest differences between
i–xi. 1 and xi. 2–xix; differences of subject-matter, thought,
and style; these are clearly brought out by Eichhorn,[1] thus:
in the first part the subject of wisdom finds constant treatment, but in the second it is mentioned only once, and that
in a somewhat quaint manner (xiv. 5–7); in the first part
the doctrine of immortality is prominent, whereas in the
second it is mentioned once only, and that without any
emphasis (xv. 3); in the first part the absence of particularism is a striking feature, while in the second it abounds;
in the first part unbelief is the cause of all wickedness, in
the second it is idolatry which is the cause of this. Then,
as to style, there are many linguistic differences, and parallelism, which runs all through the first part, is absent from the
second; in the first the historical references are made in a
simple, straightforward manner, in the second, which is full
of them, there is exaggeration and imaginary detail; "the
first part is appropriate and concise, the second inappropriate, diffuse, exaggerated and bombastic."[2] Nevertheless, striking as these differences are, Eichhorn did not maintain that they necessarily demanded the view of diversity of
authorship; the same writer may assume different attitudes
of mind at different periods of his life, and it is quite possible
that the unattractive nature of the second part was due to its
having been written in the early part of the author's life in

[1] *Einleitung in die Apokryphischen Schriften*, pp. 86 ff. (1795).
[2] *Ibid.* p. 145.

the exuberance and inexperience of youth, while the earlier part represents the maturer and more sober attitude fostered by thought and meditation.

On the other hand, it cannot be a matter of surprise that other investigators feel compelled to postulate diversity of authorship. Thus, in the eighteenth century already the French scholar Houbigant held that the book was of dual authorship, i–ix, and x–xix being their respective parts;[1] similarly Bretschneider,[2] in addition to which he regarded chap. xi as the work of a redactor; Lincke divides the book into two parts, i–xii. 8 and xii. 9–xix, each from a different writer;[3] Stevenson sees in the book a combination of four independent writings, (1) i–xi. 4; (2) xiii. 1–xv; (3) xi. 21–xii. 22; (4) xi. 5–20, xii. 23–27, xvi–xix.[4] The arguments in favour of composite authorship turn mainly on the points mentioned above.[5]

But the champions of single authorship have also a strong case; foremost among these must be reckoned Grimm;[6] his arguments have been supplemented by others; they have been conveniently enumerated by Holmes,[7] thus:

The use of certain unusual words and expressions throughout the book,[8] the same extensive vocabulary, the similar use of compound and poetical words, assonances, and the like; the rhythmical structure throughout the book, though this is not conceded by all commentators; the use of philosophic theories in both parts; the omission of proper names in both parts; and " the occurrence in both parts of the striking conception of the 'world fighting for the righteous,' which is found in v. 17, 20, xvi. 17, 24, xviii. 24 (perhaps), and xix. 6."

In placing the arguments for and against unity of authorship side by side, it will be acknowledged that it is difficult

---

[1] *Lectori ad libros Sapientiæ et Ecclesiastici* (1773).
[2] *De libri Sapientiæ parte priore* . . . (1804).
[3] *Samaria und seine Propheten,* pp. 119 ff. (1903).
[4] *Wisdom and the Jewish Apocryphal Writings,* pp. 1 ff. (1903).
[5] They are fully set forth by Holmes, in Charles, *op. cit.* i., 522 f.
[6] " Commentar über das Buch der Weisheit," in *Kurzgefasstes Exegetisches Handbuch zu den Apocryphen des Alten Testamentes,* vi. 9 ff. (1860).
[7] *Op. cit.,* pp. 521 f.
[8] The most striking of these is the word μεταλλεύω which is used in the same *erroneous* meaning in both parts (iv. 12 and xvi. 25).

to decide the question; Gregg goes too far in maintaining that " attacks upon the unity of the book have failed, and no serious effort to dispute it has recently been made." [1] Holmes sees that " there are considerable difficulties in the way of accepting the unity of authorship which have not been met by its upholders." " If," he says, " we could assume that the writer of the second part had studied the first part carefully and wished to write a supplement to it, both resemblances and differences could be accounted for." [2] Goodrick's view is an interesting one; he stands for unity of authorship, and points to the " peculiar and indeed anomalous nature " of the section included between vi. 24 and ix. 18, i.e. chaps, vii–ix. " In these three chapters are included the most peculiar, and in some respects the most objectionable, parts of the book: the references to Platonic philosophy, and the direct claims to Solomonic authorship." He does not, however, suggest that these chapters should be eliminated; " it is not necessary to eliminate them; only to point out that they possibly belong to a later period of development of the writer's ideas, and were inserted by him with a definite purpose; that they may be removed without injuring the general construction of the book; and that they contain statements in advance of, if not inconsistent with, those put forward elsewhere; " Goodrick's elaboration of this last theme is very convincing. [3]

In view of the difficult and complicated nature of the subject, much sympathy will be felt with Toy's conclusion; while he thinks that it is perhaps " not possible to decide with certainty whether the book is the production of one man," he feels that, " on the whole, it seems easier to account for the differences of matter and style under the supposition of one single author than to explain the unity under the supposition of two or more authors." [4]

---

[1] The Wisdom of Solomon, p. xxvii (1909); it is true, Holmes' commentary was published subsequently to this; but, although we may disagree with their points of view, it cannot be said that Lincke and Stevenson have made no serious effort to dispute unity of authorship.

[2] Op. cit., p. 524.

[3] The Book of Wisdom, pp. 74 ff. (1913).

[4] Encycl. Bibl. iv. 5338.

IV. Date

Jt would be wearisome to detail the various arguments of scholars whereby they support the different dates favoured, especially as many of their arguments are inconclusive. Apart from Farrar, the tendency among commentators prior to the present century was to favour a date before B.C. 100. Grimm gives a wide margin (B.C. 145 to B.C. 50), while more recent investigators—Thackeray [1] and Gregg are exceptions, and Eissfeldt [2] also allows a wide margin " during the first century B.C."—contend for a somewhat later date.

Of the various arguments put forward, two, at any rate, may be regarded as conclusive: (1) the book, for reasons already given, must have been written before the writings of Philo,—he died about 45 A.D.; (2) the mention of the worship of an absent ruler must refer to a ruler of the Roman Empire; the passage in question is xiv. 16, 17:

> Then, in process of time, the ungodly custom having grown strong, was observed as a law, and by the commands of rulers graven images were worshipped; the which, men not being able to honour in their presence because they dwelt afar off, they made a visible image of the king they honoured, that by their zeal they might flatter the absent as though present.

It has been maintained that this refers to the Ptolemies, but it is hardly possible that this can have been meant by the writer; a Jew would assuredly have made some caustic reference to the worship of a *woman* had this been the case; for what are the facts? In writing about the deification of the Ptolemaic rulers Edwyn Bevan says that the worship of Ptolemy I was instituted after his death (B.C. 282/3) by his son Ptolemy II;

> with his father Ptolemy II associated his mother Berenice on her death (soon after B.C. 279), the two being wor-

---

[1] *Grammar of the Old Testament in Greek*, p. 62 (1905).
[2] *Einleitung in das Alte Testament*, p. 657 (1934).

shipped together as θεοὶ σωτῆρες . . . When the
sister-wife of Ptolemy II, Arsinoë Philadelphus, died in
B.C. 270–271, she too was deified. And now a further
step was taken. Ptolemy II had himself put on a level
with his sister; the living king and the dead queen were
worshipped together as θεοὶ ἀδελφοί. This cult was
combined with that of Alexander. . . . When Ptolemy II
was succeeded by Ptolemy III Euergetes, the θεοὶ εὐεργέται
(*i.e.* Euergetes and his wife Berenice II) were added to
Alexander and the θεοὶ ἀδελφοί, and so on with the
other kings till the end of the Ptolemaic dynasty.[1]

Thus, almost throughout the period of the Ptolemaic
rulers a queen was associated with the king as a goddess to
be worshipped; it is quite inconceivable that this deification
of a woman should have been passed over in silence by a
Jewish writer in such a passage as xiv. 16, 17. But further,
in this passage, the deified ruler is spoken of as one who was
absent (*i.e.* from Alexandria); that could not apply to the
Ptolemaic rulers; it could apply only to a Roman emperor,
and, as will be seen, this emperor can have been none other
than Caligula who, in 40 A.D. proclaimed himself a god,
and as such demanded worship from his subjects.

That Caligula was the emperor in question is confirmed
by another consideration. There are some passages in our
book which, it is generally agreed, refer to a time of persecution; thus, in iii. 1 words of consolation are written in
regard to sufferers: " The souls of the righteous are in the
hands of God, and, of a truth, no torment shall touch them ";
similarly in v. 1: " Then shall the righteous stand forth
with much boldness before the face of him that afflicted
him, and of them that regarded his troubles of no account."
In vi. 5–9 vengeance is pronounced against persecutors:

Terribly and swiftly shall He come upon you, for stern
judgement befalleth them that are in high place. For
the man that is of low estate may be forgiven in mercy,
but the mighty shall be mightily tested. For the Lord of
all will not have respect for any man's person, neither will

[1] In Hastings' *Encyclopædia of Religion and Ethics*, iv. 527.

He reverence greatness; for He himself made small and great, and alike He taketh thought for all; but upon the mighty shall searching scrutiny come . . .

The persecution here referred to has been fully and clearly dealt with by Goodrick whose words may here, in part, be quoted:

> . . . A sore persecution had just been endured; a persecution not unto death indeed, but involving grave damage and distress. This persecution, founded in part on gross calumny, had as one of its main features the attempted enforcement of idolatry, and of idolatry in its most insane and revolting form—the worship of a living man. This living man was a prince ruling at a distance, but his commands were enforced by apostate Jews dwelling close at hand, who had surrendered their ancient belief without sincerely adopting any other, and represented no religion except that of Epicureanism, for which they sought to find their text-book in the so-called Solomon's "Preacher." This persecution had been carried on through the agency of the dregs of the populace of Alexandria, wherein were represented the superstition of ancient Egypt at its worst, combined with hereditary Greek hatred of the Jews and wild misrepresentation of their religion and ordinances. Finally, a time of temporary repose must be pictured, in which it was possible to substitute severe rebuke for furious complaint. All these conditions the period from 41 A.D. to 44 presents, and an examination of the book of Wisdom confirms the belief that it was then written.[1]

We conclude, therefore, that our book was probably written about the year 40 A.D. or a few years later.

V. THE ORIGINAL LANGUAGE OF THE BOOK

Since, as we have seen, our book was written in Alexandria, the great centre of Greek-speaking Jews, it may be assumed,

[1] *Op. cit.*, pp. 15 f.

quite apart from other reasons, that Greek was the language
in which it was written.

There are, however, further reasons for regarding the
present Greek form of the book as original. Jerome, in his
Praef. in libr. Sal., says: *Liber qui sapientia Solomonis inscribitur
apud Hebraeos nusquam est, quin et ipse stylus Graecam eloquentiam
redolet.* It is true, opinions differ considerably as to the
measure of the writer's acquaintance with Greek; thus,
Farrar thinks that " he shows a singular mastery of the
Greek language in its later epochs of mingled decadence and
development . . .," he was " a master of the Greek vocabulary." [1] Margoliouth,[2] on the other hand, protests that " so
far is the style of ' Wisdom ' from being excellent that it is
atrocious "; and on this point Freudenthal [3] agrees with
him, holding that the writer was not writing in his own
language. Similarly, Goodrick maintains that " the writer
is handling a language with which he is only half acquainted "; and elsewhere he asks:

> Is not Freudenthal right when he says that the author
> was writing in a foreign language which he really did not
> know? Is the wealth of language and the mastery of
> vocabulary anything more than what might be acquired
> by any educated hearer of a Greek rhetorician in the
> schools of Alexandria? . . . It is by no means certain
> that a native Greek would not have regarded the fervid
> outpourings of Pseudo-Solomon very much as we do the
> fervid rhetoric of the intelligent Babu. [4]

It is unnecessary to quote further from other scholars;
the great mass are in no doubt as to the language in which
the book was originally written. Nevertheless, there have
not been wanting some very able writers who maintain that
Hebrew was the original language of our book, or at any
rate, of part of it. Thus, Focke [5] holds that the first five

[1] *Op. cit.*, 404b, 405a.
[2] "Was the Book of Wisdom written in Hebrew? " in the *Journal of the
Royal Asiatic Society*, 1890, p. 266.
[3] In the *Jewish Quarterly Review* 1891, p. 734; cp. André, *op. cit.*, p. 319.
[4] *Op. cit.*, pp. 69 f. What Goodrick says here will come home with great
force to anyone who, like the present writer, has come into close personal
contact with the type mentioned, and heard him " hold forth."
[5] *Die Entstehung der Weisheit Salomos* (1913).

chapters were written in Hebrew; these were translated into Greek, and the translator then wrote the rest of the book; before him, Margoliouth (see above) championed a Hebrew original; and, much earlier, Bretschneider [1] sought to establish Hebrew as the original form of part of the book. More recently Speiser,[2] recognizing two parts of which the book is made up (i. 1–vi. 22; viii. 1–ix. 18; and vi. 22–viii. 1; ix. 1–xix), has sought to show that the first part was written in Hebrew. He believes that " while the first part was written *for Jews* (quite likely Palestinian) against *Ecclesiastes*, or at least called for by the latter, the second is directed primarily against Gentiles or hopelessly un-Jewish Jews (Egyptian)." And once more, Purinton [3] argues for a Hebrew original for i. 1–xi. 1, thus dividing the book differently from Speiser. In his final paragraph he observes that while both Wisdom and Solomon figure in the first part of the book, Solomon drops right out after xi. 1, while Wisdom is mentioned but once after that, in xiv. 5.

We cannot discuss here the many striking and ingenious illustrations which Speiser and Purinton give in support of their contention; while they are in part very suggestive, our feeling is that they do not necessarily prove that the first part of the book is a translation from the Hebrew. Since the author was undoubtedly a Jew, whether he lived in Alexandria or Palestine, whose mother-tongue was Hebrew, it is natural enough that he should have thought in Hebrew; and that as he wrote in his acquired language, Hebrew was at the back of his mind and would often reflect itself in what he was writing. This would explain, as it seems to the present writer, many passages which, it is granted, look like translations from Hebrew; but it is not only isolated passages which suffice as illustrations, the whole material must be taken into consideration, and it is at least doubtful, when this is done, whether a Hebrew original can be justly postulated for any part of the book.

---

[1] *De libri Sapientiæ parte priore* . . . (1804).
[2] " The Hebrew Origin of the First Part of the Book of Wisdom," in the *Jewish Quarterly Review*, 1924, pp. 455 ff.
[3] In the *Journal of Biblical Literature*, xlvii. 1928, pp. 276–304.

VI. Purposes of the Book

Apart from the general inculcation of wisdom common to all the Wisdom-writers (*e.g.* vi. 12–20; vii–viii) our author clearly has some specific objects in view. That he addresses himself exclusively to Jews is evident from the many allusions to past Jewish history which could have been comprehensible to Jews only. But the Jews of his environment in Alexandria were in an evil plight; those true to their faith were suffering persecution:

" Let us lie in wait for the righteous, for he is of no use to us, and is opposed to our doings " (ii. 12); " With insult and torture let us try him, that we may take knowledge of his gentleness, and that we may judge of his endurance in suffering; to a shameful death let us condemn him . . ." (ii. 19, 20).

The first object of the writer, then, was *to cheer and comfort his co-religionists* and to *strengthen them in their faith*; in the most beautiful passage in the book (iii. 1–9) he teaches them that they need not fear death, for " the souls of the righteous are in the hands of God, and of a truth, no torment shall touch them . . . their hope is full of immortality . . . and the Lord shall reign over them for ever." His teaching on immortality, which, so far as we know, he was the first of the Wisdom-writers to set forth in full development, finds expression elsewhere in the book: " God created man for incorruption " (ii. 23); " the righteous man, though he die before his time, shall be at rest " (iv. 7); " the righteous shall live for ever, and in the Lord is their reward; and the care of them is with the Most High " (v. 15).

Thus the heartening of his co-religionists by his teaching on immortality must also be regarded as one of the author's objects in writing.

But it is clear that the persecutors of these faithful Jews were themselves Jews; in ii. 12, where the persecutors of the righteous man are spoken of, they say that the latter " reproacheth us for sins against the Law, and denounceth us for our breaches of what is seemly "; that could only be said by those who were themselves Jews; they were thus

renegade Jews, and that it was not only of offences against the Law that they were guilty is seen, *e.g.*, in ii. 6–9:

> Come, therefore, and let us enjoy the good things there are, and let us make use of creation to the full as in youth; with costly wines and perfumes let us fill ourselves, and let no flower of the spring pass us by; let us crown ourselves with rosebuds ere they fade away, and let there be no glade through which our mirth passeth not; for let none of us be without his share in our proud revelry; everywhere let us leave signs of our enjoyment, for this is our portion, this is our lot.

So that these Jews, occupying high places in the Gentile world (i. 1, v. 8) were materialists, hedonists, Epicuræans; it is against such that the writer utters warnings:

> But the ungodly shall receive punishment according as they reasoned (see ii. 1 ff.), which were heedless of the right, revolting from the Lord; for he that setteth at nought wisdom and instruction is miserable; and vain is their hope, and useless their labours, and unprofitable are their works (iii. 10, 11).

Another object, therefore, was *to warn renegade Jews* in order that they might turn from their evil courses and from their unbelief.

Finally, such passages as xiii, xiv, xv. 7–17, on the folly of idolatry—and there are others—show that a further purpose of the book was *to combat the worship of idols*. Primarily this was doubtless directed against the heathen; but the danger of renegade Jews, referred to above, falling into idolatrous practices, whether from conviction or policy, was great enough; and the writer may well have had these in mind, as well as the Gentiles, in his invectives against idolatry.

Underlying all these purposes there lay quite clearly the intention both to proclaim the superiority of the Jewish faith, and also to set forth Wisdom as the highest ideal, for Wisdom and faith in God are inseparable. Thus, for those faithful Jews who were suffering for their belief such words

as the following, *e.g.*, would have given comfort and courage:
" . . . And from generation to generation, passing into holy
souls, she (*i.e.* Wisdom) maketh men friends of God and
prophets (*i.e.* inspired men). For nothing doth God love
save him that dwelleth with Wisdom " (vii. 27, 28);
" Through her (*i.e.* Wisdom) I shall have immortality, and
an eternal memorial shall I leave to those (who come) after
me " (viii. 13, cp. ix. 18, etc.). In the same way, when
speaking against the renegade Jews, the writer says: " For
into an evil-devising soul Wisdom entereth not, neither doth
she dwell in a body enslaved by sin " (i. 4); see also iii. 10,
11, quoted above. A significant passage occurs in iv. 17 ff.,
where comfort for the godly, and denunciation of the renegade Jews appear together: " For they shall see the end of
the wise man, and shall not understand what he (*i.e.* the
Lord) purposed concerning him, nor for what end the Lord
set him in safety; they shall see it (*i.e.* the end of the wise
man) and account it as nothing; and them shall the Lord
laugh to scorn. And after this they shall become a dis-
honoured carcase, and a mockery among the dead for ever; "
the passage means that the ungodly will see the death of the
wise, *i.e.* godly, man, but they will not understand that this
is God's will, for it is His purpose to set the godly man in the
safety of immortality; but the ungodly have no hope of
immortality; the passage must be read in the light of
iii. 2, 5; iv. 14 and v. 14.

As an instance of the writer's purpose of combatting
idolatry, and showing that it is the antithesis of wisdom, we
may quote xiii. 17 ff.: " And when he prayeth concerning
his goods and his marriage and his children, he is not
ashamed to address a soulless object; yea, for health he
calleth upon that which is weak, and for life he beseecheth
a dead thing. . . ."

A further object, though not all authorities seem to be
agreed on this matter, was to controvert the teaching of
Ecclesiastes (*Koheleth*).

As long ago as 1799 Nachtigal [1] discerned this intention on
the part of the writer; it has been noticed by subsequent

---

[1] *Das Buch der Weisheit* (1799) referred to by Goodrick, *op. cit.*, p. 23.

commentators, though its significance has not always received due attention, possibly because the conditions of the times have not been sufficiently taken into consideration. When, for example, Gregg says that " the resemblances between *Wisdom* and the Greek version of *Ecclesiastes* are very few and doubtful," and that " the theory that *Wisdom* was prompted by opposition to *Ecclesiastes* may be confidently rejected," [1] he expresses a view which the facts do not bear out. Goodrick, on the other hand, rightly maintains that " there is a plainly traceable attempt to controvert the teaching of the writing (or the *congeries* of writings) known under the name of *Koheleth* or *Ecclesiastes* " [2] We may also quote the words of another recent commentator (Holmes):

The first section of *Wisdom* might be said to be a polemic against the words of Eccles. vii. 15, " There is a righteous man that perisheth in his righteousness, and there is a wicked man that prolongeth his life in his evil-doing "; the passages iv. 7–9 and 17–19 read like a direct contradiction of this. That one book (continues Holmes) could be written in answer to another (both now sacred) is seen from *Ecclesiastes* itself, which was doubtless written in antagonism to the view propounded by Ezekiel and his followers that righteousness and unrighteousness were both rewarded in this life, a view which the author of *Job* also contests. *Ruth*, also, was probably written as a protest against the endeavours of Ezra and Nehemiah to enforce the Deuteronomic law (xxiii. 3) against mixed marriages. The first part of *Wisdom*, therefore, may have been written to oppose the despairing philosophy of *Ecclesiastes* and the opinions and practices of the apostates, who may have quoted it to support their views.[3]

A few illustrations may be given to show parallel thoughts and directly contradictory words:

In Wisd. ii. 1, where the writer sets forth the reasonings of the ungodly, it is said: " Short and sorrowful is our life, and there is no healing at the last end of man "; Eccles. ii. 23

---

[1] *Op. cit.*, pp. xxv. f.   [2] *Op. cit.*, p. 23.   [3] *Op. cit.*, p. 525.

P

has: " For all his days are but sorrows, and his travail is grief "; v. 17 (Sept. 16): " All his days are in darkness and in mourning, and much vexation, and sickness, and bitterness." Wisd. ii. 2: " For by mere chance were we born, and hereafter we shall be as though we had not been "; Eccles. iii. 19: (Sept.) " And is it not (a matter of) mere chance (συνάντημα) what happens unto the sons of men, and mere chance to beasts, similar (' one ') mere chance to all? " Similarly in ix. 11: " . . . time and chance happeneth to them all alike," and iii. 20: " All go unto one place; all are of the dust, and all turn to dust again." Wisd. ii. 4: The ungodly say: " And our name will be forgotten in time, and no man will remember our works . . ."; precisely the same thought occurs in Eccles. i. 11: " There is no remembrance of the former (generations); neither shall there be any remembrance of the latter (generations) that are to come, among those that shall come after "; and ix. 5: " For the living know that they shall die; but the dead know not anything, neither have they any more reward; for the memory of them is forgotten." Wisd. ii. 5: " For our life is the passing of a shadow, and there is no putting back of our latter end . . ."; Eccles. vi. 12 has: " For who knoweth what is good for man in his life, and the days of his vain life that which he spendeth as a shadow? for who can tell a man what shall be after him under the sun? " Cp. viii. 8. Wisd. ii. 6: " Come, therefore, and let us enjoy the good things there are, and let us make use of creation to the full as in youth "; similarly in Eccles. ii. 24: " There is nothing better for a man than that he should eat and drink, and make his soul enjoy good in his labour "; with the whole of Wisd. ii. 6–10 should be compared Eccl. ix. 7–9. In all these passages the parallel thoughts representing the views of the free-thinking Jews are strikingly similar, and the writer of *Wisdom* who, as a Jew, must have been familiar with *Ecclesiastes*, evidently had this book in mind.

As illustrations of direct contradictions we have, *e.g.*, in Eccles. ix. 2: " All things come alike to all; there is one event to the righteous and to the wicked; to the good and [to the evil;] to the clean and to the unclean; to him that sacrificeth and to him that sacrificeth not; as is the good, so is the sinner . . ."; against this attitude we have in Wisd. iii. 2, 3: "In the eyes of the foolish they seemed to have died, and their departure was accounted a misfortune, and their going from us (their) destruction; but they are in peace"; while in verse 10 it is said: "But the ungodly shall receive punishment according as they reasoned, which were heedless of the right, revolting from the Lord."

In another direction the views of *Ecclesiastes* are contradicted in this way: Eccles. ix. 11 has: "I returned, and saw under the sun, that the race is not to the swift, nor the battle to the strong, neither yet bread to the wise, nor yet riches to the understanding, nor yet favour to men of skill"; in reply to such one-sided pessimism Wisd. viii. 10, 11 says: "Through her (Wisdom) I shall have praise among the multitudes, and honour with elders, though (I be) young. Sharp in judgement shall I be found, and in the sight of the mighty shall I be admired." Again, in Eccles. ii. 16 it is said: "For of the wise man, even as of the fool, there is no remembrance for ever, seeing that in the days to come all will already have been forgotten"; against which Wisd. viii. 13 retorts: "Through her I shall have immortality, and an eternal memorial shall I have to those (who come) after me." And once more, whereas Eccles. i. 18 speaks thus of Wisdom: "For in much wisdom is much grief; and he that increaseth knowledge increaseth sorrow," in Wisd. viii. 16 it is said: "When I enter my house I shall find rest with her, for converse with her hath no bitterness, nor life with her pain, but gladness and joy."

These passages are not exhaustive,[1] but they are sufficient to justify the contention that the first part, at any rate, of our book had as one of its objects to combat the attitude of mind which *Ecclesiastes* represents; this being a book with which the writer of *Wisdom*, as a Jew versed in the Scriptures, must have been familiar, the conclusion presses itself upon one that it was the book which he had in mind primarily.

[1] Various other points are well brought out by Goodrick (*op. cit.*, pp. 25 f.); see also Plumptre, *Ecclesiastes, or the Preacher*, pp. 70 f. (1889).

VII. The Conception of Wisdom

This subject has been briefly dealt with in chap. v, § iv; but a little further consideration of it is called for here.

Our author conceives of Wisdom as the artificer ($\dot{\eta}$ τεχνῖτις) of all (vii. 22ᵃ, cp. Prov. viii. 30); but this does not imply that Wisdom created anything, she merely carries out God's will in His created world. In the striking passage beginning with vii. 22ᵇ, where the nature of Wisdom is described, it is said that she is a spirit (according to the reading of Cod. A), or that " in her is a spirit . . ." (according to most of the MSS.); the former reading, though less authenticated, is supported by i. 6 and ix. 17, where Wisdom is identified with God's holy Spirit. Wisdom is holy, unique, many-sided, pure, unsullied, kind, beneficent, loving, all-powerful, all-surveying, pervading the spirits of men; she is the breath of the power of God and " a clear effluence of the glory of the Almighty," therefore wholly pure; she is also " the reflection of the eternal light," the spotless mirror of the divine activity, " the image of His goodness." Being but one, she can do all things, and abiding within herself she nevertheless renews all things, and enters into holy souls, making them the friends of God and vessels of inspiration (" prophets "), for it is those who are in constant converse with Wisdom that God loves. Wisdom, it is said further, is more beautiful than the sun and the stars, more lovely than light. She lives with God, and God loves her; she has been initiated into the knowledge of God, and chooses His works,—it is difficult to understand what this last means. She is worth more than riches, and no activity is as great as hers. If a man seeks to attain to righteousness let him acquire Wisdom, for the efforts entailed generate self-control and prudence, righteousness and manliness, the things most needed in life (vii. 22ᵇ–viii. 7).

In another passage, the " Prayer of Solomon," it is said:

With thee is Wisdom which knoweth thy works, having been present (with thee) when thou madest the world; and she understandeth what is pleasing in thine eyes, and what is right in thy commandments. Send her forth out of the holy heavens, and speed her from the throne of thy glory, that, being present with me she may labour, and that I may know what is well-pleasing in thy sight. For she knoweth all things and understandeth them, and will lead me in my actions wisely, and will guard me in her splendour (ix. 9–11).

These are the most striking passages in our book regarding Wisdom; but there are a few others to be mentioned. In i. 4 it is said that " into an evil-devising soul Wisdom entereth not, neither doth she dwell in a body enslaved by sin," *i.e.* Wisdom, being of God, is altogether alien to the sinner's outlook, cp. vi. 23; similarly in iii. 11 : " He that setteth at nought wisdom and instruction is miserable. And vain is their hope, and useless their labours, and unprofitable are their works "; the ignoring of Wisdom is thus ungodly, and brings its own punishment. On the other hand, following after Wisdom brings its own reward: " For you, therefore, O rulers, are my words, that ye may learn wisdom and not fall away. . . . Earnestly desire, therefore, my words, yearn for them, and ye shall be taught."

An important passage is vi. 12–20, which is evidently based on Prov. viii, and concludes (verses 17–20) with an example of the Sorites (σωρείτης) a chain, or series, of propositions heaped one on the other:

For the truest beginning of her is the desire for instruction; and the care for instruction is love (for her); and love (for her) is the observance of her laws; and the heeding of her. laws is the assurance of incorruption (*i.e.* immortality); and incorruption is the means of coming near to God; thus, the desire for Wisdom leadeth unto a kingdom (*i.e.* dominion).

In x. 1–21, and indeed from here to the end of the book, containing an historical retrospect, Wisdom is represented as directing the heroes of old in their doings; it means here little more than good sense or prudence, though, as Deane says, " it comprises also the notion of a deep knowledge, an appropriation of the history of God's dealings with His people, and a thorough trust in the divine aid which is never refused to the prayer of the faithful." [1]

Briefly then, these various passages present Wisdom under three aspects: " We find in the first six chapters . . . a laudation of Divine Wisdom, personified at times, but certainly not hypostatised; in the next three we have something very like hypostasis; in the last ten, 'practical godliness '—the merest φρόνησις." [2]

VIII. Manuscripts and Versions

The chief MSS. of our book are אBAV; an examination of Swete's *apparatus criticus* [3] (Cod. V is not included) shows that there are not many variations of importance (see for variant readings, *e.g.* iv. 18, vi. 12, vii. 22, viii. 13, x. 18). Of the cursives, 248, containing a " Lucianic " [4] text, is the most important, like other " Lucianic " MSS. it contains some interesting variants.[5]

Of the Versions the most important is the Latin; though contained in the Vulgate, it is not Jerome's work, but the Old Latin; in his *Praefatio in libr. Sal.*, he says: *In eo libro, qui a plerisque Sapientia Salomonis inscribitur . . . calamo temperavi, tantummodo canonicas Scripturas vobis emendare desiderans.* In a few cases, *e.g.* i, 15; ii. 8, it has readings which are probably original, though not found in any of the Greek uncial MSS. On the other hand, it contains many errors owing to a misunderstanding of the original; but, says Deane, " with due allowance for these defects, it probably represents the reading of MSS. earlier than any that have come down to us, and in this respect, at any rate, is of great critical value, while its language is interesting as presenting provincialisms and phrases which point to an African origin."[6]

[1] *The Book of Wisdom*, p. 25 (1881).
[2] Goodrick, *op. cit.*, p. 54.
[3] *The Old Testament in Greek*, ii. 604–643 (1896).
[4] The revision of the Greek Bible, the " Antiochian revision," was undertaken by Lucian of Samosata; he was martyred in 311 or 312 A.D.
[5] Holmes and Parsons, *op. cit.*, v; Feldmann, *Textmaterialien zum Buch der Weisheit* (1902).   [6] *Op. cit.*, p. 4.

The Syriac Version (*Peshitta*) is closely related to the Latin, but it has many mistranslations, it is paraphrastic, and has a large number of explanatory glosses.

The Syro-Hexaphar has many variants from the Greek MSS. which are valuable.[1]

The other Versions, Arabic, Coptic, and Armenian are of less importance.

IX. Literature

For the older literature see Deane, *op. cit.*, pp. 42 f. (1881); and Schürer, *op. cit.*, iii. 509 ff. (1909).

Houbigant, *De auctore libri Sapientiae Dissertatio* (1839).

Grimm, " Das Buch der Weisheit," in *Exegetisches Handbuch zu den Apokryphen*, vi. 1 ff. (1860).

Deane, *The Book of Wisdom* (1881).

Farrar, *The Wisdom of Solomon*, in Wace, *op. cit.*, i. 403 ff. (1888).

Bois, *Essai sur les origines de la philosophie Judéo-Alexandrine* (1890).

Thielmann, *Die lateinische Uebersetzung des Buches der Weisheit* (1893).

Siegfried, *Die Weisheit Salomos*, in Kautzsch, *op. cit.*, i. 476 ff. (1900).

Feldmann, *Text-kritische Materialien zum Buche der Weisheit* . . . (1902).

André, *op. cit.*, pp. 310 ff. (1903).

Holtzmann, *Die Peschitta zum Buche der Weisheit* . . . (1903).

Lincke, *Samaria und seine Propheten* (1903).

Stevenson, *Wisdom and the Jewish Apocryphal Writings* (1903).

Friedländer, *Griechische Philosophie im Alten Testament*, pp. 182 ff. (1904).

Gregg, *The Wisdom of Solomon* (1909).

Holmes, " The Wisdom of Solomon," in Charles, *op. cit.*, i. 518 ff. (1913).

Goodrick, *The Book of Wisdom* (1913).

Jocke, *Die Enstehung der Weisheit Salomos* (1913).

See also the literature referred to in the footnotes.

---

[1] See Goodrick, *op. cit.*, pp. 423 f.

ECCLESIASTICUS

I. Title

THE variety of titles given to this book in the ancient past is somewhat curious; no other Biblical or deutero-canonical book offers a parallel in this respect. These various titles may be enumerated as follows:

The Hebrew MSS. (see below § V) only begin with the concluding words of iii. 6, so that, for the present at any rate, it is not possible to say with certainty what the original Hebrew title was. On the other hand, these MSS. give definite information regarding the name of the author, and in so far they help in determining what the original title may have been. In l. 27 the writer speaks of himself as "Simeon, the son of Jeshua the son of Eleazar, the son of Sira"; at the end of the book there is a subscription, in the third line of which these identical words occur; but in the second line of this subscription it is: "Simeon, the son of Jeshua, who was called the son of Sira." This would lead one to suppose that Simeon was the name of the author; Schechter and Taylor believe this to have been the case: " . . . it is more probable that the name of our author was Simeon. Probably he was so called after the High-priest Simeon whose younger contemporary he was—a custom usual enough among the Jews at a very early period." [1] That the author was a great admirer of this High-priest is clear from l. 1 ff., and Nestle has shown that "the name Simeon is firmly attached to the author of this book in the Syrian Church." [2] On the other hand, in the Prologue to the Greek translation made by the grandson of the writer, the translator speaks of " my

---

[1] *The Wisdom of Ben-Sira*, p. 65 (1899).
[2] In Hastings' *D.B.* iv. 550a. On the other hand, Smend holds that "Simeon the son of" was added under the influence of l. 1, 24 (Hebr.), where the High-priest Simeon is spoken of.

grandfather Jesus "; and the early Rabbis call the book
" The instruction of Ben-Sira."
   In most of the Greek MSS. the title is " Wisdom of Jesus
son of Sirach," which in Cod. B is abbreviated to " Wisdom
of Sirach "; and in l. 27 they read: " Jesus the son of
Sirach (the son of) Eleazar, the Jerusalemite," though
" Eleazar " is omitted in some cases.
   In the Syriac MSS. the usual title is " Wisdom of Bar
Sira," though " Jesus the son of Simeon " also occurs; the
Syro-Hexaplar gives the name of the author as " Jesus the
son of Sirach (the son of) Eliezer."
   . A word may here be added regarding the form *Sirach* of
the Greek MSS.; the addition of the last letter (the Greek χ)
was intended to indicate that the word was indeclinable; [1]
why this particular letter was chosen is explained by Gott-
fried Kuhn; he says:

   The Greek σιραχ is to be pronounced *Sira*, not *Sirach*.
The first (Greek) scribe who wrote down the name added
an *Alef* (א), the Hebrew character, for the want of a
corresponding Greek one: ΣΕΙΡΑא. By this means the
object was achieved of indicating that the word was not
to be regarded as a substantive of the Greek first declension
(σειρα = " chain "), but as an indeclinable foreign word.
It has a " consonant " as its final letter, the soundless
semitic א. The copyists, who could not read Hebrew
and were not familiar with the original signification of
this letter, put in place of it the Greek χ since this was
similar to the Hebrew א. Thus arose σιραχ (Sirach).[2]

Schlatter,[3] however, regards the χ as due to a scribal error;
he thinks that the original Greek text of the words " Sirach
(the son of) Eleazar " was not, as now Σειρὰχ, 'Ελεαζάρ, but
ΣΕΙΡΑ ▽ ΕΛΕΑΖΑΡ, the ▽ being an abbreviation for υἱοῦ
(" the son of "), and that this ▽ became corrupted into X.
The suggestion is very interesting.

---

   [1] Cp. *Akeldamach* ('Ακελδαμάχ) which is the reading of the best Greek MSS.
in Acts i. 19 for the Aramaic form *Akeldama*; and Josech ('Ιωσήχ Luke iii. 26)
for *Jose;* see Dalman, *Grammatik des Jüdisch-Palästinischen Aramäisch*, p. 202
note 3 (2. ed. 1905).
   [2] *Zeitschrift für die A.T. Wissenschaft*, 1929, p. 289.
   [3] *Das neugefundene hebr. Stück des Sirach* . . ., p. 4 (1897).

The Latin MSS. need not be taken into consideration, so far as the title is concerned, for they follow the Greek. But in the Vulgate, which otherwise represents the Old Latin Version (for Jerome left the Latin text of *Sirach* as he found it, see further § VII), the title is *Ecclesiasticus*; it is from this that the title in the English Bible is taken. But Jerome tells us (*Praef. in Libr. Sal.*) that he had seen a Hebrew copy of the book which had the title " Parabolae "; this is interesting, for quotations from the book occurring in later Jewish literature are twice introduced by the words " the Parabolist said ";[1] Schechter quotes, moreover, the words of Rabbi Joseph to the effect that the " Proverbs of Ben-Sira " should be read because they contain useful matter.[2]

As to the title "Ecclesiasticus," however, something further must be said. It is generally held that this title was given because the book was the " Church Book " *par excellence* among the *Libri Ecclesiastici*, i.e. books which were not admitted into the Canon, but which were regarded as edifying and therefore read in the Church. It is pointed out that this is the explanation of the title given by Rufinus (*Comm. in Symb.* 38),[3] and that it has been in use in the Western Church ever since the time of Cyprian.[4] The correctness of this explanation has, however, recently been questioned by De Bruyne[5] on the grounds that it implies that the book was not regarded as canonical at the time this title was given to it, which the evidence shows to be very improbable, and that it implies also that the book occupied an outstanding position among those which we now call deutero-canonical, which is an error; for during the early centuries of the Church it was not *Ecclesiasticus* which was the most important of this group, but the *Wisdom of Solomon*, with its prophecy of the sufferings of Christ (ii. 12-20),[6] its description of the happiness of the righteous departed (iii. 1-8), and the distress of spirit among the unrighteous (v. 1-9), and with its discourse against the

---

[1] Cp. Cowley-Neubauer, *The Original Hebrew of a portion of Ecclesiasticus*, p. xx, note x, p. xxiv, note xxxviii, p. xxvi, note liv (1897).
[2] In the *Jewish Quarterly Review*, 1900, pp. 460 f.
[3] His date is 345-410 A.D.
[4] He died in 258 A.D.
[5] In the *Zeitschrift für die A.T. Wissenschaft*, for 1929, pp. 260 ff.
[6] This was the interpretation of the passage in the early Church.

heathen (xiii 1–5); this is the book which was most quoted by the Fathers, and which was most read. De Bruyne then gives reasons for his theory as to the origin of the title "Ecclesiasticus"; to go into these would take up too much space here; but he concludes his arguments with the question: "Est il téméraire de supposer que le nom *Ecclesiasticus* est formé sur le modèle *Ecclesiastes*?" The question certainly deserves consideration, for the usual explanation given to account for the title is not convincing.

What the actual title of the original Hebrew book was can only be surmised on the basis of the Hebrew MSS. (see above) and of the titles occurring in the Versions, and on the later Rabbinical evidence; putting these together it may be said that the original Hebrew title was either: "The Instruction of Jesus the son of Sira" (מוּסַר יֵשׁוּעַ בֶּן־סִירָא) or: "The Wisdom of . . ." (. . . . . . . חָכְמַת).[1]

II. DATE

There are two main indications regarding the approximate date at which our book was written:

(1) The panegyric on the High-priest Simeon, the son of Jochanan, in l. 1. ff., and (2) the statement of the writer's grandson in the Prologue that he came into Egypt in the thirty-eighth year of Euergetes the king, and translated his grandfather's book during his sojourn there. These indications would be definite enough were it not for the fact that there were two High-priests of the name of Simeon, and two Egyptian kings of the name of Euergetes; thus:

Simeon I, the son of Onias, approximately B.C. 300–270;[2]
Simeon II, the son of Onias, approximately B.C. 225–200;[3]
Ptolemy III Euergetes I, B.C. 246–221;
Ptolemy VII Euergetes II, Physkon, B.C. 145–116; but he reigned as joint-king with Ptolemy VI Philometor from B.C. 170 to 145.[4]

---

[1] In modern works the author is frequently spoken of as Ben-Sira, while the book, for convenience' sake, is commonly referred to as *Sirach*.
[2] Josephus, *Antiq.* xii. 43.
[3] *Antiq.* xii. 224.   [4] Bevan, *The Ptolemaic Empire*, p. 285 (1927).

Josephus' description of Simeon I, " he is called Simon the Just, both because of his piety towards God, and his kind disposition to those of his own nation," would agree with what is said in xlix. 15^b, l. 1 ff., especially the opening words: " Great among his brethren, and the glory of his people," and verse 7: " He took thought for his people (protecting them) from spoliation "; the account of his ministration in the sanctuary illustrates his " piety towards God." But if we are to identify the Simeon in this passage with Simeon I it will mean that our book was written at the latest about the middle of the third century B.C.; and this cannot be reconciled with what is said in the Prologue about Ben-Sira's grandson having made his translation during his sojourn in Egypt in and after the thirty-eighth year of Euergetes; for there is, as a matter of fact, but one Euergetes who can be meant; Euergetes I reigned only twenty-five years, whereas Euergetes II reigned fifty-four altogether, so that his thirty-eighth year would be B.C. 132. Allowing something like fifty years for the period between grandfather and grandson, we should get, approximately, the year B.C. 180 as that of the composition of our book. Two subsidiary points demand notice; Josephus applies the expression " the Just " to Simeon I, which, as we have seen, is appropriate to the words written in reference to the Simeon of Chap. l; in explanation of this it may justifiably be maintained that Josephus was mistaken, and that the epithet should be in reference to Simeon II; as is well known, Josephus is not always reliable in what he writes. Then, again, Josephus— in this case rightly—speaks of Simeon as the son of Onias and this would be correct in regard to both Simeons; but the text of our book in l. 1 speaks of " Simeon, the son of Jochanan "; there was, however, no High-priest who could be thus described. The fact is, as Smend has shown,[1] that the two names Onias and Jochanan in their Hebrew form could easily have been confused; the Greek text reads Onias. In the Hebrew text " Jochanan " should be read " Onias."

For the date B.C. 180, more or less, of our book one or two

[1] *Die Weisheit des Jesus Sirach*, pp. 478 f. (1906).

indirect arguments may be mentioned. It was during the
High-priesthood of Simeon II that Antiochus the Great
(B.C. 223–187), through his great victory at Panion in B.C.
198 over the Egyptian forces, was able to incorporate the
whole of Syria within his empire. Josephus tells us that
when, in visiting his newly won territory, Antiochus came to
Jerusalem, he was well received by the Jews," " who gave
plentiful provision to all his army. . . ." [1] In recognition of
this the king rewarded the Jews in various ways; these are
recorded by Josephus in a letter of Antiochus, in which,
among other things, he writes:

> I would also have the work about the temple finished,
> and the cloisters, and if there be anything else that ought
> to be rebuilt. And for the materials of wood, let it be
> brought to them out of Judæa itself, and out of the other
> countries, and out of Libanus, tax free; and the same
> I would have observed as to those other materials which
> will be necessary, in order to render the temple more
> glorious.[2]

The carrying out of these instructions would obviously
have been under the supervision of the High-priest, so that
we can understand the words of Ben-Sira in l. 1 ff., where,
in referring to Simeon, the priest, i.e. High-priest, he says:

> In whose time the house was renovated;
> And in whose days the Temple was fortified;
> In whose time a reservoir was dug,
> A water-cistern like the sea in abundance.
> In his days the wall was built,
> (With) turrets for strength like a king's palace.

Here, therefore, we have a strong indirect piece of evidence
for the date of the book as indicated above.

Again, in x. 1 ff. there seem to be some covert references to
historical events which occurred during the lifetime of
Ben-Sira; in verse 8 he says:

> Dominion goeth from one nation to another
> Because of the violence of pride.

[1] *Antiq.* xii. 133.   [2] *Antiq.* xii. 141.

These words may well refer to the war between Syria and
Egypt which is also referred to, but with more detail, in the
somewhat later book of *Daniel*; there, in xi. 11, 12 it is said:

> And the king of the south shall be moved with choler,
> and shall come forth and fight with him, even with the
> king of the north; and he shall set forth a great multitude,
> but the multitude shall be given into his hand. And the
> multitude shall be carried away, and his heart shall be
> exalted; and he shall cast down tens of thousands, but
> he shall not prevail.

This is in reference to the battle of Raphia (B.C. 217) when
Ptolemy IV Philopator, " the king of the south," gained the
victory over Antiochus III, " the king of the north."
Ptolemy's heart was exalted, or as Ben-Sira says, was filled
" with the pride of violence "; but ultimately he did not
prevail, dominion went from the nation of Egypt to that of
Syria.

It is quite possible, moreover, that when Ben-Sira goes
on in verse 10 to say that:

> The ravage of disease mocketh the physician,
> A king to-day, to-morrow he falleth,

he is referring to the death of Ptolemy IV, which, as Bevan
says, " was wrapped in some mystery "; [1] Polybius tells us
that " after the termination of the war for Coele-Syria
Ptolemy Philopator abandoned entirely the path of virtue
and took to a life of dissipation "; [2] that may well have been
the cause of the sudden death to which Ben-Sira refers.

Finally, it is certain that our book must have been written
before the outbreak of the Maccabæan wars soon after B.C.
170, because there is no hint of this external danger to the
the country; on the other hand, there is a direct reference to
the hellenistic Jews who, later, were largely responsible for
the Maccabæan revolt because of their siding with Antiochus
Epiphanes against their own orthodox brethren; in xli.
8–10 Ben-Sira says:

[1] *Op. cit.*, p. 250.   [2] *Histories*, xiv. 12, 3.

Woe unto you, ungodly men,
Who have forsaken the Law of the Most High God.
If ye be fruitful (it will be) for harm,
And if ye bear children (it will be) for sighing . . .

The fact that Ben-Sira speaks of these without any farther reference to the critical state of affairs which their attitude helped to bring about is conclusive evidence that he wrote before the beginning of the Maccabæan era.

All these subsidiary points go to substantiate the contention that the book was written, at any rate, before B.C. 170, while the evidence of the Prologue suggests, as above remarked, a date B.C. 180 at the latest.

III. CONTENTS OF THE BOOK.

To set forth the contents of our book in the same way in which this has been done with the other books of this collection would not be found satisfactory, on account of the rather haphazard way in which the material has been written down; here and there, it is true, signs of some attempt to co-ordinate the subject-matter are discernible; but the attempts are desultory, and generally speaking the material is mixed up in disorderly fashion. The best way to gain an insight into the contents is to tabulate the various subjects, with references, under different heads, in alphabetical order, thus:

Appearances are often fallacious: xi. 2–13.
Art of ruling: ix. 17–x. 18.
Autobiographical note: xxxiii. 16–18 (xxxvi. 16a, xxx. 25–27).[1]
Conduct towards women: ix. 1–9.
Control of the tongue: Need of propriety in speech, xxiii, 7–15.
Right use of speech, v. 9–vi. 1.
Silence and speech, xx. 1–8.
The evil tongue, xxviii. 13–26.

[1] On the dislocation of the text, involving these complicated references, see below § VI.

Q

Foresight, xviii. 19–29.
Forethought, xxxii (xxxv) 18–24.
Forgiveness, xxvii. 30–xxviii. 7.
Humility, iii. 17–25; vii. 4–7.
Independence, xxxiii. 19–23 (xxx. 28–32).
Kindness, iv. 1–10.
Self-control, vi. 2–4; xviii. 30–xix. 3; xxii. 27–xxiii.
  6; xxxvii. 27–31.
Wealth: A false security, v. 1–3.
  Uses of wealth, xiv. 3–19; xxxi (xxxiv) 5–11.
  Wealth and poverty, xxxi (xxxiv) 1–4.
Wisdom: Blessedness of those who seek Wisdom, xiv. 20–27.
  Fear of the Lord is Wisdom, i. 11–21; ii. 15–18; vii.
    29–31; xxxiv (xxxi) 9–20.
  Origin of Wisdom, i. 1–10.
  Possession of Wisdom brings joy, xv. 1–10.
  Praise of Wisdom, xxiv. 1–34; li. 13–30.
  Reward of those who seek Wisdom, iv. 11–19; xx.
    27–31.
  Search for Wisdom, vi. 18–37.
  Wisdom as seen in the Creation, xvi. 24–30.
  Wisdom brings honour, x. 30–xi. 1.
  Wisdom in practice, i. 22–30.
  Wisdom opposed to craftiness, xix. 20–30.
  Wisdom true and false, xxxvii. 16–26.
Wives: A good wife, xxvi. 1–4, 13–18.
  An evil wife, xxv. 13–26; xxvi. 5–12.
  Different types of wives, xxvi. 19–27.
  The choice of a wife, xxxvi. 21–26 (26–31).
Woes of Humanity: xl. 1–17.

IV. THE AUTHOR AND HIS BOOK

No book in the canonical scriptures, nor yet in deutero-canonical writings, gives so much direct, and still more indirect, information regarding the author as the one under consideration.

That Ben-Sira was a native of Jerusalem is evident from various indications of the book; the glimpses into social life

which he gives, such as could only apply to residence in a
large city, his knowledge of traders and their ways, his
evident contact with men of different callings, the very fact
of his being a *Ḥakam* ("Wise man"), his familiarity with
the Temple and its services,—these and other indications
leave no doubt that the home of Ben-Sira was ln Jerusalem;
and this is further borne out by the fact that the Greek
Version in l. 27 speaks of him as " the Jerusalemite."

As a *Ḥakam* he would have his " lecture-room " or something equivalent to this; he, therefore, speaks of his *Beth
ha-Midrash*, " House of Learning," or " Instruction,"
where men seek Wisdom, in li. 23:

> Turn in unto me, ye unlearned,
> And lodge in my house of instruction (*Beth ha-Midrash*).

When he says further: " Get Wisdom for yourselves without
money," the words, while they may well have been prompted
by Isa. lv. 1, reflect the ambition of many zealous teachers,
whose glory it was to give teaching, whether of the Law or
Wisdom, *gratis*; this is re-echoed in the Talmud (*Nedarim*
36a): " As I have taught you without payment, saith God,
so must you do likewise."   But as a *Ḥakam*, Ben-Sira would
have been, as in earlier days, a *sopher* or " scribe "; this is
implied in xxxix. 1–11, where the dual activities of the
Wisdom-Scribe are set forth by one who evidently speaks of
his own doings (cp. xxxix. 12 ff.) [1] thus, for the purpose of
teaching others, he

> Meditateth in the Law of the Most High;
> He searcheth out the wisdom of all the ancients,
> And is occupied in prophecies;
> He preserveth the discourses of men of renown,
> And entereth into subtleties of parables;
> He seeketh out the hidden things of proverbs,
> And is conversant with the dark things of parables (1–3).

---

[1] On the dual functions of the Wisdom-Scribe see the present writer's *The
Book of Proverbs*, pp. lxviii ff. (1929).

As a result:

> He himself poureth forth words of wisdom,
> And giveth thanks to the Lord in prayer;
> He himself (*i.e.* the writer) directeth his counsel and
>   knowledge,
> And in the secrets thereof doth he meditate.
> He himself declareth wise instruction,[1]
> And glorieth in the Law of the covenant of the Lord . . .
>   (7–11).

It will be noticed here how Wisdom and the Law are identified (cp. xv. 1; xix. 20; xxi. 11; xxiv. 23; xxxiv [xxxi] 8).

The other side of the Wisdom-scribe's activities is hinted at in verse 4:

> He serveth among great men,
> And appeareth before a ruler,
> He travelleth in the land of alien nations,
> And hath tried both good and evil things among men.

This is to say, the Wisdom-scribe was still in Ben-Sira's day in some sense a state functionary; his learning and knowledge of men fitted him to go on diplomatic missions to the courts of foreign rulers (on this see further below). Doubtless it was largely these visits to other countries which opened Ben-Sira's mind, ardent Jew as he was, to extraneous influences:

> The traces of the influence of Greek modes of thought to be found in our book are not seen in definite form, but, as one would expect where the influence was at work unconsciously, they are to be discerned rather in the general outlook and conception; what is perhaps the most striking example of this is the way in which virtue and knowledge are identified; this is a distinct Hellenic *trait*, and is treated in the book as axiomatic. In the past, human and divine wisdom had been regarded as opposed,

---

[1] So the Syriac which is better than the Greek, " the instruction of his teaching."

whereas, owing to Greek influence, both in our book and in the Wisdom Literature generally, it is taught that wisdom is the one thing of all others which is indispensable to him who would lead a godly life. The evil of wickedness is represented as lying in the fact that wickedness is foolishness, and therefore essentially opposed to wisdom. On the other hand, the Jews were faithful to the Law, the ordinances of which were binding because it was the revealed will of God; and therefore, in order to reconcile this old teaching with the new teaching that wisdom was the chief requirement of the man of religion, Wisdom became identified with the Law: " The fear of the Lord is the beginning of wisdom "; by the " fear of the Lord " is meant of course, obedience to His commands, *i.e.* observance of the Law. These words express what is, in truth, the foundation-stone of the Wisdom Literature, and this identification between Wisdom and the Law formed the reconciling link between Judaism and Hellenism in this domain. Nowhere is this identification more clearly brought out than in the *Book of Wisdom* and *Sirach*. This fully explains why Ben-Sira, following therein, without doubt, many sages before him, divides mankind into two categories, the wise and the foolish, which correspond respectively to the righteous and the wicked.[1]

This extraneous influence, then, was to a large extent doubtless the result of Ben-Sira's sojournings in foreign parts, though the general atmosphere of the times will also have contributed to this. In several passages he refers to his travels; xxxix. 4 has already been quoted; when he says, clearly from his own experience, that during his travels he has " tried both good and evil things among men," he may well be thinking of one of the " evil things " of which he was the victim, during one of his journeys; to this he refers in li. 1 ff., from which it is evident that he was once in danger of his life owing to the slanderous tongue of some enemy; he thanks God for the preservation of his life:

[1] Box and Oesterley, *The Book of Sirach*, in Charles' *Apocr. and Pseudep.*, i. 269.

Thou didst preserve me from the slander of the people,
From the scourge of a slanderous tongue,
And from the lips of those who turn aside to lying,
Thou wast with me in the presence of those who rose up
    against me.
Thou didst help me, according to the abundance of
    thy mercy,
Out of the snare of those watching for my downfall.
And from the hand of those that seek my life;
Out of many troubles hast thou saved me . . .

That the reference here is to foreign enemies is clear from
the words " the slander of the people." In speaking of this
passage Ryssel pointedly remarks that " since Ben-Sira's
travels must certainly have extended to Syria and Egypt,
he might easily have been suspected by one of the kings of
these countries of conspiring in the interests of the other ";
the relations between these two countries before B.C. 198
were very strained (see further, Part I, chap. iv).

A pleasanter experience of his travels is referred to in
xxxi (xxxiv) 12 ff., where Ben-Sira gives advice to a young
contemporary as to behaviour when sitting at " the table
of some great man." [1] But however sumptuous a feast
among strangers, Ben-Sira evidently prefers his home:

Better the life of a poor man under a shelter of logs,
  Than sumptuous fare among strangers (xxix. 22).

Further, Ben-Sira claims to be in the following of the
canonical writers who had written Wisdom books; he says:

I, indeed, rose up,[2] last of all,
As one that gleaneth after the grape-gatherers;
I advanced by the blessing of God,
And filled my wine-press as a grape-gatherer (xxxiii.
  16-18 [= xxxvi. 16a and xxx. 25-27]).

---

[1] It is granted that " the table of some great man " does not necessarily
refer to a foreign noble or king; but the possibility of this must be granted in
view of, e.g., *Aboth* vi. 5 : " Lust not after the table of kings."

[2] The Hebrew word שָׁקֵד means to be awake or watchful; in later Hebrew
it has the sense of being intent upon something, or studious.

The words would almost seem to imply that Ben-Sira, in his modesty, claimed to be little more than a collector from the works of his predecessors; the study of his book, however, shows that this was far from being the case. Doubtless, he was very familiar with the earlier Wisdom books, and shows frequent identity of thought with sayings in the book of *Proverbs*; but it must be remembered that there was a large mass of Wisdom material, oral and written, which was common property; so that what may often appear to be indebtedness on the part of Ben-Sira to the writers of the book of *Proverbs*, is as likely as not to be traditional material of unknown authorship utilized by both. Apart from this, however, Ben-Sira shows plenty of individuality, and goes his own way in many particulars. To be sure, in various directions,—in thought, point of view, method of expression, etc., all the Wisdom writers are at one; allowing for this, we may make a brief examination of Ben-Sira as a teacher.

His great insight into human nature, his knowledge of and sympathy with the weaknesses of man (though never condoned), come out again and again. An interesting example of this occurs in xvi. 17–23; here Ben-Sira describes the attitude of a man who, being but one in the great mass of people, most of whom were more illustrious than himself, thinks that he is beyond the notice of God, who is so great and mighty in heaven and earth:

> I am hidden from God,
> And in the height who will remember me?
> I shall not be noticed among so illustrious a people,
> . And what am I among the mass of the spirits of all the
>   children of men?
> Behold the heavens and the heavens of the heavens
> And the deep of the earth . . .

Therefore, argues such a one:

> In truth, unto me he will not have respect,
> And as for my ways, who will mark them?
> If I sin no eye beholdeth it,

> Or if I deal untruly in all secrecy, who will know it?
> My righteous dealing, who declareth it?
> And what hope is there?   For the decree is distant.

In other words, we have here the type of man depicted,
who does not, indeed, deny the existence of God, but who
feels his insignificance in the crowd of men, so many of whom
are greatly his superiors; and, contrasting his pitiable
unimportance with the immeasurable greatness of God, he
feels that he is of no account.   But instead of this generating
in him a sense of sane and fitting humility, he prefers to
make it an excuse for indulging in sin—who cares if he does
do wrong?—the *arrière pensée* of his "righteous dealing"
either reflects the fatuous self-justification of this type of
person—a perennial type in one form or another—or perhaps
it is a touch of irony on Ben-Sira's part.   At any rate, it is
one of many illustrations which show how thoroughly in
touch Ben-Sira was with his fellow-creatures; his comment
on this kind of thing is:

> They that lack understanding think these things,
> And a man of folly thinketh thus.

Another instance of Ben-Sira's knowledge of men and their
weaknesses is afforded by his reiterated precepts regarding
control of the tongue; in xix. 4 ff., he inveighs against
thoughtless chattering and the harmfulness caused thereby;
the evil of it, as he implies, consists especially in the fact that
it tends to be about other people; and there are those who
take a positive delight in saying things about others which,
whether true or not, were best left unsaid; to such Ben-Sira
remarks:

> Hast thou heard anything?   Let it die with thee;
> Be of good courage, it will not burst thee.

A great many similar illustrations could be given; they
tell of Ben-Sira's insight into human nature, and his sound
common sense in dealing with men of all kinds.   That he
was not wanting in sympathy is certain; one instance of
this may be offered; he does not crush the sinner with bitter
invective, but exhorts him with a really helpful warning:

My son, hast thou sinned? Add not thereto;
And make supplication concerning thy former sins.
Flee from sin as from the face of a serpent;
For if thou come near it, it will bite thee.
The teeth of a lion are the teeth thereof,
Slaying the souls of men.
Like a two-edged sword is all iniquity,
From the stroke thereof is no healing (xxi. 1–3).

Ben-Sira's contact with all sorts and conditions of men was truly remarkable; in public life, already referred to, and in social life (xxxi [xxxiv] 12–xxxii [xxxv] 13), he must, on the face of it, have come across the most diverse characters; and how thoroughly in touch he was with humanity in general is abundantly seen by the way in which he sets forth the right relationships between men in all walks of life; the small man and the great; the rich and the poor (iv. 1–10; vii. 32; xiii. 21–23, etc.); household servants and their lords; slaves and masters (vii. 20, 21; xxxiii. 24 ff. xxx. 33 ff.); husband and wife (vii. 19, 26); children and parents (iii. 1–16, vii. 23–25; xxx. 1 ff.; xlii. 9 ff.); physician and patient (xxxviii. 1 ff.); guests and host (xxxi [xxxiv] 12 ff.; xxxii [xxxv] 1 ff.); buyers and sellers (xxvi. 29 ff.); lenders and borrowers (xxix. 1 ff.); frequently he speaks of the conduct of friends one to another (vi. 5–17; vii. 12, 18; ix. 10; xii. 8 ff.; xix. 13; xxii. 19 ff.; xxxvii. 1 ff.); he urges the visitation of the sick (vii. 35), the comforting of mourners (vii. 34); the very animals have his sympathy (vii. 22); he insists on the honouring of the priesthood (vii. 29–31); he warns the faithless (ii. 12–14), and encourages the god-fearing (ii. 15–18); and he lays stress on man's duties to himself, both in regard to the body (xxiii. 6; xxx. 14 ff.; xxxvii. 27 ff.) and the spirit (vii. 1–3; xxiii. 2 ff., 16 ff.; xxx. 21 ff.).

This solicitude for the welfare of his fellow-creatures receives its full significance when it is realized that it is the outcome of Ben-Sira's love of God; duty to God is the incentive of duty to one's fellow-creatures; that, in effect, though unexpressed in so many words, is the burden of his book. To illustrate fully the depth of Ben-Sira's religious feelings and convictions would call for much space; it must suffice to refer to the following more outstanding passages: (i. 11–20; ii. 1–6, 15–18; xvii. 1–14; xviii. 1–14; xxxiii [xxxvi] 7–15; xxxiv [xxxi] 9–20; xxxv [xxxii] 14–26; xxxvi. 1–17 [xxxiii. 1–13a, xxxvi. 16b–22]; xxxix. 12–35; xl. 18–27; xlii. 15–xliii. 33; li.

That he was an ardent student of the Scriptures is frequently evident, see especially xxxix. 1–3, and, above all, the long section on the Praise of the Fathers of old (xliv–l. 24); in the Prologue, too, Ben-Sira's grandson speaks of his grandsire as " having much given himself to the reading of the law, and the prophets, and the other books of our fathers. . . ."

So that with all his intercourse with humanity, bad as well as good, and with all his worldly knowledge, Ben-Sira was a man of piety and saintly disposition; of him it may be said that he was one who lived in the world, but kept himself unspotted from the world.

The doctrinal teaching of our book has been dealt with above (see chap. vii.) but a few words as to his teaching on Wisdom are called for here.

Wisdom, according to Ben-Sira, was pre-existent before the creation of the world; it proceeded from God, almost like the divine breath, and covered the earth like a mist; it is thus ubiquitous, and intended for the use of all humanity; Wisdom is made to say:

> I came forth from the mouth of the Most High,
> And as a mist I covered the earth.
> In the high places did I fix my abode,
> And my throne was in the pillar of cloud.
> Alone I compassed the circuit of heaven,
> And in the depth of the abyss I walked.
> In the waves of the sea, and in all the earth,
> And in every people and nation I gained a possession
> (xxiv. 3–6).

It is evident that extraneous influence is to be discerned

here both in the personification of Wisdom,[1] and in the conception of Wisdom walking in the depth of the abyss; for, according to Babylonian mythology, Ea, one of the most important of the Babylonian gods, dwelt in Apsu, " the deep," and was known as " the Lord of Wisdom "; [2] in the cosmogony of the Babylonians Bel is the creator of man, and Ea is the deep beneath the earth and which it encompasses, and he is the source of wisdom and culture. " Ea," says Jastrow, " the father, is the personification of Wisdom, while Bel embodies the practical action which streams forth from Wisdom.[3]

But Ben-Sira, while recognizing the presence of Wisdom among all peoples, goes on to say (Wisdom is still speaking) :

> With all these I sought a resting-place,
> And said, In whose inheritance shall I lodge?
> Then the Creator of all things gave me commandment,
> And he that created me fixed my dwelling-place;
> And he said, In Jacob let thy dwelling-place be,
> And in Israel take up thine inheritance (xxiv. 7, 8).

What Ben-Sira means by these words is that Wisdom was embodied in the Law given on Sinai (cp. verse 20), an identification between Wisdom and the Law to which reference has already been made. Elsewhere, Ben-Sira earnestly appeals to his hearers to become, as it were, the bond-slaves of Wisdom;

> Hearken, my son, and receive my judgement,
>   And refuse not my counsel;
> And bring thy feet into her fetters,
>   And into her chains thy neck.
> Bow down thy shoulder and bear her,
>   And chafe not under her bonds . . . (vi. 23–27)

For such as respond to this appeal the reward will be great :

> Her net will become for thee a stay of strength,
>   And her bonds robes of gold.

---

[1] Though Ben-Sira was undoubtedly also indebted to Prov. viii for this.
[2] Jeremias, *Handbuch der altorientalischen Geisteskultur*, pp. 352 ff. (1929) *Das alte Testament im Lichte des alten Orients*, p. 67 (1930).
[3] *Die Religion Babyloniens und Assyriens*, i. 61 (1905).

> An ornament of gold is her yoke,
>> And her fetters a cord of blue (cp. Num. xv. 38).
> With glorious garments shalt thou array thyself,
>> And with a crown of beauty shalt thou crown thyself
>> with her (vi. 29–31).

It cannot, however, be too strongly insisted upon that Ben-Sira's teaching on wisdom, whether in the domain of utilitarianism (*e.g.* xviii. 30–33), or in more exalted spheres (*e.g.* xxvii. 8–10), is based on a religious foundation; this is much more pronounced and explicitly stated than in the book of *Proverbs*; a good instance of this occurs in iv. 11–14:

> Wisdom teacheth her children,
> And taketh hold of all that give heed to her.
> They that love her love life,
> And they that seek her shall obtain grace from the
>> Lord.
> They that take her of her shall find glory from the Lord.
> They that serve her serve the Holy One,
> And God loveth them that love her (See also xxv. 10).

Instructive, too, are the words in i. 26:

> If thou desire wisdom keep the commandments,
> And the Lord will give her unto thee freely.

This expressed identity of Wisdom with religion is a noteworthy feature of our book.

Ben-Sira's general standpoint was Sadducæan; not that in his day the Pharisees and Sadducees constituted definitely opposed parties; this arose in post-Maccabæan times; none the less, the pronounced differences of opinion which in later days resulted in the formation of antagonistic parties, Pharisaic and Sadducæan, were already in evidence.

> It has been suggested (says Dr. Taylor, in reference to a hint thrown out by Kuenen), with a certain plausibility, that the book Ecclesiasticus approximates to the standpoint of the primitive *Çaduqin* (Sadducees) as regards its theology, its sacerdotalism, and its want of sympathy with

the *modern* Soferim (Scribes). The name of Ezra is significantly omitted from its catalogue of worthies; "it remains singular," remarks Kuenen, "that the name whom a later generation compared, nay made almost equal, to Moses is passed over in silence. . . . Is it not really most natural that a Jesus ben Sirach did not feel sympathy enough for the first of the Scribes, to give him a place of honour in the series of Israel's great men?" The modern *Scribe* was to Ben-Sirach an unworthy descendant of the primitive Wise.

He refers also to the significant fact that in the Babylonian Talmud (*Sanhedrin* 100b) the "Books of Sadducees" and the Book of Ben-Sira" are placed side by side on the *Index expurgatorius*.[1]

The Sadducæan standpoint is indicated in several particulars in our book. Regarding the future life, no belief in the resurrection is expressed, only the old Sheol conception (xiv. 12–16; xxx. 17; xli. 4; xlviii. 5, in this last passage the raising up of a corpse from death does not mean resurrection in the real sense). Following upon this there is no belief in angels,[2] in the sense of risen men becoming angels; that the Sadducees believed in angels in the sense of the heavenly hosts, *i.e.* angels who are such by nature, must be obvious when it is remembered that the Sadducees insisted most strongly on the superior authority of the Pentateuch, where angels are not infrequently mentioned; hence in xlii. 17 angels in this sense are spoken of. Then, again, with regard to the Law; insistence on its precepts occurs again and again, but always in reference to the Pentateuch; there is never any hint of the Pharisaic standpoint regarding the Law. The difference between the two attitudes is clearly shown by Josephus.

The Pharisees have delivered to the people a great many observances by succession from their fathers, which are not written in the laws of Moses; and for that reason it is that the Sadducees reject them, and say that we are to

---

[1] *Sayings of the Jewish Fathers, comprising Pirqe Aboth* . . ., p. 115 (1897).
[2] Cp. Acts xxiii. 8.

esteem those observances to be obligatory which are in
the written word, but are not to observe what are derived
from the tradition of our forefathers.[1]

Further, the attitude towards the Gentile world in our
book is distinctly more favourable than the Pharisaic (*e.g.* i.
9; xvii. 17. xviii. 13, " the mercy of the Lord is upon all
flesh "); this would be in accordance with the Sadducæan
outlook, who, as representatives of the wealthier classes, and
in touch with the ruling circles, would necessarily have
been brought more in contact with the outside world.

Another important point in this connexion is what is said
in the " Thanksgiving " which appears in the Hebrew text
after li. 12; in the ninth verse it is said:

> Give thanks unto him that chooseth the sons of Zadok
>   for priests,
>   For his mercy endureth for ever.

It is perhaps unnecessary to point out that " the sons of
Zadok " are equivalent to the Sadducees; so that these
words support what has been said as to the Sadducæan
standpoint of our book.

Finally, one other matter demands mention. It will be
pointed out later (§ VI), that there are two recensions of the
Greek Version of our book; the second of these, as will be
seen, is a Pharisaic recension of the book. The obvious
conclusion to be drawn from this is that in somewhat later
times, when the Pharisees, as a party, were wholly in the
ascendant, it was thought well that this popular Wisdom book
should, because of its generally Sadducæan standpoint, be
" pharisaized " by means of the addition of a number of
verses which set forth specifically Pharisaic views.

V. The Original Language of the Book and the Hebrew MSS.

Even in the Greek form of our book, which until comparatively recently had been regarded as the most authoritative form, there is ample evidence to show that it is a

[1] *Antiq.* xiii. 297.

translation from the Hebrew. To illustrate this would involve the discussion of many technical points, and comparisons between Hebrew and Greek linguistic usages, which would take up a great deal of space; investigations of this kind would be hardly appropriate here. Abundant material will be found in Smend's great work on *Ecclesiasticus*.[1]

Further, in the prologue to our book Ben-Sira's grandson writes:

> Ye are intreated therefore to read with favour and attention, and to pardon us, if in any parts of what we have laboured to interpret, we seem to fail in some of the phrases. For things originally spoken in Hebrew have not the same force in them when they are translated into another tongue . . .

Again, Jerome, in his Preface to the books of Solomon writes:

> *Fertur et* παναρετος *Jesu filii Sirach liber et alius* ψευδεπίγραφος, *qui Sapientia Salomonis inscribitur. Quorum priorem Hebraicum reperi, non Ecclesiasticum, ut apud Latinos, sed Parabolas praenotatum, cui juncti erant Ecclesiastes et Canticum Canticorum, ut similitudinem Salomonis non solum librorum numero, sed etiam materiarum genere coaequaret.*[2]

The Hebrew text was thus still in existence in Jerome's day (died 420 A.D.).

And lastly, citations in Hebrew occur in the Talmud. It was therefore certain that our book was originally written in Hebrew; but apart from the Talmudic quotations, no trace of the Hebrew original was thought to exist. Then, in 1896, a Hebrew fragment of the book was found in the " Genizah "[3] of the ancient synagogue at Cairo. More and more of these fragments were discovered as the years

---

[1] *Die Weisheit des Jesus Sirach*, pp. lxii ff. (1906).
[2] Quoted by Schürer, *op. cit.*, iii. 217.
[3] The term *Genizah* (from the root to " hide ") is applied to a room adjoining the synagogue set apart for storing disused manuscripts of the books of the Bible which had been employed in public worship, but which it was thought wrong to destroy. Manuscripts of heretical books were also deposited in the *Genizah*.

went on, all from the same home, the most recent having come to light in 1931.

This discovery (says the finder of it, Rabbi Joseph Marcus), coming more than three decades after the flush of excitement of the first discoveries, besides its own intrinsic interest and importance, filling up a large gap, will, I hope, succeed in drawing the attention of scholars to the possibility that all the Genizah material has not yet been carefully examined, and that there may yet be, awaiting the discerning eye of the scholar, hidden leaves of Ben Sira to be brought to light.[1]

For the list of publications in which all these fragments first appeared, see below, pp. 254 f.; but it will be well to append here a list of the passages which are now available in Hebrew according to the different manuscripts designated A–E:—

MS. A: ii. 18ᵈ, added after vi. 17.
iii. 6ᵃ–xvi. 26ᵇ.
xxiii. 16ᵗ, added after xii. 14.
xxvii. 5, 6, added after vi. 22.

MS. B: xxx. 11–xxxvi (xxxiii) 3.
xxxii (xxxv) 11–xxxviii. 27ᵇ.
xxxix. 15ᶜ–li. 30.

MS. C: iv. 23ᵇ, 30, 31.
v. 4–7, 9–13.
vi. 18ᵇ (in part), 19, 28, 35.
vii. 1, 2, 4, 6ᵃᵇ, 17, 20, 21, 23–25.
viii. 31ᵇ (in part).
xix. 2ᵃ, 3ᵇ.
xx. 5–7, 13.
xxv. 8, 13, 17–22, 23ᶜᵈ, 24.
xxvi. 1, 2ᵃ.
xxxvi. 24ᵃ.
xxxvii. 19, 22, 24, 26.

MS. D: xxxvi. 29–xxxviii. 1ᵃ.

MS. E: xxxii (xxxv) 16–xxxiii (xxx) 32; xxxiv. 1 mutilated.

---

[1] *The Jewish Quarterly Review*, Jan. 1931, p. 223.

It will thus be seen that for some passages two MSS. are available, and for some even three. Out of the 1616 distichs represented in the Greek text, 1090, for the most part entire, have so far been recovered in their Hebrew form. A number of complicated problems arise in regard to the relationship of these MSS to one another; for discussion on these we refer our readers to Smend's work, already referred to.[1] Here we must restrict ourselves to some general remarks about the MSS. All of them, with the exception of MS. E,[2] abound in scribal errors; letters which are similar to one another are frequently confused; many words are hopelessly corrupt, and are often in their wrong order; sometimes whole lines are misplaced.[3] Of great importance are the many doublets, variants, and marginal notes; in MS. B, especially, a number of *stichoi* are given in twofold, sometimes threefold, form; in MS. A, too, there are many doublets. Nevertheless, the careful study of these MSS. shows that, in spite of all these variations, they represent not independent types of text, but different recensions of the same archetypal text; and fragmentary as they are, they contain, as is recognized by the majority of scholars, the genuine text of Ben-Sira so far as they go.

The reconstruction of the text, it will be realized, is a difficult task; but with the help of the Hebrew of the Old Testament, the language of which Ben-Sira constantly echoes, and with the help of the Versions, especially the Greek and the Syriac, this reconstruction has been accomplished with conspicuous success by Smend.[4]

A matter of particular interest is the question of a secondary Hebrew recension. When we come to speak of the Greek Version it will be pointed out that there is a *secondary* Greek recension which owed its existence to the wish to make the book more acceptable to later orthodox, *i.e.* Pharisaic, circles. This secondary Greek recension was not due to a purely

[1] Pp. lvi–lxii.
[2] "This MS. is free from doublets, corruptions and blemishes which disfigure the other MSS. and has only one marginal gloss" (Joseph Marcus, *op. cit.*, p. 224).
[3] See the contents of the MSS. given above for one or two examples of this.
[4] *Die Weisheit des Jesus Sirach, Hebräisch und Deutsch* (1906); this is a different volume from that mentioned above.

R

Greek revision of the book, it depends upon a secondary Hebrew recension. "The phenomena of the text point unmistakably to the latter alternative; the secondary Greek text depends essentially upon, and is a translation of, a younger Hebrew recension of the book." [1] Illustrations to be given in the next section will show the significance of this recension.

VI. The Greek Version and the Secondary Greek Text

The value of the Greek Version lies not only in the fact of its being the oldest of the Versions, but still more because in many passages it has preserved a form of text more closely approximating to the original Hebrew than that of the Hebrew manuscripts which have been discovered; the latter fact makes this Version most valuable for the reconstruction of the Hebrew text, though the freedom with which the Greek translation was made—a fact hinted at in the Prologue—demands great caution when used for this purpose.

Mention must here be made of the great displacement in the Greek text; this is dealt with by Swete:

A remarkable divergence in the arrangement of the Septuagint and Old Latin Versions of Ecclesiasticus xxx–xxxvi calls for notice. In these chapters the Greek order fails to yield a natural sequence, whereas the Latin arrangement, which is also that of the Syriac and Armenian Versions, makes excellent sense. Two sections, xxx. 25–xxxiii. 13ᵃ (ὡς καλαμώμενος . . . φυλὰς Ἰακώβ) and xxxiii. 13ᵇ–xxxvi. 16ᵃ (λαμπρὰ καρδία . . . ἔσχατος ἠγρύπνησα), have exchanged places in Latin, and the change is justified by the result. On examination it appears that these sections are nearly equal, containing in B 154 and 159 στίχοι respectively, whilst ℵ exhibits 160 in each. [2]

There can be little doubt that in the *exemplar* from which,

[1] Box and Oesterley, *op. cit.*, p. 278.
[2] *The Old Testament in Greek*, ii. pp. vi ff. (1896).

so far as is certainly known, all our Greek MSS. of this book are, as Fritzsche says, "ultimately derived, the pairs of leaves on which these sections were severally written had been transposed; whereas the Latin translator, working from a manuscript in which the transposition had not taken place, has preserved the true order." [1] The displacement is sometimes apt to cause some confusion when giving references; the matter is simplified when it is remembered that in the Greek text xxxiii. 13^{bc} xxxiv. 1–xxxvi. 16^{a} must come between xxx. 24 and xxx. 25. All the Greek manuscripts, including the cursive 248 (on this see below) have this displacement.[2]

The Greek Version has come down to us in two forms; one of these is represented by the great uncials BℵA, followed by a number of cursives; it appears also in the Aldine and Sixtine editions, and is the basis for the Revised Version. This is a translation of the primary original Hebrew text.

The other form of the text is represented by a group of cursives, of which the most representative is 248, and the manuscript used by the first corrector of Cod. Sinaiticus ℵ$^{c.a}$ (seventh century); it is also reflected, more or less, in the Old Latin and Syriac Versions, in the Syro-Hexaplar, in which the passages belonging to this later recension are, for the most part, marked with the asterisk, and in the Complutensian text; it has also the support of Clement of Alexandria and St. Chrysostom in their quotations from our book. This second form represents the translation of a recension of the Hebrew text.

We have, thus, a primary and a secondary Greek text, each of which is translated from a Hebrew original.

The secondary Greek text must have come into existence at a very early period, and must at one time have received wide recognition and have been regarded as authoritative; the fact that the Old Latin Version contains a large number of passages belonging to it is evidence, apart from other things, of the favour which this secondary Greek Version

---

[1] *Kurzgefasstes exegetisches Handbuch zu den Apokryphen*, v. 169 f. (1851–1860).
[2] See Smend, *Die Weisheit des Jesus Sirach*, p. lxxvii.

must have enjoyed at one time. The text of this Version
is characterized by a large number of additions to the
original text; the manuscripts belonging to the 248 group
contain nearly 150 additional *stichoi*, besides which ninety
others have been preserved in different manuscripts of the
Old Latin Version.[1] At the same time, it must be added
that although some half-dozen Greek MSS. represent this
secondary Greek text, there is no one MS. now extant which
contains this text as such; all that can be said is that the
248 group have to a larger or smaller extent been influenced
by it. The cursive MSS. of the other group mentioned
above which follow, in the main, the great uncials representative of the primary text, were originally based on the
secondary text, for they contain traces of it, according to
Ryssel, and are therefore the descendants of MSS. which
were corrected on the basis of the great uncials; this cor-
rectional process must, of course, belong to considerably
later times.

To sum up, then: The course of the *early history of the
Greek text*, or rather texts, can perhaps be best described
in this way: There was an original Hebrew text; a Greek
translation of this was made by the writer's grandson.
Later there was a revised Hebrew text, made for reasons
of which we shall speak below; a Greek translation was
likewise made of this; so that both Greek translations were
made direct from two Hebrew originals, respectively. One
was made from the Hebrew text of the author, the other
from a Hebrew text which embodied a large number of
additions to the original text.

That the two Greek translations owe their origin to two
independent Hebrew texts is shown by the following facts:
(1) in the Talmud, and some other Jewish writings, there
are Hebrew quotations from our book which differ from the
text of the great uncials, but which are represented in the
secondary Greek text reflected in the 248 group, in the Old
Latin Version, and in the quotations which occur in the
writings of Clement of Alexandria and St. Chrysostom;

[1] These have all been gathered together and conveniently tabulated by
Smend, *op. cit.*, pp. xcix–cxviii.

(2) in a certain number of instances the secondary Hebrew recension which, as we have seen, is sometimes preserved in the Hebrew MSS now available, has been incorporated in the 248 group, but not in the great uncials; and (3) many of the additions found in this 248 group can, on account of their form, be explained only on the supposition of their having been translated from the Hebrew. It is, therefore, evident that the additions in the 248 group are not interpolations in the Greek text, but are based, as a whole, on a secondary Hebrew original.[1]

Now, as to the object of this secondary Greek text and its Hebrew original,—while in some instances the additions are intended to explain the Hebrew and to make its meaning clearer, yet this is only a subsidiary purpose; the real object is to be sought in another direction. It will be found that in most of them " there is a tendency to emphasize spiritual religion as distinct from practical religion; love to God, hope in Him, the desire to please Him and to give glory to Him; the thirst for righteousness; the need of repentance; the recognition of the divine recompense; a developed belief regarding the Hereafter,—these are the main characteristics to be observed in the additions." [2] These are all the precepts of Pharisaism at its best. In his minute and well-balanced investigation into the contents of the additions, Hart has shown that " they are fragments of the Wisdom of a Scribe of the Pharisees, and contain tentative Greek renderings of many of the technical terms and watchwords of the sect." [3]

VII. The Other Ancient Versions

The *Syriac Version* is not a translation from the Greek, but from some form of the original Hebrew; it is, according to Smend, " the worst piece of translation in the Syriac Bible "; though, as he adds, in many cases it is uncertain

---

[1] Cp. the present writer's *The Wisdom of Jesus the son of Sirach, or Ecclesiasticus*, p. xcviii (1912).   [2] *Ibid.*
[3] *Ecclesiasticus : the Greek Text of Codex 248* (1909) p. 274; the examination of the additions will be found on pp. 275-320, and there is much else in this book of great interest.

whether its defects are due to the fault of the translator, or to the Hebrew text he had before him, or are to be put down to the vicissitudes of the handing down of the Syriac text. It reveals a great number of omissions; compared with the Hebrew and Greek texts there are 370 *stichoi* wanting, *i.e.* about one-ninth of the book, though in some cases such omissions are due to Christian influence, *e.g.* in xvii. 27, where it is said that the dead can no more praise God, xliv. 9 according to which the ungodly when they die are as though they had never been born,—and many others.[1]

But though the Syriac Version is a translation from the Hebrew there are many passages which are directly translated from the Greek; this is the case, *e.g.*, with xxvi. 19–27, xliii. 1–10; it is not necessary to regard these passages as having been added at a later time, because the influence of the Greek Version is to be discerned throughout; and, as Smend shows by a number of examples, the Syriac text has been corrected from the Greek.

In spite of the many defects of the Syriac Version, it is of great value both from the fact that it is translated from the Hebrew, and also because it contains a number of passages which are found elsewhere only in the Hebrew MSS., or in isolated Greek MSS., or in the Old Latin.[2] It has already been pointed out that in this Version the displacement of the text does not occur.

The *Latin Version* has come down to us in an even worse condition than the Syriac; this is due not only to accidents in transmission, but still more owing to the fact that it was translated from a Greek text which was in a worse state than that represented by any extant Greek MSS. Nevertheless, as Smend points out, it must be regarded as a piece of good fortune that it was not ousted by a translation of Jerome, for it contains many ancient elements which are more than likely to have been obliterated had Jerome made a translation of his own.

The *Syro-Hexaplar*—the name given to the Syriac Version

---

[1] Smend, p. cxxxvii.
[2] For the valuable estimate of this Version see Smend, pp. cxxxvi–cxlvi.

made by Paul of Tella (616 A.D.) from the Septuagint of
of Origen's Hexapla [1]—is of considerable value owing to the
excellence of many of its readings; but it has suffered,
according to Smend, from the hand of a corrector. "If
we retain the designation Syro-Hexaplar" says Nestle, "we
must bear in mind that Sirach had no place in Origen's
Hexapla; but in one particular respect this Syriac Version
reminds us of the Hexapla; one of the critical marks of
Origen, the asteriscus, appears also in Sirach, at least in its
first part up to Chap. xiii." [2] There are altogether forty-
five asterisks, about twenty of which are placed against words
and sentences belonging to the secondary Greek text.

There are a number of other Versions: The Sahidic,
Ethiopic, Armenian, Slavonic, and Arabic. These are of
much less importance. The *Sahidic* is based on a text closely
related to the Greek uncials, and is therefore of some value
for text-critical purposes. The *Ethiopic* is full of paraphrases intended to explain the Greek from which it is
translated. The *Armenian* is translated from the Latin,
but apparently worked over on the basis of the Greek. The
Slavonic "follows a text similar to that of the Complutensian
edition, but with only a portion of the additions." [3] The
Arabic is a translation from the Syriac, it is full of paraphrases,
and has evidently been influenced by the Greek.[4]

VIII. Literature

Fritzsche, *op. cit.*, v., pp. ix ff., 1 ff. (1859).
Edersheim, in Wace, *op. cit.*, ii. 1 ff. (1888).
Schechter and Taylor, *The Wisdom of Ben-Sira* (1899).
Lévi, *L'Ecclésiastique ou la sagesse de Jésus fils de Sira* (1898,
　　1901).
Ryssel, in Kautzsch, *op. cit.*, i. 226 ff. (1900).
Knabenbauer, *Commentarius in Ecclesiasticum* . . . (1902).
Peters, *Der jüngst wieder aufgefundene hebräische Text des Buches
　　Ecclesiasticus* . . . (1902).

[1] See Swete, *Introduction to the Old Testament in Greek*, pp. 112 f.
[2] In Hastings' *D.B.* iv. 544.
[3] Margoliouth, quoted by Nestle, Hastings' *D.B.* iv. 544.
[4] For all these Versions see Smend, *op. cit.*, pp. cxxix ff.

Peters, *Ecclesiasticus Hebraice* (1905).

Strack, *Die Sprüche Jesus des Sohnes Sirachs* (1903).

André, *op. cit.*, pp. 271 ff. (1903).

Smend, *Die Weisheit des Jesus Sirach* (1906) (Introduction and Commentary).

—— *Die Weisheit des Jesus Sirach, Hebräisch und Deutsch* (1906) (Text and translation).

—— *Griechisch-syrisch-hebräischer Index zur Weisheit des Jesus Sirach* (1907).

Fuchs, *Textkritische Untersuchungen zum Hebräischen Ekklesiastikus* (1907).

Hart, *Ecclesiasticus, the Greek Text of Codex 248* (1909).

Oesterley, *The Wisdom of Jesus, the son of Sirach, or Ecclesiasticus* (1912).

Box and Oesterley, in Charles, *op. cit.*, i. 268 ff. (1913).

Oesterley, *The Wisdom of Ben-Sira in " Translations of Early Documents "* (1916).

The publications of the Hebrew Fragments:

Schechter, " Ecclesiasticus xxxix. 15–xl. 8," in *The Expositor* for July (1896).

Cowley-Neubauer, *The Original Hebrew of a Portion of Ecclesiasticus* (xxxix. 15–xlix. 11) (1897).

Halévy, in the *Revue sémitique*, v. 147 ff. (1897).

Schechter, " Genizah Specimens " (xlix. 12–l. 22) in *The Jewish Quarterly Review*, x. 197 ff. (1898).

Schechter and Taylor (as above).

Halévy, " Eccles. xlix. 12–l. 22 " in *Revue sémitique*, v. 148 ff., 193 ff. (1897).

Margoliouth, " The Original Hebrew of Eccl. xxxi. 12–31; xxxvi. 22–xxxvii. 26 " in *J.Q.R.*, xii. 1 ff. (1900).

Schechter, " A Further Fragment . . ." (iv. 23–v. 13; xxv. 8–xxvi. 2), in *J.Q.R.*, xii. 456 ff. (1900).

Adler, " *Some Missing Fragments of Ben-Sira* " (vii. 29–xii. 1), in *J.Q.R.*, xii. 466 ff. (1900).

Lévi, " Deux nouveaux manuscrits hébreux de l'Ecclésiastique " (xxxvi. 24–xxxviii. 1) in the *Revue des études juives*, xi. 1 ff. (1900).

Gaster, " *A New Fragment of Ben-Sira* " (xviii. 31–33, etc.),
   in *J.Q.R.*, xii. 688 ff. (1900).
Marcus, " *A Fifth Manuscript of Ben-Sira* " (xxxii [xxxv] 16–
   xxxiii 32; xxxiv. 1) in *J.Q.R.*, xxi. 223 ff. (1931).
G. R. Driver, " Hebrew Notes on the Wisdom of Jesus Ben-
   Sirach," in *The Journal of Biblical Literature*, 1934, 273 ff.

Editions of texts other than the Hebrew :

Greek: Swete, *The Old Testament in Greek*, vol. ii. (1896).
Syriac: Lagarde, *Libri Veteris Testamenti Apocryphi Syriace*
   (1871).
Latin: the text of the Vulgate; Lagarde, *Codex Amiatinus*,
   in *Mittheilungen* . . . i (1884).

The superb English edition, edited by A. D. Power, and
published by the Ashendene Press, must also be mentioned
here.

BARUCH

I. Title

In the Septuagint the title is simply "Baruch," and this is followed in the Syro-Hexaplar; but in the ordinary Syriac Version it is: "In addition the Second Epistle of Baruch the Scribe," or in another MS. more simply "The Second Epistle," the "second" referring "by implication to the earlier preceding Epistle in the Syriac addressed by Baruch to the nine and a half tribes beyond the Euphrates." [1] Both Latin Versions (see below, § VII) have: "Prophecy of Baruch" as title; the Coptic Version has: "Baruch the Prophet," and the Armenian: "Epistle of Baruch." The title in the R.V. thus follows the Septuagint. In some lists of the Church Fathers, as well as in references to it in their writings, it is cited, together with the *Epistle of Jeremy* and *Lamentations*, as "Jeremiah"; the three "form a kind of trilogy supplementary to the prophecy." [2] In the *Apostolic Constitutions* v. 20 (but not in the Syriac *Didascalia*) [3] the book is referred to simply as "Baruch." [4]

II. Contents of the Book

Our book consists of two distinct parts, each of which contains two main subdivisions; Part I: chap. i. 1–iii. 8; Part II: chap. iii. 9–v. 9. The former of these is in prose, the latter is poetry, which, unfortunately, is not indicated in the R.V.

Part I: i. 1–14, an historical introduction, according to which Baruch wrote the book in Babylon, "in the fifth year, and in the seventh day of the month," clearly a

---

[1] Whitehouse, in Charles, *op. cit.*, i. 583.
[2] Swete, *Introduction to the Old Testament in Greek*, p. 274 (1900); see also Thackeray, *The Septuagint and Jewish Worship*, p. 80 (1921).
[3] Connolly, *Didascalia Apostolorum*, p. 191 (1929).
[4] For other books bearing the name of Baruch, see Charles, *The Apocalypse of Baruch*, pp. xvi–xxii (1896).

mistake for " the fifth month " (II Kgs. xxv. 8), at the time when the Chaldæans took Jerusalem, *i.e.* in the nineteenth year of Nebuchadrezzar (B.C. 586). It was read in the hearing of Jeconias (Jehoiachim) and the rest of the exiles in Babylon (verses 1–4). The people wept, and fasted, and prayed. Then a collection of money was made, which was sent to Jerusalem, in order that offerings might continue to be made on " the altar of the Lord our God "; the altar is thus thought of as still standing (cp. Jer. xli. 5, Lam. i. 4). The people in Jerusalem are enjoined to pray for Nebuchadrezzar and for his son Belshazzar (!), in order that the exiles may dwell in peace; prayers are also asked for these latter, whose punishment for their sinfulness is recognized (verses 5–13). In verse 14 the writer continues: " And ye shall read this book which we have sent unto you, to make confession in the house of the Lord, upon the day of the feast and on the days of the solemn assembly " (on this see below, § VI).

i. 15–iii. 8: The long confession which follows falls into three subdivisions: the confession proper (i. 15–ii. 10); a prayer that, in spite of the sins of the people, God will have mercy on them; the Almighty is reminded of His promise to the patriarchs, and of the new covenant of later days: " And I will make an everlasting covenant with them to be their God, and they shall be my people; and I will no more remove my people of Israel out of the land that I have given them " (ii. 11–35). These last words are clearly based on Jer. xxxi. 31–34. A final prayer, with further confession of sin, concludes this part (iii. 1–8).

PART II: iii. 9–iv. 4: The poetical portion begins here with a homily on Wisdom, largely influenced by the Wisdom literature, and more especially by *Proverbs* and *Job*. Israel is bidden to hearken unto Wisdom, for it is only because of her having forsaken " the fountain of Wisdom " that she is in exile; had she not done this she would have dwelt in peace for ever (iii. 9–13). All those who have not sought Wisdom, the rich, the worldly wise, and the mighty, vanish and go down to the grave and perish (iii. 14–28). Wisdom is the possession of the Almighty alone, but He has given it to Jacob His servant, and to Israel His beloved (iii. 29–37). The identification of Wisdom with the Law which endures for ever; Israel is happy, for the things that are pleasing to God are made known to her (iv. 1–4).

iv. 5–v. 9: this consists of four sections, each beginning with, " Be of good cheer," followed by three others addressed particularly to Jerusalem. " These seven subdivisions may be classified again," as Thackeray points out, " according to the speaker; in two groups. The first three cantos, part penitence, part hope, are addressed by mother Zion to her exiled children. The last four, all consolation, are God's response, through the seer's mouth, to the bereft mother, —promises of retaliation on her foes with glorious visions of a return to Palestine under his leadership." [1] The sub-divisions are: iv. 5–20; 21–26; 27–29; 30–35; 36–37; v. 1–4; 5–9.

III. The Historical Background and Date

We have seen that the historical background is represented as being the early period of the Exile; Jerusalem has been burned, and the exiles are settled in Babylon. Baruch, the faithful friend and follower of Jeremiah, is among the deported exiles. The epistle which he writes is read first to Jehoiachin, the dethroned Judæan king, and his fellow-exiles, and is then sent to those of his countrymen who had been left in Jerusalem, together with some money to enable them to offer sacrifices; they are also bidden to pray for the life of Nebuchadrezzar and his son Belshazzar in order that the exiles might live in peace under their rule.

There is a mixture here of statements which are partly historical, partly doubtfully so, but partly quite unhistorical. Thus, we know from II Kgs. xxv. 9 that Jerusalem and the Temple were burned; but the destruction was not so complete as to make the city uninhabitable, or as to preclude the possibility of worship in the Temple; for we read in Jer. xli. 5 that eighty pilgrims from Shechem, Shilo, and Samaria came as mourners for the destruction of Jerusalem,

---

[1] *Op. cit.*, p. 101. On the liturgical use of our book see Thackeray, *op. cit.*, pp. 91 ff.

and brought oblations and frankincense to the house of the Lord; and further, from what is said in Lam. i. 4 it is evident that in spite of the desolation of the city priests were dwelling in it. In these particulars, therefore, the book records historical facts. On the other hand, however, it may be questioned whether the dethroned king would have been permitted to dwell among the exiles; there is no mention of his presence among the elders who assembled in the house of Ezekiel (Ezek. viii.. 1), which might well have been the case had he been at large; moreover, in Jer. lii. 31 it is definitely said that not until the thirty-seventh year of his captivity did Evil-Merodach bring him forth out of prison. Again, there is no evidence that Baruch was ever among the exiles in Babylon; at the time in question, at any rate, he was in Palestine (cp. Jer. xliii. 3); and according to Jer. xliii. 6 f. both Jeremiah and Baruch were carried off to Egypt by Johanan the son of Kareah. Baruch was not likely to have forsaken Jeremiah; had he ever been among the Babylonian exiles it is reasonable to expect that the fact would have been mentioned either by Jeremiah or Ezekiel. It is also worth mentioning that in the Syriac Version it is said that Baruch sent his letter *to* Babylon.[1]

Quite unhistorical, finally, is the statement that Belshazzar was the son of Nebuchadrezzar, and that they were contemporaries. The same mistake is made in Dan. v. 2, 11, 13, 18, 22. Belshazzar was the son of Nabonidus, the last king of Babylon, and was never king himself.[2] This dependence of our book on *Daniel*[3] is important, for, since the date of *Daniel* is B.C. 166–165, it is obvious that the purported historical background of our book is merely a literary device adopted for the purpose of disguising the actual historical background; the reason for the disguise being to avoid offending the powers that be, while those for whom the book was written would have no difficulty in seeing through the disguise. But further, throughout our

---

[1] Rothstein, in Kautzsch, *op. cit.*, i. 213.
[2] In the " Nabonidus Chronicle " No. 2 he is always called Crown Prince.
[3] This is by no means the only instance of its dependence on *Daniel* (see § V); the idea that *Daniel* may have been dependent on *Baruch* will be seen by what is said in § IV to be out of the question.

book the purported background is, as we have seen, the destruction of Jerusalem and the leading away of the captives into exile; since our book is later than *Daniel*, its earliest possible date is the Maccabæan period. This does not, however, help us much in fixing the date of our book, for the disguised historical background must offer parallels with some actual historical background, otherwise the whole proceeding is pointless. There are three episodes which have been pointed to as offering, in some sort, parallels to the events of B.C. 586: the first is the occasion on which the Jews joined a Phœnician revolt, in B.C. 351, against their suzerain, Artaxerxes III Ochus; they were severely punished by the Persian king, and many Jews were carried away captive to Hyrcania, on the shores of the Caspian sea; but the episode is not a real parallel, since, while Jericho was burned, Jerusalem did not suffer. The second is when Pompey captured Jerusalem in B.C. 63; but this is still less a parallel, for neither was Jerusalem burned, nor was there any carrying away into captivity. Far more likely is the third, namely, the destruction of Jerusalem in 70 A.D., for on this occasion Jerusalem did suffer from conflagration,[1] and masses of Jews were carried captive in the train of Titus, while many thousands were sold as slaves in different parts of the world.[2] In this case Vespasian would be identified with Nebuchadrezzar, and his son Titus with Belshazzar. With this as the actual historical background of our book, the date assigned to it would be some time soon after 70 A.D. But while this may apply to the book in its *final* form, there are strong reasons for believing that it cannot apply to all the individual parts of which the book is made up. To this we must direct our attention next.

IV. COMPOSITION OF THE BOOK

That our book is not a unity becomes evident as soon as the sections into which the book is divided (see § II) are examined and compared. We have seen that, to begin with, a difference in literary structure divides the book into two

---

[1] Josephus, *Bell. Jud.* vi. 228, 230, 232–235. [2] *Ibid.*, vii. 24.

parts, i. 1–iii. 8 (of which i. 1–14 is introductory), being in prose, and iii. 9–v. 9 in poetry; the latter, however, treats of two such different subjects in iii. 9–iv. 4 and iv. 5–v. 9, respectively, that they must be regarded as independent pieces. There are, thus, three different, self-contained sections of which our book is made up; and we must now point to reasons which will show that all three are of different authorship.

The first thing that must strike us is the different point of view between the sections i. 1–iii. 8 and iii. 9–iv. 4. In the former, which is largely a confession of sin, it is recognized that, in spite of divine mercies, Israel sinned against God, and that therefore all the evils which befel the nation in the past, as well as the present state of captivity, are the result of disobedience to God, and of refusing to walk in the way of His commandments. Yet it is just through punishment that the people have been brought to repentance: "For, for this cause thou hast put thy fear in our hearts, to the intent that we should call upon thy name; and we will praise thee in our captivity, for we have put away from our heart all the iniquity of our fathers that sinned before thee" (iii. 7). In the other piece (iii. 9–iv. 4) the question is asked why it is that Israel is suffering in exile, and the reason given is: "Thou hast forsaken the fountain of wisdom" (iii. 12); but by taking hold of wisdom happiness and prosperity become the lot of Israel; and God in His mercy has granted divine wisdom to Israel. It is then declared that wisdom appeared upon earth, and was conversant with men (*i.e.* Israel); and it continues: "This is the book of the commandments of God, and the law that endureth for ever; all they that hold it fast (are appointed) to life; but such as leave it shall die. Turn thee, O Jacob, and take hold of it; walk towards her shining in the presence of the light thereof . . . O Israel, happy are we, for the things that are pleasing to God are made known unto us" (iii. 37–iv. 4).

Two such utterly different points of view cannot possibly have come from the same mind; in the former it is the mind of the prophet that is revealed, in the latter that of the Wisdom-writer; and this receives strong emphasis when it is seen how in the former the writer is influenced by *Jeremiah, Ezekiel,* and the book of *Deuteronomy*; the latter mainly by *Job, Proverbs,* and *Ecclesiasticus,* though here and there he is indebted to *Deutero-Isaiah.*

Further, in comparing the first section (i. 1–iii. 8) with the third (iv. 5–v. 9) a striking contrast is again observable, though of a different nature.

In i. 11–13 the people are bidden to pray for Nebuchadrezzar and Belshazzar " that their days may be as the days of heaven above the earth; and the Lord will give us strength and lighten our eyes . . . and we shall serve them many days, and find favour in their sight." In ii. 20 ff. also it is said: " Bow your shoulders to serve the king of Babylon . . .," in accordance with the word of the Lord as spoken by the prophets. The rulers to whom Israel is subject are looked upon as benefactors, and Israel lives in peace under them. But a very different picture is presented in the third section (iv. 5–v. 9), where the rulers are represented as tyrannous and cruel, and whose destruction is foretold:

> My children, suffer patiently the wrath that is come upon you from God; for thine enemy hath persecuted thee; but shortly thou shalt see his destruction, and shalt tread upon their necks. My delicate ones have gone rough ways; they were taken away as a flock carried off by the enemies . . . Miserable [1] are they that afflicted thee, and rejoiced at thy fall. Miserable are the cities which thy children served; miserable is she that received thy sons. For as she rejoiced at thy fall, and was glad of thy ruin, so shall she be grieved for her own desolation . . . (iv. 25–35).

How could two such entirely opposed attitudes have been presented by one and the same writer?

We find, moreover, that the influence of Old Testament books as seen in the two sections, respectively, is different; we have seen that in i. 1–iii. 8 pre-exilic prophetism is that which influenced the writer; in iv. 5–v. 9 it is the exilic

---

[1] The Greek δείλαιοι means rather being in a state of terror.

prophet Deutero-Isaiah, to whom the writer is mainly indebted.

The conclusion may, therefore, be legitimately drawn that the three literary pieces of which our book is composed are of different authorship. The question of their respective dates must be our next enquiry.

V. Dates of the Component Parts of the Book

It has been pointed out above that the book in its final form as we now have it must be assigned to a date at any rate subsequent to the destruction of Jerusalem in 70 A.D.; but this does not necessarily apply to the three independent literary pieces of which the book is made up; at the same time, whatever the date or dates of these latter, it is not unreasonable to assume that the final redactor may have added some words of his own here and there in each of them.

It must, however, be confessed that it is exceedingly difficult to come to definite conclusions regarding the dates of these different pieces, and, in any case, they can only be approximate and tentative.

As to the first section (i. 1–iii. 8), the disguised historical background portrayed in i. 1–14 is, as we have seen, the critical period which culminated in 70 A.D.; but this is meant to apply to the whole book, and must, in its present form, be assigned to the final redactor; though this is not to say that an earlier form of an introduction did not exist. That the section as a whole is not earlier than the second half of the second century B.C. may be regarded as highly probable on account of its dependence on *Daniel* for its unhistorical statements referred to above, and also on account of the use made of Dan. ix. 4–19;[1] this part of *Daniel* was interpolated, according to Charles, about the year B.C. 145.[2] To put it as late as the end of the first century A.D. may be thought improbable in view of the doctrine of immortality expressed in ii. 17, 18: ". . . for the dead that are in the grave, whose breath is taken from their bodies,

[1] Almost every verse in Bar. i. 15–ii. 29 is based on Dan. ix. 4–19.
[2] *A Critical Commentary on the Book of Daniel*, pp. 222, 226 f. (1929).

8

will give unto the Lord neither glory nor righteousness ";
by the end of the first century A.D. it may be urged, a more
developed doctrine of immortality had become general
among the Jews. Nevertheless, it must be conceded that
this date is, at the least, a possible one; the undeveloped
belief in immortality is not conclusive against this date as
the New Testament contains sufficient indication that not
all Jews shared the belief in the resurrection of the body in
the first century A.D. While the great difference of tone and
outlook in the different sections of our book makes it evident
that they cannot have come from a single author, it is,
nevertheless, quite possible that they were written, more or
less, within the same period. There is, moreover, much in
this section which is particularly appropriate to the time
soon after 70 A.D.: the advice to be submissive to Babylon
(Rome) was the known point of view of a school of thought
among the Jews at this time; the attitude of gloomy prostra-
tion that pervades the whole, and the references to the
sufferings of the siege, and even to cannibalism, are under-
standable, as are the references to the scattered captives.
We suggest, therefore, that this section belongs to a time
soon after the destruction of Jerusalem in 70 A.D.

The approximate date of the second piece (iii. 9–iv. 4) is
suggested by the following considerations: Its indebtedness
to Ecclus. xxiv would make it, at any rate, later than *circa*
B.C. 180; but it may, of course, be much later than this;
the doctrine of immortality in iii. 10, 11 (". . . thou that
art defiled with the dead, thou art counted with them that
go down to the grave ") would accord with this date, more
or less; so, too, the indication in iii. 10 of Israelites having
dwelt in the Dispersion for a considerable time: "How
happeneth it, O Israel, that thou art in thine enemies' land,
that thou art waxen old in a strange country?" This
might, it is true, refer to the time of widespread Roman
dominion; but it could equally apply to the time before
this when Israelite communities existed in Babylonia, Egypt,
and Asia Minor; the former is however, more likely; and the
end of the first century A.D. would again be quite possible.
A date during the Maccabæan period is unlikely, as in this

case some definite allusions to the conditions of that time would rightly be looked for.

The third section (iv. 5–v. 9) contains several allusions which point to some time after the destruction of Jerusalem in 70 A.D. In iv. 8–10 we read: ". . . ye grieved also Jerusalem that nursed you . . . for God hath brought upon me great mourning; for I have seen the captivity of my sons and daughters . . ."; the first part of this passage may well refer to the internecine strife among the Jewish parties during the siege of Jerusalem, and the second part to the immense numbers of Jews who were sold into slavery (see above § III). In iv. 15, 16 it seems certain that Rome is alluded to: "For he hath brought a nation upon them from far, a shameless nation, and of a strange language, they neither reverenced old man, nor pitied child. And they have carried away the dear beloved sons of the widow, and left her that was alone desolate of her daughters." Rome must also be meant in iv. 31–35, quoted above, where calamity and destruction, it is declared, shall be her lot. On the other hand, the repeated phrase, "Be of good cheer," and the words of encouragement in v. 1 ff. show that some time must have elapsed since the catastrophe occurred, and that new hope had arisen. This is in accord with what we know of the history of the time, for Hegesippus records that during the reigns of Vespasian, Domitian, and Trajan, hopes of the advent of the Messianic king were entertained. In v. 1–9 the Messianic kingdom is quite obviously heralded.

When it was that these three pieces were joined together, and our book received its present form, it is not possible to say.

VI. THE ORIGINAL LANGUAGE OF THE BOOK

While, according to the opinions of many, though not all, of the older critics, Greek was the original language of our book, later scholars are convinced that part of it, at least, was written in Hebrew.[1] Most authorities are agreed that

[1] In the Syro-Hexaplar the note " this is not in the Hebrew " occurs three times (Schürer, op. cit., iii. 464).

the first section (i. i–iii. 8 in its original form) was originally in Hebrew; others hold that this applies also to the second piece (iii. 9–iv. 4), but that the last one (iv. 5–v. 9) was Greek. Whitehouse makes out a strong case for this, based largely on the close parallels between the Greek of the *Psalms of Solomon* xi and Bar. iv. 36–v. 9.[1] Cornill's contention that the two last sections present a Greek too elegant to be a translation,[2] is answered by Rothstein to the effect that this shows the skill of the translator, but does not militate against the two pieces being translations; he has his doubts, moreover, as to the Greek being really so elegant.[3] The strongest advocate for a Hebrew original of all three pieces is Kneucker,[4] and his retranslation of them into Hebrew gives great weight to his opinion, in which he has many followers. If, as Thackeray's investigations seem to prove[5] the book in its final form—or part of it previously —was used for liturgical purposes, then it must have been in Hebrew; that its place of origin was Palestine is generally acknowledged.

There are, thus, differences of opinion on this subject; we believe, however, that, upon the whole, the balance of probability favours a Hebrew original for the whole book. That nothing of the book has survived in a Hebrew form need not cause surprise; changes in the Liturgy which have taken place from time to time would fully account for its disappearance; with the case of *Ecclesiasticus* before us there is always the possibility that fragments may yet come to light.

VII. Manuscripts and Versions

Our book is contained in the uncials BAQV and in a number of cursives; it does not appear in *Cod. Sinaiticus*, nor in Cod. C.

The Syriac Version exists in two forms: the *Peshitta* and the *Syro-Hexaplar*;[6] the former " was based on the Hebrew

[1] In Charles, *op. cit.*, i. 572 ff.; though Charles, in an editorial note, disagrees.
[2] *Einleitung in das Alte Testament*, p. 273 (1896).
[3] In Kautzsch, *op. cit.*, i. 215.
[4] *Das Buch Baruch* (1879). [5] *Op. cit.*, pp. 91 ff.
[6] See Whitehouse's valuable notes on this, *op. cit.*, i. 577 ff.

original as well as on the Septuagint Version," [1] so far as
the first two pieces are concerned, but not so with regard to
the third, which, according to Whitehouse, is based on the
Greek original.

The Latin Version also exists in two forms; both are
translations of the Greek, which is also the case with the
other Versions, Coptic, Ethiopic, Armenian, and Arabic.

VIII. LITERATURE

Fritzsche, *op. cit.*, i. 167 ff. (1851).

Reusch, *Erklärung des Buches Baruch* (1853).

Kneucker, *Das Buch Baruch, Geschichte und Kritik, Uebersetzung und Erklärung* (1879).

Herbst, *Das apokryphische Buch Baruch aus dem Griechischen im Hebräische übertragen* (1886).

Grätz, " Abfassungszeit und Bedeutung des Buches Baruch," in *Monatsschrift für Geschichte und Wissenschaft des Judenthums*, iii. 5 ff. (1887).

Gifford, in Wace, *op. cit.*, ii. (1888).

Knabenbauer, *Commentarius in Danielem prophetam, Lamentationes, et Baruch* (1905).

Rothstein, in Kautzsch, *op. cit.*, i. 213 ff. (1900).

André, *op. cit.*, pp. 245 ff. (1903).

Schneedorfer, *Das Buch Jeremias, des Propheten Klagelieder, und das Buch Baruch erklärt* (1903).

Whitehouse, in Charles, *op. cit.*, i. 569 ff. (1913).

Harwell, *The Principal Versions of Baruch* (1915).

Thackeray, *The Septuagint and Jewish Worship*, Lecture III (1921).

[1] Whitehouse, *op. cit.*, i. 578.

THE EPISTLE OF JEREMY

I. Title

In Codd. BA the title is "Epistle of Jeremiah," in Cod. Q simply "Epistle"; but in some Greek MSS. it follows *Baruch* without a break, and is therefore without a title; similarly in the Vulgate, where it forms chap. vi of *Baruch* without any title. The R.V. title is thus taken from the Septuagint.

II. Contents of the Book

This rambling and unedifying fragment does not lend itself to a clear analysis of its contents; but some attempt must be made to describe these.

The Epistle purports to have been written by the prophet Jeremiah to the exiles in Babylon; this is stated in the superscription, which is evidently not an original part of the Epistle; according to it the people are not yet in exile. The name of Jeremiah never occurs in the Epistle itself.

The prophet tells his people, who are represented as still in Palestine, that because of their sins they are to be carried captive to Babylon. The captivity will last for seven generations, and then the exiles will be brought out in peace (vv. 2, 3). A description is then given of the idols, silver, golden, and wooden, of Babylon, of their inability to hear or help their worshippers, and therefore the folly of serving them (vv. 4–27). A further emphasis on the impotence of idols follows, together with an exposure of their priests (vv. 28–39). How, it is asked, can such impotent images be called gods? And how can men be so foolish as to worship what their own hands have fashioned? Better to be a king who shows his manhood, or even a household utensil which is at any rate useful, than to be such a god

268

(vv. 40–59). Sun, moon, stars, lightning, wind, and clouds all fulfil their offices, but these gods can do nothing. " Better, therefore, is the just man that hath none idols; for he shall be far from reproach " (vv. 60–73).

III. Purpose and Date of the Epistle

The purpose for which the epistle was written is clear enough; it is to shame idolaters for their foolish worship, and to call them to wiser courses. But to whom does the writer address himself? The epistle was evidently inspired by Jer. x. 1–16 and Isa. xliv. 9–20; these prophets were denouncing Gentile idolaters, but their denunciations had the further object of warning their own people, lest they should be tempted to join in such worship. We may postulate the same in the present case. But while in the case of the earlier prophets we know to what particular generation they were speaking, and where their hearers were living, the period and locality in the present instance are not so certain. Babylon, as we have seen in *Baruch*, may be a mark for some other city, and the period at which the epistle was written is difficult to determine. It has been held that Egypt is meant by " Babylon," and that the date of the epistle is the middle of the second century B.C. Large colonies of Jews were settled at this time both in Babylonia and Egypt. There are, however, indications in the epistle from which it would appear that Babylon is to be taken literally; in verse 4 the procession of gods is referred to: " But now shall ye see in Babylon gods of silver, and of gold, and of wood, borne upon shoulders "; such processions are known to have been customary in Babylon; [1] the custom mentioned in verse 43 is spoken of by Herodotus as prevalent in Babylon.[2] Evidently, therefore, the purpose of the writer was to warn his people living in Babylonia against idolatry, see verses 2 ff., and verses 5, 6: " Beware therefore that ye in nowise become like unto the strangers. . . . But say in your hearts, O Lord, we must worship thee."

[1] See, *e.g.*, the relief portraying such a procession in Gressmann, *Altorientalische Bilder zum alten Testament*, Plate 136 (1927).
[2] *Hist.*, i. 199, 200.

As to the date of the Epistle, it is well known that many Jews of the Dispersion were attracted to alien cults throughout the Greek period (B.C. 300 onwards),[1] so that the warning contained in the epistle would be appropriate at any time during that period; but the words in verse 3, "So when ye be come into Babylon, ye shall remain there many years, and for a long season, even for seven generations; and after that I will bring you out peaceably from thence," may well indicate a closer date, as Ball has pointed out: "Seven generations," he says, "allowing forty years to the generation, according to Old Testament reckoning, would cover 280 years. If we count from the exile of Jechonias (B.C. 597), this brings us to the year B.C. 317, or, counting (as the author may have done) from B.C. 586, the year of the final captivity, we arrive at B.C. 306, some thirty years after the arrival of Alexander in Babylon."[2]

IV. The Original Language of the Epistle

It has been mostly held that the epistle was originally written in Greek; "it hardly admits of doubt," says Rothstein, "that this epistle was originally composed in Greek";[3] similarly Schürer says: "This small literary piece is certainly Greek in origin."[4] If the date suggested, the end of the fourth century B.C., be accepted, it is highly improbable that the Epistle can originally have been written in Greek. But apart from the question of date, Ball has conclusively proved that Hebrew was the original language: "Almost every verse exhibits peculiarities which suggest translation, and that from a Hebrew original . . . there are places where the strange phraseology of the Greek can only be accounted for by assuming that the writer of it supplied the wrong vowels to some Hebrew word which he was translating, or mistook some Hebrew consonant for another resembling it . . ."; the examples given are wholly convincing. Eissfeldt also believes it to have been

---

[1] *E.g.* the cult of Sabazios in Asia Minor, see *The Labyrinth* (ed. Hooke, pp. 115–158 [1935]).
[2] In Charles, *op. cit.*, i. 396.
[3] In Kautzsch, *op. cit.*, i. 226.
[4] *Op. cit.*, iii. 467.

written in Hebrew originally.[1] The Greek version would be considerably later, probably about the middle of the second century B.C.

V. LITERATURE [2]

Fitzsche, *op. cit.*, i. 205 ff. (1851).

Rothstein, in Kautzsch, *op. cit.*, i. 226 ff. (1900).

André, *op. cit.*, pp. 263 ff. (1903).

Nestle, *Septuagintastudien*, iv. 16. ff. (1903).

Ball, in Charles, *op. cit.*, i. 599 ff. (1913).

Naumann, *Untersuchungen über den apokryphischen Jeremiasbrief* (1913).

Thackeray, *Some Aspects of the Greek Old Testament*, pp. 53 ff. (1927).

[1] *Einleitung in das alte Testament*, p. 652 (1934).
[2] For MSS. and Versions see under *Baruch*.

THE SONG OF THE THREE HOLY CHILDREN

WHICH followeth in the third chapter of *Daniel* after this place,—*fell down bound into the midst of the burning fiery furnace.*— Verse 23. That which followeth is not in the Hebrew, to wit, *And they walked*—unto these words, *Then Nebuchadrezzar*— verse 24.

I. TITLE

The title is presumably taken from that occurring in some late Greek cursives, " *Hymn of the Three Children.*" It is an inadequate title, for the piece consists of three sections: (*a*) The Prayer of Azariah, verses 24-45 (R.V. 3-22); (*b*) A narrative portion, verses 46-51 (R.V. 23-27); (*c*) The Hymn of " the Three," verses 52-90 (R.V. 28-68).

In the canonical *Daniel* iii. 23 it is said: "And these three men, Shadrach, Meshach, and Abednego, fell down bound into the midst of the burning fiery furnace," after which comes (Theodotion's Version): "And they walked in the midst of the fire, praising God, and blessing the Lord," followed by the three sections just mentioned; and the Septuagint has: "Therefore thus prayed Ananias and Azarias, and Misael, and they praised the Lord when the king had ordered them to be cast into the furnace." There is thus no title either in Theodotion's Version or in the one existing MS. of the Septuagint (see § V). But in the Greek ecclesiastical Canticles added as an appendix to the Psalter, Cod. A (fifth century) has the title " Prayer of Azarias " to verses 24-45 (R.V. 3-22), and the title " Hymn of our fathers " to verses 52-90 (R.V. 28-68), for this latter Cod. T and the cursive 55 have " Hymn of the Three Children." [1]

---

[1] Swete, *Introduction to the Old Testament in Greek*, p. 261 (1900): " It will be noticed that Cod. A recognizes two distinct Canticles; but a sixth-century text shows us that the African Church at this time possessed a collection of Canticles which did not differ much from that of the Greek Church "; in this text the two parts of the Canticle are not separated (Cabrol, *Dict. d'Archéol. Chrétienne et de Liturgie*, Fasc. xiv. 661 (1908).

The narrative portion, verses 46–51 (R.V. 23–27), does not, of course, find a place in the appendix. The Syriac Version (Peshitta) has the title: " Prayer of Hananiah and his companions " for the whole of the Addition. The Vulgate also treats the whole of the Addition as a single piece; it gives no title, but prefaces it with the words: *Quae sequuntur in Hebraeis voluminibus non reperi,* and at its conclusion adds: *Hucusque in Hebraeo non habetur, et quae posuimus de Theodotionis editione translata sunt.*

II. CONTENTS OF THE ADDITIONS

As already pointed out, this Addition to *Daniel,* consists of three separate pieces; their contents are as follows:

(1) *The Prayer of Azariah* (verses 24–45 = R.V. 3–22).

An ascription of praise to God (3, 4; the verses are according to the R.V.); a recognition of God's justice, in accordance with which misfortune has fallen upon Jerusalem owing to the sins of the people (v. 5); confession of sin (vv. 6, 7); justice of the divine punishment (vv. 8–10); prayer for deliverance for the fathers' sake (vv. 11–13); the present plight of the people, but in penitence and promise of amendment God's mercy is entreated, and the downfall of the enemy is besought (vv. 14–22).

(2) *The Narrative Portion* (verses 46–51 = R.V. 23–27).

An account of the heating of the furnace; the fury of the fire destroys the Chaldæans who are about the furnace. An angel appears in the furnace who " smote the flame of the fire out of the furnace," so that the fire becomes like " a moist whistling wind," and Azarias and his companions remain uninjured.

(3) *The Song of the Three Children* (verses 52–90 = R.V. 28–68).

General introductory Benedictions (vv. 29–34); introductory words to the Song or Hymn, itself, calling upon all the works of Creation to bless the Lord (v. 35). The Hymn is divided into three main portions, comprising three themes: in the first portion (vv. 36–52) [1] the theme is the "Heavens"; all that is in any way connected with the Heavens is called upon to praise and exalt the Lord. In the second portion (vv. 53–60) [2] the theme is the "Earth," and all that belongs to it; here similarly everything is called upon to praise and exalt the Lord. In the short third portion (vv. 61–65) "Israel" is the main theme; priests, servants of the Lord, the spirits of the righteous, and all that are "holy and humble of heart," are bidden to praise and exalt the Lord. The Hymn concludes on the note of thanksgiving (vv. 67, 68). Verse 66 evidently does not belong to the original form of the Hymn; it may be conjectured that it was inserted in order to bring the Hymn into more immediate relation with the context into which it was inserted.

III. THE PROBLEM OF THE ADDITIONS

The question arises as to whether these three literary pieces which in the Septuagint follow after Dan. iii. 23, but which do not figure in the canonical *Daniel*, are later insertions; and whether they were inserted before or after the translation was made? Opinions on these matters differ. Some scholars [3] maintain that the Additions formed an original part of the canonical book, their main argument being that there is otherwise an unaccountable gap after iii. 23, and that without the Additions the verses which follow read strangely since the reason for Nebuchadrezzar being "astonied" is not given until later. Of the existence of the gap between iii. 23 and 24 there can be no doubt; Rothstein [4] accounts for it by suggesting that verses 23–27 in the Septuagint (the Narrative portion) formed part of the original text, which is likely enough, as it would certainly fill in the gap; the Hymn he regards as a later addition,

---

[1] In the R.V. verses 36, 37 are misplaced; the misplacing consists really in transposition, for the R.V. is here following Theodotion, the reverse order being found in the Septuagint.

[2] In the R.V. verses 45, 46, 49 are omitted.

[3] *E.g.* v. Gall, *Die Einheitlichkeit des Buches Daniel*, p. 23 (1895).

[4] In Kautzsch, *op. cit.* i. 173; see also Jahn, *Das Buch Daniel nach der LXX hergestellt*, pp. 32 f. (1904).

to which, still later, the Prayer of Azarias was prefixed—this is suggested by the textual confusion of verse 24 in the Aramaic, *i.e.* the logical gap between verse 23 and this verse. Rothstein holds to the possibility, however, that both the Prayer and the Hymn stood in the original text.[1]

There are, on the other hand, some strong grounds for doubting whether the two main Additions formed part of the original text: Dan. iii is a self-contained narrative; the Additions are not only unnecessary, they are intrusive, and break the otherwise even flow of the story. Moreover, they have no bearing on the narrative itself; as will have been seen from the contents of the Prayer, it would have been quite inappropriate in the mouth of Azarias, and the same is true of the Hymn. Apart from the introductory words (verses 1, 2) to the Prayer, and to the Hymn (verse 28), the absence of which would not make the slightest difference to either, there is only one reference to the narrative in the canonical *Daniel* iii, namely verse 66, and this has quite obviously been inserted after the composition of the Hymn, for it cuts off the concluding thanksgiving from the rest of the Hymn. The Narrative portion (vv. 23–27), as already pointed out, may well have formed part of the original narrative in *Daniel* iii, though why it is not found in the canonical *Daniel* is difficult to say excepting on the assumption that the Prayer and the Hymn were inserted in the original text, and afterwards deleted, but preserved in the Greek translation. In this case, the Narrative portion would have been torn from its context when the Additions were first inserted. Kuhl[2] denies that the Narrative portion formed part of the original text; he does not regard the " gap " after iii. 23 (canonical *Daniel*) as such, but merely a break, purposely made, as a literary device to enhance the interest of the narrative; so that, according to him, there

---

[1] The question of the original language of the canonical *Daniel* arises here; but into this we cannot enter. Rothstein and others contend for a Hebrew original for the whole of the Additions, but as they belong to the Aramaic portion of *Daniel* one might expect, though not necessarily, that they would have been written in Aramaic originally. Charles holds that both the Prayer and the Hymn " were written in Aramaic and inserted at an early date in some manuscripts of *Daniel*, but not in others "(*A Critical Commentary on the Book of Daniel*, p. 73 [1929]).

[2] *Die Drei Männer im Feuer*, pp. 86 ff., 105 f. (1930).

is no need to suppose that the Narrative portion ever formed part of the original text. He holds, however, that all three Additions were inserted in the original text before the Septuagint translation was made.

A good deal turns on what the original language of the Additions was; here again, opinions differ,[1] though the general tendency inclines towards a Hebrew original. Kuhl seems to us, however, to have settled the question definitely; his re-translation of the Additions into Hebrew compels the conviction that this, and neither Aramaic nor Greek, was the original language.[2]

The object of the Additions is fairly obvious; the Prayer of Azarias was added, in the first place, to show that Azarias, the servant of God, was not forestalled by Nebuchadrezzar in recognizing and blessing the God of Israel (canonical *Daniel* iii. 28, 29); a second reason was to show that the deliverance from the fire was in answer to prayer (v. 20 in the Additions). The Hymn was added as an expression of praise and thanksgiving to the Creator.

That neither the Prayer nor the Hymn was composed for insertion in the text of *Daniel* is evident because there is no point of contact between them and the context in which they stand. The Hymn, at any rate, will have belonged to some collection of hymns traditionally handed down, just as there were numerous collections of psalms; the similarity in many respects between our Hymn and Ps. cxlviii has often been pointed to.

IV. DATES OF THE ADDITIONS

If we are right in contending that the Additions were inserted in the text of the canonical *Daniel* before it was translated into Greek, their approximate dates are not diffi-cult to determine. Both the Prayer and the Hymn belonged to traditional material, and the latter must, in all probability,

---

[1] See, *e.g.*, Bludau, *Die alexandrinische Übersetzung des Buches Daniel*, pp. 157 f. (1897); Gaster contends for an Aramaic original (*Proceedings of the Soc. of Bibl. Arch.*, xvi. 280 ff., 312 ff., xvii. 75 ff. [1894, 1895]); but the mediæval Aramaic MS. published by Gaster seems to be a translation of Theodotion's Version.

[2] *Op. cit.*, pp. 128–133, 150–155.

be earlier than the canonical *Daniel*, written circa B.C. 166.
The words in the Prayer: "Neither is there at this time
prince or prophet, or leader, or burnt-offering, or sacrifice,
or oblation, or incense or place to offer before thee, and to
find mercy" (R.V. v. 15), point to a somewhat later date
than the Hymn, for these words clearly reflect the conditions
a few years after the accession of Antiochus IV Epiphanes
to the Syrian throne in B.C. 175, *i.e.* approximately B.C. 168.
The Hymn would appear to be older; as marks of its
relatively early date Kuhl points to "the strict adhesion
to the form of the type to which it belongs, its systematic
arrangement down to the smallest details, the absence of
ordinary forms of speech, the sobriety and realism of its
contents, and the entire self-oblivion of the singer." [1]

V. TEXT AND VERSIONS

The Septuagint of the book of *Daniel* containing the
Additions exists in one manuscript only, the cursive 87
(*Cod. Chisianus*, in the library of the Chigi family at Rome).
"The handwriting appears to belong to the Calabrian
school of Greek calligraphy, and the date usually assigned
to it is the ninth century." [2] It contains also Theodotion's
Version; the Septuagint form is somewhat fuller. [3]

Theodotion's Version, made in the first half of the second
century A.D., displaced the Septuagint at a very early date.
In addition to the uncials BAVQ and others of later date,
there are a number of cursives which contain this Version. [4]
It seems probable that "there were two pre-Christian
versions of *Daniel*, both passing as the 'LXX,' one of which
is preserved in the Chigi MS., while the other formed the
basis of Theodotion's revision." [5]

Only fragments of the Old Latin Version are extant; [6]

[1] *Op. cit.*, p. 99.
[2] Swete, *The Old Testament in Greek*, iii. p. xi (1899), p. xii in 1905 edition.
[3] Swete gives both on opposite pages (*op. cit.*, iii. 514 ff. for the Additions).
[4] They are enumerated by Swete, *Introduction to the Old Testament in Greek*,
pp. 165 ff. (1900).
[5] Swete, *Intr.*, p. 48, and see further p. 423.
[6] Sabatier, *Bibl. Sacr. Latinæ Versiones antiquæ*, II (1751); Burkitt, *The
Old Latin and the Itala*, pp. 18 ff. (1896).

they are mainly translated from Theodotion's Version, but Burkitt shows that before the time of Jerome both the Septuagint and Theodotion's Version existed in Latin Versions. In the Vulgate of *Daniel*, translated from the Aramaic–Hebrew, the Additions are included, being translated from Theodotion's Version.

The *Syriac Version (Peshitta)* is likewise translated from Theodotion, but differs both from it and the Septuagint in many instances; whether this is due merely to arbitrariness and textual corruption, or whether some other form of the Greek was laid under contribution cannot be said.

The *Syro-Hexaplar* is " a literal translation of the LXX of the Hexapla in which the Origenic signs were scrupulously retained " in the sections which contain these additions; [1] the Syro-Hexaplaric *Daniel* "is divided into ten chapters, each headed by a full summary of its contents." [2]

All the other Versions, Coptic, Sahidic, Ethiopic, Arabic, Armenian, and Slavonic, are translations from Theodotion's Version.

Two very late Aramaic texts, based on Theodotion's Version, are not of much value. [3]

VI. LITERATURE

Fritsche, *op. cit.*, i. (1851).

Brüll, " Das Gebet der drei Männer in Feuerofen," in *Jahrbuch für jüdische Geschichte und Literatur* for 1887, pp. 22 ff.

Ball, in Wace, *op. cit.*, ii. 305 ff. (1888).

v. Gall, *Die Einheitlichkeit des Buches Daniel* (1895).

Bludau, *Die alexandrinische Übersetzung des Buch Daniel*, pp. 155 ff. (1897).

Rothstein, in Kautzsch, *op. cit.*, i. 172 ff. (1900).

André, *op. cit.*, 208 ff. (1903).

[1] Swete, *Intr.*, p. 112; it is, therefore, of considerable value as supplementing or correcting the text of *Cod. Chisianus*.

[2] *Ibid.*, p. 356.

[3] See Gaster, " The Unknown Aramaic Original of Theodotion's Additions to the Book of Daniel," in *Proceedings of the Soc. of Bibl. Arch.*, xvi. 280 ff. 312 ff. (1894), and xvii. 75 ff. (1895); Neubauer, in *The Jewish Quarterly Review* for 1899, xi. 364 ff.

Jahn, *Das Buch Daniel nach der LXX hergestellt* (1904).
Daubney, *The Three Additions to Daniel* (1906).
Goettsberger, *Das Buch Daniel* (1928).
Charles, *A Critical Commentary on the Book of Daniel*, pp. 72 ff. (1928).
Christie, " The Strophic Arrangement of the Benedicite," in the *Journal of Biblical Literature* for 1928, pp. 188 ff.
Kuhl, *Die Drei Männer im Feuer* (1930).
For editions of the text see Schürer, *Geschichte des jüdischen Volkes* . . . iii. 453 ff. (1909).

T

THE HISTORY OF SUSANNA

Set apart from the beginning of *Daniel*, because it is not in the Hebrew, as neither the Narration of Bel and the Dragon.

I. TITLE

IN the one extant MS. of the Septuagint (*Cod. Chisianus*), which gives also Theodotion's Version, *Susanna* forms chap. xiii of *Daniel*, and it has the title Σουσαννα α' σ' θ' (= Aquila, Symmachus, Theodotion). The Vulgate and the Syro-Hexaplar also place it at the end of *Daniel* as chap. xiii, though without any title; but the latter has a note at the end: " Completed is Daniel according to the tradition of the Seventy," so that it evidently regarded *Susanna* as part of the canonical book. In Theodotion's Version, represented by all the Greek MSS., and by the other Versions, the title varies. In the great uncials BAQ *Susanna* follows immediately after the title of the whole book, " Daniel " [1] (Q: " Daniel according to Theodotion "), but without any special title for *Susanna*; similarly the Old Latin Version; Cod. A, however, has the subscription: ορασις α'. Some Greek MSS. have the title " Susanna," others, " The History of Susanna," yet others, " The Judgement of Daniel "; fuller titles are given in the cursives 232, " Visions of the prophet Daniel concerning the elders and Susanna," and 235, " Vision of the very wise Daniel concerning Susanna." In *Cod. Chisianus* Theodotion's Version is headed το ειρ αγρυπνος Δανιηλ,[2] and *Susanna* appears as chap. xiii. Kay refers to a Codex from mount Athos which has the

---

[1] But there are reasons for thinking that *Susanna* did not originally occupy this place, see Bludau, " Die Alexandrinische Uebersetzung des Buches Daniel und ihre Verhältniss zum Massoretischen Text," pp. 166 f. (in Barden-hewer's *Biblische Studien*, ii. Bd., Heft 2 und 3 [1897]).

[2] το ειρ is explained as = the Hebrew עִיר "the Watcher," so that this title would mean " Daniel the sleepless Watcher."

title: ορασεις ενδεκα του προφητου Δανιηλ deinde sequitur περι του Αββακουμ. His omnibus praemittitur περι της Συσαννης; and states that chap. xiv of *Cod. Chisianus* has the superscription; εκ προφητειας Αμβακουμ υιου Ιησου εκ της φυλης Λευι.[1] It would thus appear that the story was sometimes associated with the name of Habakkuk (cp. *Bel and the Dragon,* verses 33 ff.).

II. CONTENTS

Susanna, " a very fair woman " and devout, having been brought up by god-fearing parents, was the wife of Joakim, a wealthy and honourable man, who dwelt in Babylon. Among the many visitors who frequented Joakim's house were two elders who held influential positions, being consulted by numbers of those who had law-suits. Surrounding Joakim's house was a large garden, in which his wife Susanna was accustomed to stroll about after the departure of the daily visitors at noon. Attracted by her beauty the two elders would watch her as she wandered in the garden; and unlawful desires towards her possessed them. Though conscience-stricken, they deliberately directed their thoughts away from what was right; and while both were consumed with unholy lust, neither durst, for very shame, impart to the other his feelings and intent. One day, having ostensibly departed each to his home for the mid-day meal, they both slunk back again, and met! This necessitated a mutual explanation, and they confessed one to the other their evil intent towards Susanna. Thereupon they agreed to seek an occasion on which they might find her alone. Not long after they succeeded in this; for as Susanna, according to her wont, was walking in the garden with her two maids, she determined to bathe, for the day was warm, and nobody, as she thought, was present in the garden; therein, however, she was mistaken, for the two elders had beforehand concealed themselves there. All unconscious of this, Susanna bade her maids close the garden gates against intrusion,

[1] In Charles, *op. cit.,* i. 638.

and bring her what she needed for her bath. No sooner had the maids disappeared than the two elders emerged from their hiding-place and approached Susanna with lustful intent, threatening her at the same time that if she would not consent to do their will, they would accuse her of having had a young man with her and of having sent her maids away on that account. In despair Susanna cried: "I am menaced on every side, for if I do your will, death will be my lot; and if I refuse I shall not escape your malice; better will it be for me to refuse you and to suffer at your hands, than sin against the Lord by a wicked act." And then she called aloud for help. But when the elders heard her cry, they, too, set up a shout, and one of them ran to open the garden gate. Then the maids, hearing this noise in the garden, hastened back to find out the cause; but when the elders told them their tale, that a young man had been with their mistress, they were greatly shocked, for no word of scandal had ever before been breathed against Susanna's virtue. The next day, in the presence of Susanna's husband, her parents, children, and kindred, the two elders publicly charged her with having committed adultery with a young man in the garden, affirming at the same time that they had been witnesses of the act, and that the young man had escaped their hands when they attempted to detain him. The accusation, being made by two such highly respected elders, was believed to be true; Susanna was condemned to death. But, conscious of her innocence, she lifted up her voice in prayer to God; nor did she pray in vain, for as she was being led to her death God stirred up the spirit of a youth named Daniel who was to be her deliverer. Standing in the midst of the people he cried: "Are ye so without understanding, ye sons of Israel, that without examination or knowledge of the truth ye have condemned a daughter of Israel?" Then he commanded them all to return to the hall of justice, "for," said he, "these have borne false witness against her." Thereupon all returned to the hall of justice, and Daniel was invited to examine Susanna's accusers. This he did by questioning them separately; as a result, their evidence was contradictory, for one said that the sinful act had taken place under a mastick tree, while the other affirmed that it had been under a holm tree. The falseness of the accusation having thus been clearly set forth, the guilty elders were put to death, and the innocent blood was saved. All Susanna's kindred thereupon praised God that no wrong had been found in her; and Daniel was thenceforth " held in high estimation in the sight of the people."

III. Purpose of the Story

The story itself suggests several purposes, for any one of which it may have been written, viz: to illustrate the triumph of virtue; or to show that God will not forsake the innocent victim of slander; or to teach the efficacy of prayer. André points to the moral added in the Septuagint text (verse 62), and says that " the Jews utilized the story of Susanna and the two licentious elders to warn young men of the dangers of carnal desires," but rightly adds that there is nothing to show that this was the purpose which the original writer had in view. Again, when in the last verse of the story, according to Theodotion's version, it is said that " since that day onwards Daniel was held in high estimation in the sight of the people," one might infer that Theodotion believed the story to have been written for the purpose of eulogizing Daniel; but this again would not necessarily indicate the original writer's object; besides, the name of Daniel did not, in all probability, appear in the original form of the story.

While it seems probable that our story was, in the first instance, composed simply for the sake of story-telling without any further object, it was doubtless utilized for the driving home of moral lessons; and there are good grounds for believing that its most important use, involving no doubt some slight modifications in the text, was that pointed to by Ball. There is every reason to believe that in its present form the story belongs to the former half of the last century B.C.; it was during this period that the Pharisees finally

asserted their supremacy over the Sadducæan party.[1]
At that time Simeon ben Shetach was the leader of the
Pharisaic party, and his most notable achievement was to
supersede the Sadducæan interpretation of the Law by
that of the Pharisees; hence his title of "Restorer of the
Law."[2] His rigorous insistence on upholding the Law
resulted on one occasion in his sentencing to death for
sorcery eighty women of Ashkelon; in revenge for this
the relatives of the victims brought an accusation against
his son involving the death-sentence. The accusation was
false, and on his way to execution the condemned man
protested his innocence with such effect that his accusers
confessed their crime. Thereupon the judges were prepared to release him; but in his zeal for the Law he pointed
out to the judges that, according to the Law, a witness who
withdraws his accusation may not be believed; in consequence, the accusation stood, and Simeon's son had to
suffer death.[3] It was owing to this miscarriage of justice,
caused by the witnesses not having been rigorously examined
in the first instance, that Simeon ben Shetach pronounced
the precept preserved in *Aboth* i. 9: "Examine the witnesses
thoroughly (lit. 'be redundant in examining'); and be
cautious with thy words lest from them they learn to bear
false witness."

This episode, then, Ball believes to have been the object
for which *Susanna* was utilized, a scribe having given another
shape to pre-existing material, and, as it now stands, the
conception of Daniel as judge "constituted the kernel of the
whole narrative." It is, he says, "a contrast between
two kinds of criminal procedure, which are represented,
not by a dry general description, but by a concrete instance
of their actual working. The author's aim is to portray
certain deplorable effects inherent in the administration
of justice in his own time, and to suggest a radical cure."[4]

[1] We have definite knowledge regarding the attitude of the Sadducees and
Pharisees towards each other as opposed parties as early as the reign of John
Hyrcanus (B.C. 134/3–104/3); it was during the reign of Alexandra (Salome)
B.C. 75/4–67/6 that the Pharisees became finally dominant.
[2] Bab. Talmud, *Kiddushin* 66a.
[3] Jerusalem Talmud, *Sanhedrin* vi. 23b.
[4] In Wace, *op. cit.*, ii. 328 f.

This theory regarding the purpose of *Susanna* in its present form we believe to be thoroughly sound.

IV. ORIGINAL LANGUAGE AND THE TWO FORMS OF THE GREEK TEXT

Greek is usually held to be the original language of both the Septuagint and of Theodotion's Version of the story; but Kay adduces some telling arguments which lead him to conclude rather that "from internal evidence both Greek texts are versions dependent on a Hebrew original. . . . Apart from idioms in either text, the identity, the nature of the resemblances, and the divergences, suggest the dependence of translators."[1] He believes, in order to account for the difficulties presented, that there was, in the first instance, a Hebrew form of the story; from this a Greek translation was made, *i.e.* the original Septuagint Version; then, there appeared later a revision of the Hebrew, which was the source of both the enlarged form of the Septuagint and of Theodotion's Version; but each used this source independently.

The striking differences between the Septuagint and Theodotion's Version cannot blind us to the fact that the story told by each is, in its essence, one and the same; but the differences are not such as would suggest that Theodotion merely modified and enlarged the Septuagint form, for a comparison of the two texts gives rather the impression that each is the product of an independent manipulation of an identical original,—in this case, as already remarked, of a Hebrew original.[2] To illustrate this we should have to place a number of passages from each text side by side.[3]

In the case of a popular folk-tale such as the *History of Susanna* it is altogether in the nature of things that it should, in transmission, whether in writing or by word of mouth,

[1] In Charles, *op. cit.*, i. 641 f.; "the Semitic idioms in the Greek texts in many cases favour a Hebrew rather than an Aramaic source" (*ibid.*, p. 644).
[2] Cp. Bludau, *op. cit.*, pp. 178 ff.
[3] A full English translation of both texts is given by Kay, in Charles, *op. cit.*, i. 647 ff.

have undergone modification, for one reason or another, and extension at the hands of those who repeated it.

V. Date

Since the story of *Susanna* is a folk-tale it may well be earlier than any written form, whatever the language. We have seen reason for believing that both the original, as well as the modified form of the written story, were written in Hebrew; the modified form must belong, approximately, to b.c. 80, the original form considerably earlier than this, but some time after the canonical *Daniel* was written (b.c. 166–5). When the Greek translation was made it is impossible to say; we only know that the entire Greek Canon was in existence during the Apostolic Age,[1] approximately; Theodotion's Version was made before 180 a.d.

VI. Manuscripts and Versions

What has been said about these under " The Song of the Three Holy Children " applies here too.

VII. Literature

Fritzsche, *op. cit.*, i. 113 ff., 132 ff. (1851).
Brüll, " Das apokryphische Susanna–Buch," in *Jahrbücher für jüdische Geschichte und Litteratur* for 1877.
Ball, in Wace, *op. cit.*, ii. 323 ff. (1888).
Bludau, *op. cit.*, pp. 165 ff. (1897).
Rothstein, in Kautzsch, *op. cit.*, i. 176 ff. (1900).
André, *op. cit.*, pp. 222 ff. (1903).
Kay, in Charles, *op. cit.*, i. 647 ff. (1913).
Baumgartner, " Susanna, die Geschichte einer Legende," *Archiv für Religionswissenschaft*, pp. 259 ff. (1926), 187 f. (1929).

[1] Swete, *Intr.*, pp. 26 f.

BEL AND THE DRAGON

I. Title

As this Addition follows immediately after Dan. xii. 13 at the end of the book of *Daniel* it has no title in most of the manuscripts; but in Codd. AQ it is treated as the last of the visions of Daniel with the title " Vision xii " (ὅρασις ιβ').[1] In the Septuagint MS. *Cod. Chisianus*[2] and in the Syro-Hexaplar it is headed: " From the prophecy of Habakkuk, the son of Jesus of the tribe of Levi "; and in the *Peshitta* the title is: " Bel the idol," and at verse 23, where the Dragon Story begins, there is the second title: " Then follows the Dragon."

II. Contents

This Addition consists of two distinct pieces: (1) *The Story of Bel* (verses 1–22), and (2) *The Story of the Dragon* (verses 23–42).

(1) *The Story of Bel.* According to Theodotion's Version Daniel was the chief friend of Cyrus the Persian, and lived with him. Cyrus worshipped the god Bel, the great Babylonian god who was supplied daily with " twelve great measures of fine flour, and forty sheep, and six firkins of wine " (about 54 gallons). But Daniel worshipped his God. It displeased Cyrus that Daniel would not worship Bel, for that he was a living god was proved by the amount of food and drink that he consumed daily. But Daniel laughed at this, and bade the king not to be deceived, for, said he, this idol " is but clay within, and brass without, and did never eat or drink anything." This aroused the anger of the king; so he called the seventy priests of Bel,

---

[1] In Theodotion's Version the whole of *Daniel* is divided into twelve Visions.
[2] See above, p. 277.

and inquired about the matter, threatening them with death, if they could not explain where all this food went to, but declaring that Daniel should die if they could show that Bel consumed it. The king and Daniel then proceeded to the temple of Bel. In the meantime, the priests took counsel. They then desired the king to have the food set forth as usual on the god's table, saying that if it was not all consumed by Bel by the next morning they would be prepared to die, but if it was all consumed, then Daniel must die; not that they feared anything for themselves, because they had a trap-door under the table through which they were in the habit of entering the temple and carrying off the food and drink. They then retired, and the king caused the table of Bel to be spread. But Daniel, with the king's permission, had the floor of the temple strewn with ashes. This done, and the door of the temple having been sealed with the king's signet, they departed. During the night the priests, according to their wont, came with their wives and children, and ate and drank all that was set before Bel.

The next morning the king came with Daniel, and found the seal intact; then they entered the temple, and the king seeing that the food was all gone, cried out: "Great art thou, O Bel, and with thee is no deceit at all." But Daniel laughed once more, saying: "Behold now the pavement, and mark well whose footsteps are these." And when the king saw that they were the footsteps of men, women, and children, he was greatly enraged, and compelled the priests to show him how they entered the temple. As a result they were put to death, but the image of Bel was handed over to Daniel who destroyed the idol and his temple.

(2) *The Story of the Dragon.* In contrast to the Bel idol, which was made of clay and brass, there was another object of worship among the Babylonians, namely a great dragon, more correctly a great serpent. That this was living was obvious for it could be seen to eat and drink. Daniel is, therefore, invited by the king to worship it. This, of course, Daniel refuses to do; but he undertakes to slay the animal without the aid of weapons, and thus to show that it is no

god. The king gives him leave to do so. Thereupon Daniel
boils a mixture of pitch, hair, and fat, which he gives the
creature to eat; nothing loth it swallows this, and bursts in
consequence. Then Daniel taunts the Babylonians for
worshipping a god like that. The Babylonians, however,
are greatly incensed at the death of their god, and they
conspire against the king, who, as they say, has become a
Jew under the influence of Daniel. They demand, therefore,
the person of Daniel, or else threaten to kill the king and all
his house. In this predicament the king delivers Daniel up
to them to be thrown into a den of lions. Here he remains
for six days, the lions not attempting to harm him. By
this time, having had nothing to eat in the den of lions,
Daniel was getting hungry. Thereupon an angel went to
Palestine and saw the prophet Habakkuk carrying out food
to the reapers; the angel bids the prophet go to Babylon
and give this food to Daniel. The prophet protests that he
does not know where Babylon is, still less where the den of
lions is located; so the angel takes him by the hair, and
with the blast of his breath sets him down in Babylon right
over the den. Habakkuk then bids Daniel eat the dinner
which God had sent him. Daniel, having given thanks to
God, has his dinner; Habakkuk is then transported home
again. Then, it being the seventh day that Daniel had been
in the lions' den, the king came to bewail him, and, lo, he
finds Daniel sitting there uninjured; so the king gives glory
to the God of Daniel, who is released; but they who had
sought his destruction are thrown into the den, and devoured
in the presence of Daniel.

III. ORIGIN AND PURPOSE OF THE STORIES

Both stories as we now have them are variations, respectively, of episodes narrated in the book of *Daniel* itself. The
background of the first is Dan. iii., the worship of the golden
image; that of the second is Dan. vi., Daniel in the lions'
den. The obvious purpose of both stories is to illustrate the
folly of idolatry, especially of identifying the god with his
image; and also to show forth the power of the One and

only God and His solicitude for His faithful servant; this latter, it is true, occupies only a subordinate place. It is, however, evident that some older traditional material has also been placed under contribution; the references to Habakkuk in the opening verse of the first story in the Septuagint text, as well as in the body of the second story in both the Septuagint and Theodotion's Version, point to this; similarly, the tradition about Daniel being a priest and the son of Habal, in verse 2 of the Septuagint text. Most authorities, moreover, hold that the dragon in the second story is Tiamat, the primeval monster slain by Marduk; if so, this would be another piece of ancient traditional material utilized.[1]

Now, with regard to the main purpose of both stories, namely the denunciation of idolatry, it is not beside the mark to inquire against whom it is directed: had the writer in mind Gentile idolaters to whom he wished to prove the superiority of the Jewish religion? In other words, are these stories to be regarded as polemic-apologetic writings? Or were there those of his own race against whom the writer felt compelled to raise his voice? In favour of the former view there is the fact that a good deal of apologetic literature was put forth by Jewish writers during the last two pre-Christian centuries which was successful in making many proselytes; in favour of the latter is the mention of Habakkuk, of whom Gentiles were not likely to have heard. The mention of Daniel is somewhat different; his name would doubtless have been likewise unknown to Gentiles, but as the hero of the stories that would not matter; whereas Habakkuk's *rôle* is quite subordinate.

But there is another reason for believing that these stories were written against Jews; and this raises a subject of some importance. Before coming to this, however, it is necessary

---

[1] See, *e.g.*, Gunkel, *Schöpfung und Chaos in Urzeit und Endzeit*, pp. 320 ff. (1895). In the text of our story it is evidently a living serpent to which reference is made, and which was worshipped; but this does not militate against Gunkel's contention that the prototype of our story is the Tiamat myth, for in transmission a myth takes on all kinds of variations; moreover, there are later recensions of our story (see Ball, in Wace, *op. cit.*, ii. 345 f., 357) which embody other original details. The central point of the slaying of the dragon in our story is that Daniel slays it " without sword or staff "; in the Tiamat myth the same *trait* occurs.

to say a word as to the place of origin of the stories. *Data* for deciding this question with any certainty are wanting, we have therefore to be guided by the probabilities of the case. Alexandria, Babylon, and Palestine have been suggested. If the stories were written for renegade Jews Palestine is highly improbable; there was but little danger of idolatry among the Jews there; it was in the lands of the Dispersion that Jews were subject to this temptation. Babylon is more likely, especially if, as some authorities maintain, the stories were originally written in Hebrew; in their Greek form, on the other hand, their home was probably Alexandria. These are all suppositions, for definite evidence is wanting. But there are some considerations which tend to support the opinion that the stories were originally written in Hebrew as a protest against idolatrous Jews living in Babylonia, and that at a somewhat later time the Greek translation was made in Alexandria for the similar purpose of arousing shame among Jews in different parts of Egypt who were guilty of idolatrous practices.

The first thing to which attention must again be drawn is that religious syncretism, world-wide in its ramifications, was characteristic of the period extending from the time of Alexander the Great to well into the Christian era; it was a movement by which the Jews, as is proved by abundant evidence, were deeply affected. " The time of Alexander the Great and his successors," writes Bousset, " was one of general intermingling. The frontiers between countries disappear, peoples begin to speak a common language, both as a tongue in the ordinary sense, and intellectually. Identical thoughts course through the minds of all; religious beliefs run into one another. Is it likely that Judaism alone should have been exempt from the effects of this process? It is true that ever since the Maccabæan era efforts in the direction of a narrow exclusiveness held sway; but the drawing together of Judaism and the surrounding world, brought about during the preceding centuries, the results of which appear clearly and ominously at the end of the pre-Maccabæan period, could not be broken off and obliterated as though it had never existed."[1] The Jews of Palestine, the centre of orthodox Judaism, were, naturally enough, not affected to anything like the same extent as those of the Dispersion. While Jewish communities flourished in every country of the world as then known,[2] the two most important centres of the Dispersion were Babylon and Alexandria. It would take us much too far afield to deal with the various forms of idolatry and snake-worship both in Babylon and Egypt, nor is this necessary since much has been written about each;[3] but knowing of the existence of this and of the settlement of Jews in the midst of surroundings in which these things were in vogue, realizing also the syncretistic tendencies characteristic of the time, we feel justified in believing that many Jews both in Babylon and Alexandria, as well as in other parts of Mesopotamia and Egypt, were tempted to assimilate much of what they saw going on around them; and that, therefore, the stories under consideration were written with the purpose of exposing the folly of this among those of the author's race, thereby recalling them to a better frame of mind.

IV. The Original Language of the Stories

The unanimous opinion of the older authorities, as well as some later ones, is that the original language of our stories was Greek. A few modern scholars believe that they were originally written in Aramaic, while others contend for a Hebrew original. A discussion on the subject cannot well find a place here as it would involve dealing with many technicalities; these have been well dealt with by Witton Davies both in his Introduction to the stories and in his notes

[1] *Die Religion des Judentums im späthellenistischen Zeitalter*, p. 473 (1926); see in general, also Bertholet, *Das religiongeschichtliche Problem des Spätjudentums* (1909), and Wendland, *Die hellenistisch-römische Kultur* . . . (1912).
[2] Cp. *Sib. Orac.* iii. 271, "Every sea and every land is full of thee." For one of the most remarkable instances of religious syncretism among the Jews see the present writer's essay, "The Cult of Sabazios" in *The Labyrinth* (ed. by S. H. Hooke, 1935).
[3] E.g. Sayce, *Lectures on the Religion of the Ancient Babylonians* (1887); Oldham, *The Sun and the Serpent*, esp. chap. xi (1905); Scott-Moncrieff, *Paganism and Christianity in Egypt*, esp. chap. i (1913); Jeremias, *Das alte Testament im Lichte des alten Orients*, passim (1930); etc. etc.

in the commentary; and his contention for a Hebrew original is convincingly upheld.[1] Quite apart from this, however, from what has been said above there is an *à priori* reason for assuming either an Aramaic or a Hebrew original, of which the Greek is a translation; in view of Witton Davies' arguments the latter is far more likely.

V. MANUSCRIPTS AND VERSIONS

What has been said regarding these in the other Additions to *Daniel* applies here (see pp. 277 f., above).

VI. LITERATURE

Fritzsche, *op. cit.*, i. 113 ff., 146 ff. (1851).
Brüll, " Die Geschichte von Bel und dem Drachen," in *Jahrbücher für jüdische Geschichte und Litteratur*, viii. 28 f. (1887).
Ball, in Wace, *op. cit.*, ii. 344 ff. (1888).
Bludau, *op. cit.*, pp. 189 ff. (1897).
Rothstein, in Kautzsch, *op. cit.*, i. 178 ff. (1900).
Witton Davies, in Charles, *op. cit.*, i. 652 ff. (1913).

[1] In Charles, *op. cit.*, i. 652 ff.

THE PRAYER OF MANASSES

King of Judah, when he was holden captive in Babylon.

I. TITLE

IN Cod. A and many cursives the title is "Prayer of Mannasseh" (Προσευχὴ Μανασσή); but in Cod. T (*Turicensis*, in the Municipal Library of Zürich) it is: "Prayer of Manasseh the son of Hezekiah" (Προσευχὴ Μανασσὴ τοῦ υἱοῦ Ἐζεκίου). The R.V. title is from the Vulgate: "*Oratio Manassæ regis Iuda cum captus teneretur in Babylone.*"[1] In the *Didascalia Apostolorum* (see below) it is simply *Oratio Manassis*.

II. CONTENTS [2]

An address to the Almighty, with an ascription of praise for His works of creation, His power, glory, and mercy (verses 1–7, ending with the words: "For thou art the Lord Most High, of great compassion, longsuffering, and abundant in mercy, and repentest of bringing evils upon men)." A confession of sins (verses 8–12, ending with the words: "I have sinned, O Lord, I have sinned, and I acknowledge mine iniquities"). A prayer for pardon (verse 13, ending with the words: "For thou, O Lord, art the God of them that repent"). An expression of trust in God's mercy (verse 14, ". . . for thou wilt save me, that am unworthy, according to thy great mercy"). A final ascription of praise (verse 15: "And I will praise thee for ever all the days of my life; for all the host of heaven doth sing thy praise, and thine is the glory for ever and ever. Amen").

---

[1] But it is not the work of Jerome (see below § VI).
[2] The verse-divisions, which are not given in the R.V. or in the Vulgate, are from Swete's text, *The Old Testament in Greek*, iii. 824–826 (1899).

III. ORIGIN OF THE PRAYER

In view of the various other additions inserted in the Septuagint text of canonical books it might have been expected that this Prayer would have been added after II Chron. xxxiii. 13, for that this Prayer is meant to be that which was uttered by Manasseh is obvious when it is compared with what is said in II Chron. xxxiii. 19, and this in spite of the fact that the name of Manasseh is nowhere mentioned in our Prayer. In II Chron. xxxiii. 1 ff., we are told of how, by his idolatrous practices, Manasseh led the people of Judah astray, in consequence of which, by the will of Yahweh, the Assyrians came and carried him off in chains to Babylon; then in verses 12, 13 it continues: "And when he was in distress, he besought Yahweh his God, and humbled himself greatly before the God of his fathers. And he prayed unto him, and he was intreated of him, and he heard his supplication, and brought him again to Jerusalem into his kingdom. Then Manasseh knew that Yahweh he was God." After these words the Prayer would have come in appropriately;[1] but as a matter of fact it never has formed part of the Septuagint text. In II Chron. xxxiii. 18, 19 it is said: "Now the rest of the acts of Manasseh, and his prayer unto his God, and the words of the seers that spake to him in the name of Yahweh, the God of Israel, behold, they are written among the acts of the kings of Israel. His prayer, also, and how (God) was intreated of him, and all his sin and his trespass, and the places wherein he built the high places, and set up the Asherim and the graven images, before he humbled himself; behold they are written in the history of *Hozai*."[2] From this it would appear that the Prayer had been preserved in a Hebrew historical record. But there are convincing reasons against accepting the Chronicler's statements here: the records of the reign of a king of Judah are not likely to have been preserved in "the acts of the kings of Israel"; in II Kgs. xxi. 17 they are, naturally enough, written in

[1] Cp. the prayer, or rather psalm, added to the text in Jon. ii. 1 ff.
[2] For this proper name, which never occurs elsewhere, the Septuagint reads *Hozim*, "seers," referred to in verse 18.

U

the book of the Chronicles of the kings of Judah. More important is the fact that in the account of Manasseh's reign in II Kgs. xxi. 1–18 there is not a word about his repentance; and in many other particulars it differs from the *Chronicles* record. In view of the unreliability of so much that is written in *Chronicles*, and of its generally tendencious character,[1] it cannot be doubted that the *Kings* record is to be preferred. More particularly is this so in the present case where the purpose which the Chronicler had in view in recording Manasseh's repentance is obvious; this was in order to explain the anomaly that a wicked king should have reigned so long—fifty-five years. According to the traditional doctrine of retribution it is only the righteous whose days are prolonged; but since Manasseh repented he could be pointed to as an example of God's mercy towards a penitent sinner; that the repentance did not take place until after many years of a wicked life would presumably have been explained on the principle of divine prescience. This also tells us why the Prayer was originally written, namely to reveal the state of heart of a true penitent.

But while the Chronicler's statement that the Prayer was preserved in an ancient Hebrew record cannot be accepted, it is likely enough that a redactor was acquainted with some writing of later date in which it appeared, and added it to the text of *Chronicles*; that the text has been worked over by some later hand is evident, verse 19 is clearly a doublet. Many legendary details about the life of Manasseh were current; they occur in both Jewish and Christian writings; [2] though these are of late date, the traditional material incorporated in them is much older. Thus II Chron. xxxiii. 13, 14, 18, 19 would be the work of a later scribe, and they reflect details embodied in some early writings, though of later date than *Chronicles*.

[1] See Oesterley and Robinson, *An Introduction to the Books of the Old Testament*, p. 118 (1934).
[2] See Fritzsche, *op. cit.*, i. 158; Ball, *op. cit.*, ii. 362 ff.; Charles, *The Apocalypse of Baruch*, pp. 107 f. (1896); Friedlander, *Pirke de Rabbi Eliezer*, pp. 339 f. (1916); Connolly, *Didascalia Apostolorum*, pp. 68 ff. (1929).

IV. Date of Composition

The books of the *Chronicles* belong to about B.C. 300, while the Prayer itself occurs for the first time in literature in the *Didascalia Apostolorum*[1] *circa* 200–250 A.D.[2] We have seen reason to believe that the passages in *II Chronicles* in which mention is made of the Prayer are considerably later than the book itself. On the other hand, its incorporation in the *Didascalia* points to an earlier date than this work, for it will hardly be contended that it was composed by the author of the *Apostolic Constitutions*.[3] The writer was, without doubt, a Jew; the references to the Patriarchs, and their sinlessness, the forms of expression, and the general mode of thought, stamp it as Jewish; at the same time, such unbiblical phrases as " the God of the just," and " the God of them that repent," point to a post-biblical time. The devotional spirit of the Prayer would suggest that it was composed by a *Ḥasid*.[4] Ryssel thinks it may have been composed, like other apocryphal literary pieces, during the Maccabæan period, with the object of bringing home to the Jews the lesson that by repentance they would be delivered from their present dire peril, however much on account of their sins they were suffering according to their deserts. The date of composition may, therefore, be tentatively given as the middle of the second century B.C. That the Prayer does not appear in literary form until some centuries after this would not necessarily militate against this date; it is too short and unimportant a piece of literature to have attracted much notice, and may well have lain hidden for long before it was brought to light.

[1] Connolly, *op. cit.*, pp. 72 f. It may here be pointed out that the third century *Didascalia*, a manual giving detailed information about an ancient Christian community, was originally written in Greek, but the Syriac translation is the only form in which it now exists in its entirety, though many fragments are found in an ancient Latin translation. But many portions of the Greek are embedded in the first six books of the *Apostolic Constitutions*, a Church Order belonging to the fourth century. This latter must not be confused with the *Apostolic Canons* and the *Apostolic Church Order* (= the *Didachê*); see Maclean, *The Ancient Church Orders*, pp. 25 ff. (1910). The *Prayer of Manasseh* is preserved in lib. ii. 21 of the *Didascalia*.

[2] Funk, *Die Apostolischen Konstitutionen*, p. 50 (1891); Connolly, *op. cit.*, pp. lxxxvii ff.

[3] This was the contention of Fabricius, *Libri Veteris Testamenti apocryphi*, p. 208 (1694), referred to by Ryssel, in Kautzsch, *op. cit.*, i. 167.

[4] See I. Macc. vii. 13–15.

V. The Original Language of the Prayer

If the date tentatively suggested be accepted we should expect the Prayer to have been originally written either in Aramaic or Hebrew, more probably the latter in the case of a literary piece. Ball contends strongly for a Hebrew original, and Charles gives a convincing piece of evidence for this.[1] But the majority of scholars favour a Greek original; Ryle, *e.g.*, while recognizing the difficulty of giving a certain answer in the case of so short a piece, feels, nevertheless, that " the general impression produced by the flexible style and ample vocabulary favours the view that Greek is the language in which it was composed." [2] The suggested date would not necessarily have to be modified in this case; we have seen other instances of apocryphal literature of approximately the same date having been originally written in Greek.[3]

VI. Manuscripts and Versions

The *Prayer of Manasses* is not contained in any Greek MSS. of *II Chronicles*, where we should expect to find it; doubtless, its preservation among the Canticles appended to the Psalms in Codd. AT and a number of cursives is due to the fact that it was put to liturgical use. Portions of the Greek text, " too often, only in an approximate form " of the *Apostolic Constitutions* are extant.[4]

In most of the printed editions of the Septuagint the Prayer does not appear, though there are a few in which it does; [5] it is also given by Swete, in *The Old Testament in Greek*, iii. 824–826 (1899).

The Syriac Version is contained in a manuscript which Ryssel has used for his commentary, and which he describes as a " very good text "; it has not been published.[6] This version is also contained in four Syriac MSS. of the

[1] *Op. cit.*, i. 614 f. (editorial footnote).
[2] *Op. cit.*, i. p. 615.
[3] See above, pp. 114, 191.
[4] Connolly, *op. cit.*, p. xi, and the textual notes on pp. 72 ff.
[5] For details see Ryle, *op. cit.*, i. 616.
[6] *Op. cit.*, i. 168.

Didascalia,[1] the earliest of which belongs to the eighth or ninth century.[2]

The Latin Version [3] is of unknown date, but it is much later than the time of Jerome and cannot, therefore, be called Old Latin; as the Prayer was not contained either in the Hebrew or Greek Bible, it found no place in the Vulgate itself, but was added in later days after *II Chronicles*. The Prayer is not contained in any Latin MS. earlier than the thirteenth century.

The Armenian Version follows the Greek Version in placing the Prayer among the Canticles after the *Psalms*. Similarly in the Ethiopic Version of the *Psalms* the Prayer is given in the appendix to these; it is also contained in the Ethiopic Version of the *Apostolic Constitutions*. According to Howorth, the Prayer occurs in the old Slavonic Version.[4] An Arabic Version of the Prayer is also found in Arabic MSS. of the *Apostolic Constitutions*.[5]

VII. Literature

Fritzsche, *op. cit.*, i. 157 ff. (1851).

Ball, in Wace, *op. cit.*, ii. 361 ff. (1888).

Ryssel, in Kautzsch, *op. cit.*, i. 165 ff. (1900).

André, *op. cit.*, pp. 237 ff. (1903).

Ryle, in Charles, *op. cit.*, i. 612 ff. (1913).

[1] They are described by Connolly, *op. cit.*, pp. xi ff.; see also Ryle, *op. cit.*, i. 617.

[2] *Cod. Sangermanensis* (ed. by Lagarde, [1854]). Like the other Syriac MSS. it contains the part of verse 7 which has fallen out of the Greek text; the R.V. has added it: "Thou, O Lord, according to thy great goodness hast promised repentance and forgiveness . . . that they may be saved." For another Syriac MS. see Mrs. Gibson in *Horæ Semiticæ* (1903).

[3] Edited by Sabatier, *op. cit.*, iii. 1038 ff.

[4] *Proceedings of the Soc. for Bibl. Arch.*, xxxi. 89 ff. (1909).

[5] Ryssel, *op. cit.*, i. 168.

THE FIRST BOOK OF MACCABEES

I. TITLE

In the Septuagint MSS. the title is Μακκαβαίων α′; the book figures in two uncials (א A), otherwise only in cursives. Cod. B contains none of the books of the Maccabees since it follows the Canon of Athanasius in which they are not included.[1] Origen, in his list of Biblical books (Eusebius, *Hist. Eccl.*, vi. 25, 2), gives the title as τὰ Μακκαβαϊκά, *i.e.* the Maccabæan Acts, and he adds ἅπερ ἐπιγέγραπται Σαρβηθ Σαβαναιέλ; if we may suppose the last word to be a corruption of " Israel " the words would represent the Hebrew שַׂר בֵּית יִשְׂרָאֵל, " a prince of the house of Israel ";[2] the meaning, however, of Σαρβὴθ Σαβαναιέλ must be regarded as very uncertain.[3]

II. THE ORIGINAL LANGUAGE OF THE BOOK

Origen's title would suggest that the book was written in Hebrew, and this is definitely stated by Jerome to have been the case, for in the *Prologus Galeatus* he says: *Machabæorum primum librum Hebraicum reperi.* This is entirely borne out by the study of the Greek text which again and again betrays translation from the Hebrew; and many curious expressions in the Greek are fully accounted for on the supposition of a Hebrew original. Moreover, Hebrew, rather than Aramaic, would be the natural language to be employed for a literary purpose by a Palestinian Jew, especially in this case, where the writer's intention was to follow the pattern of the Old Testament historical books.

[1] Swete, *Introduction to the Old Testament in Greek*, pp. 203 f. (1900).

[2] Cp. xiv. 27, 28. Asaramel = Saramel, in Hebrew שַׂר עַם אֵל " prince of the people of God "; it is true, the MSS. have ἐν before the name, but this must be an error on the part of some copyist who thought that it was a place-name, not realizing that it was a title given to Simon. The Syriac Version has " a prince of Israel."

[3] See further, Hastings' *D.B.*, iii. 188 note.

III. DATE

The approximate date of our book is not difficult to determine. It must have been written before the capture of Jerusalem by Pompey in B.C. 63 as there is no hint in the book of Roman enmity or overlordship; on the contrary, the friendly relationship existing between Rome and the Jews is taken for granted. On the other hand, since the history is brought down to the death of John Hyrcanus in B.C. 104/3 (xvi. 24) it was written after that date. Not only so, but it must have been some time after this year that it was compiled, since it is a *written account* of the reign of John Hyrcanus that is mentioned in xvi. 24; so that some years must have intervened to allow time for this Chronicle to have been compiled. It must also be added that the general impression conveyed by the book is that it was written some appreciable time after the events recorded; see, *e.g.*, xiii. 30: " This is the sepulchre which he made at Modin, (and it is there) unto this day." The approximate date may therefore be given as B.C. 90–70, the later limit being the more probable. This is, however, not to deny that some portions of the book have been interpolated at a much later date (see further § IV).[1]

On the other hand, it is only right to point out that, while this date is widely accepted, some scholars hold a different view, notably Torrey, who says: " The theory best accounting for all the facts—and no really plausible argument can be used against it—would seem to be, that the greater part of this history was composed and written under the inspiration of Simon's glorious reign, and that it was finished in the early part of the reign of John Hyrcanus. That is, the book was probably written between B.C. 140 and 125." [2] To say that " no really plausible argument can be used against " this view is an over-statement; we recognize the strength of his own arguments, which would take up too much space for quotation here, but we are not wholly convinced by them.

[1] On the coins of the Maccabæans see Willrich in *Z.A.T.W.*, 1933, pp. 78 f.
[2] *Encycl. Bibl.* iii. 2860.

IV. Sources

Inasmuch as the history of our book covers a period of over seventy years—apart from the references to Alexander the Great in the introductory verses—and that it was not compiled, in all probability, until some twenty or thirty years after the death of John Hyrcanus in B.C. 104/3, it is evident that the compiler must have made use of written documents. He may well have utilized the reminiscences of some who had lived during the troublous times, and he may himself have witnessed some of the occurrences which happened towards the end of the period; but there can be no doubt that he was mainly indebted to written sources for his compilation.

For the most part, we have no means of knowing what these sources were, but some few indications there are.

Direct mention is made of one source in xvi. 24, already referred to, viz. the Chronicles of John Hyrcanus' High-priesthood; true, the compiler made no use of this, but the mention of it shows that the utilization of sources was in his mind. A possible source may be implied in ix. 22 where it is said: " And the rest of the acts of Judas, and his wars, and the valiant deeds which he did, and his greatness, they are not written," by which the writer may have meant unrecorded acts as distinguished from those which had been written down; the fact that he uses the phraseology of the Old Testament, which in this connexion is always used in reference to written sources, would support this. But more definite, though of a different kind, are the sources mentioned in xi. 37, xiv. 18 ff., 27.

It is also possible that excerpts from sources of a yet different character may be discerned in such passages as: i. 25–28, 36–40; ii. 8–12, 44; iii. 3–9, 45; ix. 41; xiv. 6–15; these are clearly poetical pieces; and while it is, of course, possible that they were the work of the compiler himself, their very different character and style from the rest of the book point rather to their being quotations from some popular collections of lyrics or religious poems; that in one instance this can be proved to have been the case supports this, for vii. 17 is a quotation from Ps. lxxix. 2, 3.

But, quite apart from what has been said, there are a larger number of what purport to be original written documents, or rather copies of these. Before discussing these important sources, it will be well to enumerate them; they fall into different categories:

I. *Documents relating to internal Jewish affairs :*
- (*a*) A letter from the Jews in Gilead to Jonathan and his brethren (v. 10–13).
- (*b*) The decree making the High-priesthood hereditary in the Hasmonæan family (xiv. 27–45).

II. *Documents concerning the relations between the Jews and Rome :*
- (*a*) A letter from the Roman Senate to the Jewish people (viii. 23–32).
- (*b*) A circular letter from the Romans " to the kings and to the countries " (xv. 16–21).

III. *Documents concerning the relations between Sparta and the Jews :*
- (*a*) A letter from Jonathan to the Spartans (xii. 6–18).
- (*b*) A letter from the king of Sparta to the High-priest Onias I (xii. 20–23).
- (*c*) A letter from the Spartans to Simon (xiv. 20–23).

IV. *Documents purporting to be communications from the Syrian kings to the Jewish High-priests :*
- (*a*) Demetrius I to Jonathan (x. 3–6).
- (*b*) Alexander Balas to Jonathan (x. 18–20).
- (*c*) Demetrius I to Jonathan, representing the Jewish people (x. 25–45).
- (*d*) Demetrius II to Jonathan (xi. 29–37).
- (*e*) Demetrius II to Simon (xiii. 36–40).
- (*f*) Antiochus VII Sidetes to Simon (xv. 1–9).

Regarding the first two of these there is every reason to

believe in their authenticity. But as to those under II some difficulties present themselves. The first purports to contain the details of a " league of amity and confederacy " between Rome and " the nation of the Jews "; the date is B.C. 161, and it is Judas who is said to have taken the initiative in proposing the pact (viii. 1, 17), although he represented only a section of the Jews, and that in opposition to the recognized Jewish government. One would have expected the negotiations for a league of this kind to have been conducted and concluded with the official head of the nation, the High-priest; that he, together with the governing body and their following, were called the " ungodly " by the Maccabæan revolters would not have been likely to have affected the Roman Senate. So that an initial suspicion is raised regarding this document. It must also be objected that for Rome to recognize the independence of the Jewish State would have meant war with the Syrian power. It is true that Rome had given Timarchus " verbal recognition, but no material help," [1] so that it might be said that Rome merely recognized Jewish independence in order to embarrass Demetrius, without intending to go to the length of fighting on behalf of the Jews. To this, however, it must be said that the two cases are hardly parallel; there is a great difference between the " verbal recognition " of Timarchus and a formal written engagement in which it is definitely stated that Rome will fight " by sea and by land " on behalf of the Jews (viii. 32). So that the objection holds good that for Rome to have recognized the independence of the Jewish State would have meant war, for it is evident that *at this period* Rome had no intention of becoming embroiled in a Syrian war. It must also be pointed out that the reference to ships in viii. 26, 28, and therefore harbours, is quite inappropriate during the leadership of Judas. These objections, dealt with by Willrich, support his contention that while, in itself, the document in question may be genuine enough, it does not belong to this period of Jewish history; [2] it was inserted in the text at a much later time

[1] *The Cambridge Ancient History*, viii. 521 (1930).
[2] See further, Willrich, *Urkundenfälschung in der hellenistisch-jüdischen Literatur;*

with the object of enhancing the *prestige* of the Maccabæans.
Chap. ix follows logically after chap. vii.

The second document under II (xv. 16–21), containing the
circular letter from Rome, has also been inserted in the text for
a similar reason, as can be seen from Josephus, *Antiq.* xiv. 143 ff.;
it really belongs to the time of Hyrcanus II (B.C. 75/4–40).

The third class of documents, which deal with the supposed relations of the Jews and the Spartans, cannot be
regarded as authentic, and for these reasons: it must first
be noted that the three passages concerned are obviously
not an indispensable part in their respective contexts,
thereby suggesting the possibility of their having been
subsequently interpolated. The letter from Jonathan to
the Spartans (xii. 6–18) is, on the face of it, pointless in its
present connexion. As to the letter of Areus, the Spartan
king, to the High-priest Onias (xii. 20–23), it is sufficient,
apart from other objections, to point to what is said in
verse 21 about the Spartans and the Jews being all descended from Abraham, in order to see that the letter cannot
be genuine. The letter from the Spartans to Simon (xiv.
20–23) must likewise be regarded as a later insertion;
in the preceding verses, which purport to explain the reason
why this letter was sent, reference is made (verse 18) to a
previous " confederacy," said to have been made between
the Spartans and Judas; but there is no earlier reference
to this; if such a treaty had ever been entered into it would
undoubtedly have found mention. Further, it is said in
verse 22 that Numenius came to renew friendship; but,
according to verse 24, it was only after the letter had been
received that Simon sent Numenius to Rome.

The irrelevances and inconsistencies of these letters make
it highly improbable that they belonged to the book as
originally written.

As to the fourth class, comprising letters purporting to
have been written by Syrian kings to the Maccabæan
leaders, Willrich [1] has subjected these to a rigorously critical

---

pp. 44 ff. (1924). It is also to be noted that the subject is not mentioned in
II Macc.; but see Josephus, *Antiq.* xii. 414–419.

[1] *Op. cit.*, pp. 36–44.

examination; to go into the details of this here would take
up too much space; it must suffice to say that his arguments
are most convincing, and it is difficult to see how they can
be refuted; with his conclusions we must confess ourselves
to be in entire agreement; all these letters, and to them must
be added the correspondence with the Spartans, are, in all
probability, excerpts from the work of Jason of Cyrene
(see below, p. 315), and were interpolated into the text
of *I Maccabees* by a scribe at a later period; his object was,
doubtless, that to which reference has already been made,
viz.: the glorification of the Maccabæan leaders.

Our conclusion, then, is that the compiler of *I Maccabees*
relied, in the first instance, on one or more written sources,
of which, otherwise, we have no knowledge; the extracts
from these he supplemented by details gathered from the
reminiscences and accounts of eye-witnesses of some of
the events which he records. It is probable, further, that
the compiler inserted here and there quotations from
familiar collections of religious poems in order to enhance
the effect of his accounts. In at least two instances he
quotes from Jewish documents (v. 10–13; xiv. 27–45).

The other official documents quoted (and this applies
especially to the communications from some of the Syrian
kings to the Maccabæan leaders) do not belong to the
original form of the book; they were added in later times
by one who desired to glorify the first heroes of the Maccabæan family; his probable purpose, though unexpressed,
was to contrast them with the later degenerate scions of the
Hasmonæan dynasty.

V. CHARACTERISTICS OF THE BOOK

The way in which the history is presented invites confidence in its general veracity; the narrative is sober and
straightforward; there is, as a rule, a noticeable absence of
exaggeration, and especially of the miraculous element
which is so marked in *II Maccabees*. The compiler was
concerned with stating the facts in their bare simplicity;
and they were, in truth, from the Jewish point of view,

sufficiently remarkable not to need embroidery of any kind. The reliability of the record is confirmed by the numerous dates which are given.[1]

The writer was a loyal adherent of the Law, though not in the later, Pharisaic sense. While evincing an ardent belief and trust in God (iii. 53, 60; iv. 8–11, 30–33; ix. 46; xii. 15 and elsewhere), it is noteworthy that he never ascribes the victories of the Maccabæan leaders to any act of divine interposition; success in battle is due to good generalship and political foresight; that the name of God is never mentioned in the book is far from implying any lack of religious belief; it is simply due to the conviction that if men play their part faithfully in the affairs of the world an over-ruling divine guidance will aid them; that is implicit; there is no need to talk about it.

Another characteristic appearing throughout the book is the writer's glorification of the Maccabæan family; the outstanding achievements emphasized are: the securing of religious freedom, gained by Judas, the acquisition of territory owing to the genius of Jonathan, and the yearned-for position of political independence achieved by Simon. These are the culminating events of the Maccabæan struggle which in each case receive due emphasis, showing the special tendency on the part of the writer.

VI. Contents of the Book

A brief summary of the contents of the book:

I. Introductory (i. 1–64).

Alexander's conquest of the Persian empire; his death, and the division of his world-empire among his generals (i. 1–9), cp. II. Macc. iv. 7.

The accession to the Syrian throne of Antiochus IV Epiphanes; his Egyptian campaign. The plundering and

---

[1] Regarding these dates it must be pointed out that Kolbe (*Beiträge zur syrischen und jüdischen Geschichte* [1926]) has proved that the Seleucid era began in the spring of B.C. 311 (not B.C. 312 as has been hitherto held), so that the dates given in the margin of the Revised Version must be put forward one year. See also Schürer, *Geschichte des jüdischen Volkes*, i. 32 ff. (1901), Nowack, *Hebräische Archäologie* i. 218–220 (1894).

desecration of the Temple in Jerusalem. The attempt on the part of Antiochus, aided by the hellenistic Jews in Jerusalem, to stamp out the religion of the Jews (i. 10–64), cp. II Macc. v. 11–21.

II. The beginning of the Maccabæan revolt (ii. 1–70).

Mattathias, a priest of the house of Asmonæus, initiates the revolt (ii. 1–70, *Antiq.* xii. 265–285).

III. The leadership of Judas, called Maccabæus [1] (iii. 1.–ix. 22).

The victories of Judas over the Syrian forces under Apollonius and Seron (iii. 1–26; *Antiq.* xii. 287–292; cp. II Macc. viii. 1–7). Antiochus Epiphanes, having gone into Persia, appoints Lysias to take charge of affairs in Syria during his absence (iii. 27–37; *Antiq.* xii. 293–297; cp. II Macc. v. 1). Lysias commissions Ptolemy, Nicanor, and Gorgias to attack Judas (iii. 38–60; cp. II Macc. viii. 8–29; x. 14; xi. 1–15; *Antiq.* xii. 298–304, II Macc. viii. 8, 9, 23–29). The victory of Judas over Gorgias (iv. 1–25, *Antiq.* xii. 305–312).

Lysias is defeated by Judas (iv. 26–35; cp. II Macc. xi. 1–13; *Antiq.* xii. 313–315).[2] The re-dedication of the Temple, and the inauguration of the feast of Hanukkah (iv. 36–61; cp. II Macc. i. 18, viii. 31 f., x. 1–8; *Antiq.* xii. 316–326).

Judas punishes the Idumæans, the Bæans, and the Ammonites (v. 1–8; cp. II Macc. x. 15–23; *Antiq.* xii. 327–329).

The Jews in Gilead entreat the help of Judas against the Gentiles; Judas sends his brother Simon against the latter; he, with his brother Jonathan, goes to Gilead; both are successful in subduing the Gentiles (v. 9–54; *Antiq.* xii. 330–340).

During the absence of Judas and his brothers, two " rulers of the host," Joseph and Azarias, who had been charged to defend Judæa (see v. 18, 19), " thinking to do some exploit,"

---

[1] Usually explained as meaning the " Hammerer."
[2] Kolbe (*op. cit.*, pp. 79 ff.), by a careful comparison between I Macc. iv. 26–35 and II Macc. xi. 1–15, as well as between I Macc. vi. 28–63 and II Macc. xiii. 1–26, concludes that Lysias undertook one campaign only, that mentioned below (I Macc. vi. 28–63).

moved towards Jamnia with their forces to attack Gorgias; but they are defeated (v. 55–62; *Antiq.* xii. 350–352; II Macc. xii. 1, 2). Further successes of Judas in the south of Palestine (v. 63–68; *Antiq.* xii. 353). An abortive attempt on the part of Antiochus Epiphanes to plunder Elymais, a rich city in Persia; he returns to Babylon (vi. 1–13; cp. II Macc. i. 12, 13; *Antiq.* xii. 354, 355). News is brought to him there of the defeat of Lysias by Judas; he is represented as having been so affected by this that he died, after having first repented for having robbed the Temple in Jerusalem and having caused the death of so many Jews (vi. 1–13; cp. II Macc. i. 14–17, x. 9; *Antiq.* xii. 356–359).

Philip, having been appointed regent by Antiochus Epiphanes before he died, during the minority of Antiochus Eupator, is ousted by Lysias, who himself assumes the regency (vi. 14–17; *Antiq.* xii. 360–361).

Judas besieges the citadel in Jerusalem (vi. 18–27; *Antiq.* xii. 362, 363).

Lysias, who is accompanied by the boy-king Antiochus Eupator, undertakes another campaign [1] against Judas. Lysias is successful; but being called back to his own country owing to the threatening attitude of Philip, he makes a treaty of peace with Judas (vi. 28–63; cp. II Macc. xiii. 1–26; *Antiq.* xii. 366–382).

Demetrius I becomes king of Syria; Antiochus Eupator and Lysias are put to death (vii. 1–4; II Macc. xiv. 1, 2; *Antiq.* xii. 389–390).

Alkimus, at the head of the Jewish hellenistic party, seeks the High-priesthood; he is appointed to the office by Demetrius I; Bacchides is sent with an army to Judæa to support him (vii. 5–9; II Macc. xiv. 3–14; [2] *Antiq.* xii. 385, 393).

The treachery of Bacchides and Alkimus; Bacchides returns to Antioch (vii. 5–20; *Antiq.* xii. 394–397).

Judas and Alkimus; the latter again appeals to the Syrian king for help (vii. 21–25; *Antiq.* xii. 398–401).

[1] See footnote 2 on p. 308.
[2] But the course of events is confused in *II Macc.*

Nicanor is sent to Judæa by Demetrius I; he attacks
Judas; the battle of Adasa; Nicanor is defeated and slain
(vii. 26–50; II Macc. xv. 1–36; *Antiq.* xii. 402–412).

The course of the narrative is broken by the insertion of
an account of a treaty between Judas and the Romans
(viii. 1–32).

The history is taken up again; Demetrius I, hearing of
the death of Nicanor, sends Bacchides into Judæa again;
the battle of Elasa; the death of Judas (ix. 1–22; *Antiq.*
xii. 420–434).

IV. The Leadership of Jonathan (ix. 23–xii. 53).

The evil plight of the orthodox party on the death of
Judas; Jonathan is chosen in his place (ix. 23–31; *Antiq.*
xiii. 1–6).

The conflict between Bacchides and Jonathan; initial
successes of the former (ix. 32–53; *Antiq.* xiii. 7–21).

The death of Alkimus (ix. 54–56; *Antiq.* xii. 414).

Bacchides makes peace with Jonathan, and returns to
Antioch (ix. 57; *Antiq.* xiii. 22).

Two years of peace, after which Bacchides, stirred up by
the hellenistic Jews, again attacks Jonathan; Bacchides is
worsted by Simon, in consequence of which a peace is
arranged; Bacchides returns to Antioch; " and Jonathan
began to judge the people, and destroyed the ungodly out
of Israel " (ix. 57–73; *Antiq.* xiii. 22–34).

Alexander Balas aspires to the Syrian throne; thereupon
Demetrius I seeks the support of Jonathan, promising him
various privileges (x. 1–14; *Antiq.* xiii. 35–42).

Alexander Balas outbids Demetrius I by appointing
Jonathan to the High-priesthood (x. 15–21; *Antiq.* xiii.
43–46). Demetrius I makes a further bid for the support
of Jonathan by offering him extravagant privileges; these
Jonathan spurns as being unworthy of credence; he remains
faithful to Alexander Balas (x. 22–47; *Antiq.* xiii. 47–57;
Josephus does not refer to Jonathan's refusal of the terms).

The battle between Demetrius I and Alexander Balas;
death of the former (x. 48–50; *Antiq.* xiii. 58–61, a more
detailed account).

The treaty between Alexander Balas and Ptolemy VI, king of Egypt (x. 51–58; *Antiq.* xiii. 80–82).

The favour shown by Alexander Balas to Jonathan (x. 59–66; *Antiq.* xiii. 83–85).

Demetrius II, the rightful heir to the Syrian throne, appears in Syria to make good his claim; he is supported by Apollonius, who threatens Jonathan as the partisan of Alexander Balas (x. 67–73; *Antiq.* xiii. 86–90).

The struggle between Apollonius and Jonathan, in which the latter is victorious; he is rewarded by Alexander Balas (x. 74–89; *Antiq.* xiii. 91–102).

The alliance between Demetrius II and Ptolemy VI against Alexander Balas (xi. 1–15; *Antiq.* xiii. 109–115).

The death of Alexander Balas, followed by that of Ptolemy VI; Demetrius II becomes undisputed king of Syria (xi. 15–19; *Antiq.* xiii. 117–119, 120).

Jonathan besieges the citadel at Jerusalem; the hellenistic Jews appeal to Demetrius II; this move is countered by Jonathan; he gains the favour of Demetrius II, who grants him privileges (xi. 20–37; *Antiq.* xiii. 121–128).

Tryphon, a military adventurer, champions the cause of the son of Alexander Balas, Antiochus (VI), as a claimant to the Syrian throne (xi. 38–40; *Antiq.* xiii. 131).

Demetrius II seeks the help of Jonathan; this is granted; but soon after Jonathan transfers his allegiance to Tryphon; for this he is rewarded by Tryphon (xi. 41–62; *Antiq.* xiii. 133–153; Josephus gives a more detailed account).

Demetrius II sends an army against Jonathan; victory of the latter; (xi. 63–74; *Antiq.* xiii. 154–162).

Jonathan's renewal of the league of friendship with Rome, and with the Spartans (xii. 1–23; *Antiq.* xiii. 163–170).

Jonathan successfully attacks the army of Demetrius II (xii. 24–38; *Antiq.* xiii. 174–178).

Tryphon, fearing the growing power of Jonathan, sends an army against him; a battle is avoided, but Jonathan is treacherously murdered (xii. 39–53; *Antiq.* xiii. 187–196, 209).

x

V. The Leadership of Simon (xiii. 1–xvi. 24).

Simon is chosen as leader in place of his brother (xiii. 1–11; *Antiq.* xiii. 197–201). Tryphon determines to attack Simon, but thinks better of it, and retires (xiii. 12–24; *Antiq.* xiii. 203–209).

Simon erects a monument in honour of Jonathan (xiii. 25–30; *Antiq.* 211, 212). Tryphon murders Antiochus VI and assumes the diadem (xiii. 31–34; *Antiq.* xiii. 218, 219).

Demetrius II [1] grants independence to Simon, and confirms him in the High-priesthood (xiii. 35–42; this is not mentioned by Josephus).

Further successes of Simon (xiii. 43–53, not mentioned by Josephus).

Demetrius II makes an expedition into Parthia; he is captured by king Arsaces (xiv. 1–3; this section is clearly out of place; see *Antiq.* xiii. 184–186).

A period of peace for the Jews (xiv. 4–15; cp. *Antiq.* xiii. 227).

Renewal of the league of friendship with Rome, and with the Spartans (xiv. 16–24; cp. *Antiq.* xiii. 227).

The High-priesthood made hereditary in the Hasmonæan family (xiv. 25–49; not mentioned by Josephus, though Simon's High-priesthood is referred to in *Antiq.* xiii. 213).

The letter of Antiochus VII Sidetes, to Simon, granting him various privileges (xv. 1–9; with this contrast what is said in *Antiq.* xiii. 223, 224).

Antiochus VII attacks Tryphon, and besieges him in Dor (xv. 10–14; *Antiq.* xiii. 223).

A circular letter from the Romans to Simon and other rulers (xv. 15–24; not mentioned by Josephus).

Antiochus VII continues the siege of Dor; Simon offers him support, but this is refused; Antiochus VII breaks his friendship with Simon, and sends Athenobius to receive tribute; this Simon refuses (xv. 25–37; not mentioned by Josephus).

Antiochus VII sends Kendebæus against Simon; he is defeated by Simon's sons, Judas and John (xv. 38–xvi. 10; *Antiq.* xiii. 225–227).

---

[1] He had been taken prisoner by the Parthians in whose hands he was held, though well treated, from B.C. 139/8–129, when he once more ruled in Syria.

The murder of Simon (xvi. 11–22; *Antiq.* xiii. 228).

A reference to the reign of John Hyrcanus (xvi. 23, 24; *Antiq.* xiii. 229, 230).

VII. THE GREEK TEXT AND THE VERSIONS

The Greek text of I Macc. is contained in three uncials: Cod. ℵ (fourth century), Cod. A (fifth century), and Cod. V (eighth or ninth century),[1] and in fifteen cursives, ranging from the fifth to the fourteenth centuries.[2]

Where the text, in essentials, has been so well preserved there is not much to choose among the three uncials, though, upon the whole, those of ℵ and V, especially the former, are better than A; there can be no doubt that all three are the offspring of a single Greek MS., which must belong to a time soon after the original Hebrew was written.

Probably the most important of the cursives is that numbered 55; this MS. in a number of instances has retained a better form of text than the uncials or other cursives (*e.g.* in iii. 47, 48, 49; iv. 61; v. 22, 67; vii. 7, 38); it may well represent some early MS. differing from that which was the parent of the three uncials. The cursive numbered 71 is also interesting for a different reason, viz. its omissions, which are evidently not due to carelessness, but of set purpose, for they do not disturb the course of the narrative; on the contrary, the text is not infrequently improved by the omission. This may represent an attempt at abbreviation; or it may be the echo of some early Greek recension. Together with the cursives numbered 19, 64, and 93, this MS. is Lucianic in character, a curious fact, inasmuch as Lucianic MSS. tend to contain additions rather than omissions.

There are only two Versions, which come into consideration:[3]

(i) The Syriac: this exists in two forms; that contained

---

[1] Swete, *The Old Testament in Greek*, iii. 594–661 (1899), gives the text of Cod. A with the various readings of Codd. ℵV.

[2] See Holmes and Parsons, *Vetus Testamentum Graecum cum variis lectionibus* . . . v. (1827) for the variant readings of these.

[3] On the absence of *I, II Macc.* in the Ethiopic Version see Rahlfs in *Z.A.T.W.* for 1908, pp. 63 f.

in the *Peshitta*, which, following the cursives 19, 64, 93, represents the Lucianic recension;[1] and that which is represented in the sixth-century *Cod. Ambrosianus*;[2] this follows, in the main, the text of the Greek uncials; it is preserved only up to I Macc. xiv. 25ª.

(ii) *The Latin*: this is also preserved in two forms; that contained in the Vulgate, and a text represented in *Cod. Sangermanensis* (up to the beginning of chap. xiv); both these are forms of the Old Latin, *i.e.* pre-hieronymian;[3] and they are translated from the Greek.

VIII. LITERATURE

Grimm, in *Kurzgefasstes Exeget. Handbuch* . . . iii. pp. i ff. and 1 ff. (1853).

Bissell, in Lange-Schaff's *Commentary* . . . (1880).

Rawlinson, in Wace, *op. cit.*, ii. 373 ff. (1888).

Zöckler, *Die Apokr. des Alten Testamentes* . . . (1891).

Fairweather and Black, *The First Book of Maccabees* (1897).

Weiss, *Judas Makkabäus* (1897).

Kautzsch, *op. cit.*, i. 24 ff. (1900).

Schürer, *op. cit.*, i. 32–40 (1901), iii. 192–200 (1909).

André, *op. cit.*, pp. 65 ff. (1903).

Knabenbauer, "Commentarius in duos libros Machabæorum" (in *Cursus scripturæ sacræ*) (1907).

Bevenot, in Feldmann und Herkenne, *Die heilige Schrift des Alten Testamentes* (1931).

[1] Edited by Lagarde, *Libri vet. test. apocryphi Syriace* . . . (1861).
[2] Edited by Ceriani in photographic facsimile 1876. See G. Schmidt, "Die beiden syrischen Übersetzungen des 1. Makkabäerbuchs," in *Z.A.T.W.* for 1897, pp. 1 ff. 233 ff.
[3] Edited by Sabatier, *Bibl. sacra Latinæ versiones antiquæ*, ii. 1017 ff. (1743, etc.); see also De Bruyne-Sodar, *Les anciennes traductions latines des Machabées* (1932).

THE SECOND BOOK OF MACCABEES

I. Title, Author, and Characteristics of the Book

In the two uncials A and V the title is Μακκαβαίων β', and this is followed in all the cursives. As pointed out above, Cod. B does not include any of the books of the *Maccabees; II Maccabees* does not figure in Cod. ℵ. *II Maccabees* is not a continuation of *I Maccabees*, but deals with part of the history contained in this latter. That, unlike *I Maccabees*, our book was originally written in Greek is generally acknowledged.

The main part of the book is said to be an abbreviation of the history of Jason of Cyrene (ii. 23). The truth of this is borne out by the way in which the material is presented; the narrative consists of broken pieces, thrown down in a somewhat haphazard fashion, without historical sequence. An author writing his own work would not be guilty of such literary slovenliness; the difficulty which the Epitomist experienced in making his extracts must be his excuse for this; he says it was a " painful labour," a matter of " sweat and watching " (ii. 26). Whether the irritating verbosity, so characteristic of the book, was imitated from Jason, or whether this is the style of the Epitomist, it is certainly an unattractive element in the work.

A striking thing about the book is its Pharisaic spirit and general tendency; this was long ago convincingly shown by Geiger:[1] Sabbath observance is noted in I Macc. ii. 32–38, but it is abrogated in case of need during war time (ii. 40, 41), and it would appear that even the *Ḥasidim* acquiesced in this; but in *II Maccabees* the whole spirit of its observance is different (v. 25, viii. 26, xii. 38; xv. 1 ff.; the last reads almost like a protest against I Macc. ii. 40, 41);

[1] *Urschrift und Uebersetzungen der Bibel*, pp. 219 (1857).

315

it is the later, specifically Pharisaic, attitude. Again, belief in the resurrection was ardently taught by the Pharisees, and we have a striking instance of this in the story of the martyrdom of the seven sons and their mother (vii); thus in verse 9 one of the martyrs cries: " . . . the King of the world shall raise us up, who have died for his laws, unto an eternal renewal of life" (see also verses 14, 23, 29, 36). The Pharisaic attitude is further seen in the long drawn-out account of the martyrdom of Eleazar, "one of the principal scribes" (vi. 18 ff.); the scribes were predominantly members of the Pharisaic party.

From the point of view of the history of Jewish parties during the last pre-Christian century this pro-Pharisaic bias is of special interest because of its strongly anti-Has-monæan animus which is both subtly implied as well as explicitly set forth. In x. i, e.g., it is said that "Macca-bæus and they that were with him, the Lord leading them on, recovered the temple and the city"; the words, "the Lord leading them on" are evidently intended as an implicit rebuke, since in the parallel narrative in I Macc. iv. 36 ff. it is Judas and his brethren, with never a hint of divine help, who accomplish this. Again, in xv. 1 ff., where it is a question of fighting on the Sabbath, Nicanor is made to ask whether there is a Sovereign in heaven that had commanded to keep the Sabbath day; the reply is: "There is the Lord, living himself a Sovereign in heaven, who bade us observe the seventh day"; it is then added that Nicanor was not able to execute his purpose of fighting against the Jews on the Sabbath. Here we have another implicit hit at the Hasmonæans who, according to I Macc. ii. 40, 41, decided that fighting on the Sabbath was justified under certain circumstances.

In addition to these covert rebukes there are one or two instances of a more direct kind; thus, in x. 20 ff. Simon is charged with covetousness, and the Maccabæan brothers with their followers are represented as having fallen out; whether this was historically true or not there is not a word about it in *I Maccabees*. And, once more, in xiv. 17 Simon is said to have suffered a reverse at the hands of Nicanor;

but in the much fuller account of Nicanor's fighting, in I Macc. vii. 26 ff., nothing is said of any reverse overtaking Simon. It is possible that *II Maccabees* has here preserved a detail wanting in the older book; nevertheless, the far more reliable history of *I Maccabees* makes it more probable that this is merely an anti-Hasmonæan thrust on the part of the Pharisaic writer. The most significant fact, however, about this attitude is the protest of the writer of *II Maccabees* against the exclusive claims of the Hasmonæans and their Sadducæan partisans, expressed in the words: "Now God, who saved all his people, and restored the heritage to all, and the kingdom, and the priesthood, and the hallowing, even as he promised through the law,—in God have we hope, that he will quickly have mercy on us, and gather us together out of all the earth into the holy place . . ." (ii. 17, 18). There can be no shadow of doubt as to what is implied by these words.[1]

One thing is, however, noteworthy in this connexion; although *II Maccabees* must be regarded as definitely anti-Hasmonæan, there is never a word said against Judas; indeed, in so far as the book is concerned with the Maccabæan struggle, *his* exploits alone are dealt with, so that there would have been ample scope for seeking anything against him had such been the wish of the writer. The reason why Judas is not only not found fault with, but is placed in the position of *the* Maccabæan, to the exclusion of his brothers, brings us to another characteristic of the book connected with Pharisaism. This is connected with the two feasts mentioned in the book, in regard to each of which Judas appears as the really important person concerned, viz. the feast of Ḥanukkah, and the feast of Nicanor.

It is doubtless of set purpose that these feasts are described at the close of each of the two divisions, respectively, of our book; the intention being by this means to stress their importance. As religious institutions they would naturally have appealed to the Pharisaic Epitomist.

[1] For the antagonism between the Pharisees and the Hasmonæans with their Sadducæan following, which began as early as the reign of John Hyrcanus, (B.C. 134/3–104/3), see Oesterley and Robinson, *A History of Israel*, ii. 282 ff. (1933).

Regarding the feast of *Ḥanukkah* it is said in x. 6–8:
"And they kept eight days with gladness in the manner of
(the feast of) Tabernacles. . . . They ordained also with
a common statute and decree, for all the nation of the
Jews, that they should keep these days every year." Further-
more, in his long Preface, the Epitomist is almost entirely
concerned with this feast and with what he regards as
precedents in justification of its inauguration.

Then as to the feast of Nicanor, which is, naturally
enough, of far less importance, after Judas' defeat of the
Syrian forces, it is said: "And they all ordained with a
common decree in no wise to let this day pass undistin-
guished, but to mark with honour the thirteenth day of
the twelfth month. . . ." (xv. 36).

It is hardly necessary to say that neither of these feasts
had Biblical authority; and yet they were evidently very
popular, and the former at any rate, has been observed
ever since.[1] But feasts which were of Hasmonæan origin,
and without the sanction of the Law can hardly have been
regarded with favour in Pharisaic circles. To abrogate
them was out of the question for they had become settled
institutions; the only thing to be done, therefore, was to
discover some point of attachment between the feasts in
question and feasts of Biblical authority. Hochfeld[2] points
to the expression in II Macc. i. 9, 18, σκηνοπηγία τοῦ
χασελεῦ μηνός ("the feast of tabernacles of the month Chislev") as a description of the feast of *Ḥanukkah*, and the
reference in connexion therewith to the feast of Tabernacles
proper (*Sukkôth*) in x. 6; what was needed, he says, was a
Biblical feast by means of which *Ḥanukkah* could be brought
into the circle of the feasts of ancient tradition. For this
purpose *Sukkôth* commended itself both because chrono-
logically they were close to one another (*Sukkôth* 15 Tishri
onwards, *Ḥanukkah* 25 Chislev onwards), and also because
of their similar duration of eight days; perhaps, moreover,
because the dedication of Solomon's temple (I Kgs. viii. 2)
also took place during *Sukkôth*. Thus, a point of attachment

[1] Nicanor's Day was not observed after the seventh century.
[2] In *Z.A.T.W.* for 1902, pp. 276 f.

was found for the feast of *Hanukkah* and a feast of the Law whereby it could be made acceptable to the Pharisees in spite of its origin; but the method of doing this was characteristically Pharisaic, and offers further support to the contention that the Epitomist was a Pharisee.

Regarding Nicanor's Day the process was not so successful; it is said in xv. 36: " . . . but to mark with honour the thirteenth day of the twelfth month (it is called Adar in the Syrian tongue) "; then the addition of the words " the day before the day of Mordecai " seems to be an attempt to connect it with the feast of *Purim* (see Esther ix. 17–19).

One other characteristic of the book to be noted is the love of the miraculous and of supernatural apparitions. The Epitomist prepares us for these in his Preface, where he speaks of " the manifestations that came from heaven unto those that vied with one another in manful deeds for the religion of the Jews " (ii. 21), as among the things which he is about to relate in his abridged form of Jason of Cyrene's work.

The first of these manifestations is described in chap. iii, where Heliodorus is prevented from robbing the Temple by the appearance of " a horse with a terrible rider upon him "; he is accompanied by two young men of great strength who stand on either side of Heliodorus and scourge him unceasingly, whereby he is made " to recognize the sovereignty of God." Presently the rider appears again, bidding Heliodorus give thanks to God that his life had been spared; this Heliodorus does, and all is well.[1]

The next description is much shorter, and somewhat pointless—perhaps due to the abridgement: for forty days, nearly, " throughout the city " armed horsemen appear in the sky, drawn up in battle array; they attack and retreat; but nothing definite happens (v. 2, 3). Whether in Jason's work this was in some way connected with the campaign of Antiochus Epiphanes in Egypt, which is referred to at the beginning of the section, it is impossible to say.

The next apparition described (x. 24–31) occurs in answer

[1] See, further, Nestle in the *Z.A.T.W.* for 1905, pp. 203 f.

to prayer; Judas Maccabæus is about to fight Timotheus; but he first joins with his soldiers in prayer that God will be " an enemy to their enemies and an adversary to their adversaries." They then enter into the battle, when five riders appear out of heaven, two of whom take Judas between them, cover him with their armour, and guard him from wounds, while they attack the enemy with arrows and thunderbolts with terrible effect. The victory is with Judas.

Finally, we have the account of how, on the approach of Lysias with his army, Judas and all the people prayed that the Lord would " send a good angel to save Israel." Thereupon they sallied forth to meet the enemy; and " there appeared at their head one on horseback in white apparel " ; this so heartened them that they fell upon the enemy like lions, and won a great victory (xi. 1–14).

While it must be acknowledged that there is an air of unreality about all these stories, it is only right to recognize that a genuine piety prompts the composer of them, whether Jason of Cyrene or the Epitomist; in nearly every case the apparition is the result of prayer; evidently, therefore, the narrator believed in the possibility of such apparitions in times of special stress; in so far as this testifies to a trust in divine protection it witnesses to deep religious conviction; if the ideas of the mode of divine interposition in the affairs of men strike us as *naïve*, it must be recognized that that is not the fault of the writer, but of his age. The credulousness of an unenlightened age should not be allowed to detract from the sincerity of the individual.

II. Date of the Book

An important factor in considering the date of our book is the question as to whether the writer was acquainted with *I Maccabees*; and the matter is complicated further by the uncertainty as to how far the Epitomist relied solely on Jason of Cyrene, and how far he added material of his own.[1] This, unfortunately, is not a question which can be answered with any certainty.

From what has been said in the previous section it will have been seen that there are strong grounds for the contention that the existence of *I Maccabees* is assumed in *II Maccabees*. It must also be asserted that the strongly marked Pharisaic tendency of the book, spoken of above, is too deep-seated to be regarded as belonging to the Epitomist alone; it was Jason of Cyrene himself who represented this attitude. As to the date of *I Maccabees*, we have seen reasons for regarding this as approximately B.C. 90–70 (see above, p. 301); therefore, on the present view, *II Maccabees* must at the earliest be later than this date, and this will apply to Jason's work equally with the book as we now have it. The breach between the Pharisees and the Hasmonæans took · place towards the end of the reign of John Hyrcanus, in the year B.C. 106; [2] some time must have elapsed before the breach had assumed such proportions as to find expression in written documents. On the other hand, our book was known to Philo (*Quod omn. prob. liber*, ii. 459 [Mangey]), who died about 40 A.D. A nearer date than, approximately, the middle of the last pre-Christian century for Jason's work hardly seems possible; nor is there anything to show how much time elapsed before the Epitomist undertook his work; it is certain only that it was written well before the death of Philo.

It is, however, necessary to point out that there is considerable difference of opinion as to the date both of Jason's work and of the book in its present form. An exhaustive list of opinions is not called for, but a few of those of well-known writers may be given.

Niese[3] believes that it was written before *I Maccabees*, an opinion with which very few scholars agree. Hochfeld, following Geiger, puts the year B.C. 106 as the *terminus a quo*, and the time of Herod, or the beginning of the Christian era, as the *terminus ad quem*. Schürer thinks that Jason wrote

[1] As Schürer says (*op. cit.*, iii. 485): " We do not know how much belongs to the Epitomist and how much to the original writer."
[2] Josephus, *Antiq.* xiii. 288–298.   [3] See literature, § VI.

not long after the year B.C. 161, while as to the Epitomist
" it can only be said that he is earlier than Philo." Kamphausen [1] dates the book in its present form as belonging
to " about the beginning of the Christian era "; and
Moffatt [1] holds that Jason's work may be dated " roughly
after B.C. 130," while " the epitome falls not later than the
first half of the first century B.C."

These few opinions, of a much larger number, are of
course the outcome of solid arguments; but to deal with
these here would take up far too much space. The question is undoubtedly a difficult one to decide within close
limits, but the main argument in coming to a decision must
rest, we believe, on the Pharisaic element in the book.

III. Historicity of the Book

Even more pronounced than the differences of opinion
regarding the date of our book are those held about its
historical value. Some scholars, such as Schlatter [1] and
Niese, place, as it seems to us, far too great a reliability on
its historical trustworthiness; others [2] depreciate it, perhaps
unduly. That *II Maccabees* has preserved some historical
data not recorded in *I Maccabees* may well be the fact; that
II Maccabees has distorted history in certain directions is
demonstrable; so that there is something to be said for each
of these two positions. But, upon the whole, it is probable,
we believe, that the depreciatory attitude is nearer the truth
than that which would place an exaggerated value on the
historical records of our book; and for these reasons:

(1) The marked contrast between the sober, straight-
forward, historical presentation of *I Maccabees*, and the exaggerated, often fantastic, statements in *II Maccabees*, together
with its chronological disorder, creates an unfavourable
impression regarding the reliability of this latter. (2) The
divergence between the two books must as a rule, though
there may be some exceptions, be decided in favour of
I Maccabees, a fact which detracts from the reliability of

---

[1] See literature, § VI.   [2] *E.g.* Willrich, Kosters.

II Maccabees. (3) The tendency of *II Maccabees* to subordinate the facts of history to the interests of Pharisaic propaganda must arouse suspicion as to the *bona fides* of *II Maccabees.*[1] (4) There are a number of historical mistakes in *II Maccabees* (iv. 21, ix. 2, 9; x. 11; xiii. 22, cp. I Macc. vi. 47; xv. 33, 37); whether due to ignorance, or other cause, such things undermine confidence.[2]

Thus, facts compel one to regard with considerable suspicion the historical reliability of *II Maccabees*, though it must be recognized that in some instances historical details which are peculiar to *II Maccabees* are based upon facts (*e.g.* chap. iii in parts), and in so far our book has a value for the study of the history of the period.

IV. CONTENTS OF THE BOOK

Introductory Letters (i. 1–ii. 18).

The Jews of Palestine send greetings to the Jews of Egypt. God's blessing is invoked on the latter. The sore trials through which the Palestinian Jews had passed are briefly referred to, special mention being made of the evil perpetrated by Jason and his following. The greeting concludes with an exhortation to the Egyptian Jews to observe the feast of Tabernacles in the month Chislev, *i.e.* the festival of the Dedication of the Temple (i. 1–10[a]).

A second letter from the Palestinian Jews to the Jews of Egypt, in which the exhortation to observe the feast oɪ Tabernacles in the month Chislev is repeated (verses 13–16 are in parentheses). Precedents from past history regarding the re-kindling of the altar fire (i. 10[b]–ii. 18).[3]

---

[1] See Geiger, *op. cit.*, pp. 219 ff.; Wellhausen, *Die Pharisäer und Sadduzäer*, p. 82 (1874).

[2] See further, Willrich, *Urkundenfälschung* . . ., pp. 44–57.

[3] Willrich, *Juden und Griechen vor der makkabäischen Erhebung*, pp. 76 f. (1895); Büchler, *Das Sendschreiben der Jerusalemer an die Juden in Aegypten* . . . in "Monatschr. f. Gesch. u. Wissensch. des Judenthums," pp. 481–500, 529–554 (1897); Torrey, "Die Briefe ii. Makk." i. 1–18, in the *Z.A.T.W.* for 1900, pp. 225–242; Herkenne, "Die Briefe zu Beginn des Zweiten Makkabäerbuches," in Bardenhewer's *Biblische Studien*, viii. 4 (1904); Laqueur, *Kritische Untersuchungen zum zweiten Makkabäerbuch*, pp. 52 (1904); Wellhausen, "Ueber den geschichtlichen Wert des zweiten Makkabäerbuchs . . .," in *Nachr. der Gött. Ges. der Wissensch.*, Phil.-hist. Kl., pp. 117–163 (1905).

The Epitomist's Preface (ii. 19–32).

The record of the events about to be recounted is taken from the large work of Jason of Cyrene; the writer says that he intends to offer only an abridged form of the work before him (ii. 19–32).

Pre-Maccabæan History (iii. 1–vii. 42).

The attempt of Heliodorus, envoy of the Syrian king Seleucus IV, to plunder the Temple. He is induced to undertake this owing to the report of Simon, " the guardian of the Temple," concerning the immensity of the Temple treasure. The miraculous way in which the attempt was frustrated (iii. 1–40).

Onias, the High-priest, seeks the intervention of the Syrian king in order that the strife between him and Simon may be ended (iv. 1–6).

Antiochus IV Epiphanes succeeds to the Syrian throne. Jason, through bribery, receives from him the High-priest's office; his encouragement of the hellenistic Jews (iv. 7–22).

Menelaus, by offering a higher bribe, supplants Jason in the High-priesthood; he causes Onias, the real High-priest, to be murdered by Andronicus, who is punished by the king for his act (iv. 23–38). Lysimachus, with the connivance of Menelaus, commits many sacrilegious acts; he is killed by the mob (iv. 39–42).

Menelaus, in spite of his wicked deeds, succeeds in retaining the High-priesthood (iv. 43–50).

An account of a miraculous appearance of warriors in the sky (v. 1–3). Jason's attack on Jerusalem in the hope of regaining the High-priesthood; his death (v. 4–10).

Antiochus Epiphanes, under the impression that Jason's attack had been a revolt of the Jews, takes a terrible vengeance on the city. Judas Maccabæus is mentioned for the first time (v. 11–27).

The Temple is desecrated at the command of Antiochus Epiphanes (vi. 1–11).

Parenthetic Legendary Material (vi. 12–vii. 42).

The doctrine of retribution (vi. 12–17).

The martyrdom of Eleazar the scribe (vi. 18-31).
The martyrdom of the seven sons and their mother (vii. 1-42).

The Maccabæan Rising (viii. 1-xv. 36).

Judas Maccabæus musters a following (viii. 1-7).
The victory of Judas over Nicanor (viii. 8-29).
The victory of Judas over Timotheus and Bacchides (viii. 30-33).
The humiliation of Nicanor (viii. 34-36).
The terrible sufferings of Antiochus Epiphanes; his repentance and his letter to the Jews; his death (ix. 1-29).
The clearing of the Temple under the guidance of Judas; the inauguration of the feast of Dedication (x. 1-9).
Antiochus V Eupator becomes king; the death of Ptolemy Macron, satrap of Cœle-Syria (x. 10-13).
Judas defeats the Idumæans (x. 14-23).
The victory of Judas over Timotheus owing to the miraculous appearance of five heavenly horsemen (x. 24-38).
Lysias, the regent, is defeated by Judas after the miraculous appearance of a rider in white apparel who rides at the head of the Jewish forces. A treaty of peace between the Syrians and the Jews is concluded (xi. 1-38).
The peace is broken by Timotheus and his followers in Joppa and Jamnia; they are punished by Judas, who also defeats the Arabians. The city of Caspin is captured (xii. 1-25).
Further successes of Judas (xii. 26-37).
Judas makes a propitiation on behalf of those who have fallen (xii. 38-45).
The death of Menelaus (xiii. 1-8).
The unsuccessful campaign of Antiochus Eupator and Lysias against Judas. A peace is arranged (xiii. 9-26).
Demetrius, being now king, is urged by Alkimus, "who had formerly been high-priest" to send Nicanor against the Jews. Nicanor, however, makes peace with Judas. Alkimus misrepresents Nicanor's action with unfortunate results (xiv. 1-36).
The tragedy of Razis, an elder of Jerusalem (xiv. 37-46).

Nicanor's attack on the Jews; his defeat and death; the institution of " Nicanor's day " (xv. 1–36).

The concluding words of the Epitomist (xv. 37–39).

V. The Greek Text and the Versions

In general, see under *I Maccabees* (p. 314); in most of the MSS. the two books are found together, so that their textual history is similar. There are a certain number of corruptions, sometimes serious, in the text; difficulties occur, *e.g.* in iv. 34; viii. 33; ix. 14, and in many other places. Several Latin Versions, or portions of them, are in existence. The Old Latin is preserved in the Vulgate; a different Latin Version is represented in a MS. (Cod. Ambrosianus), published by Peyron, *Ciceronis orationum pro Scauro* . . ., pp. 73–117 (1824), and another in Codex Complutensis (Berger, *Notices et extraits de la Bibl. Nat.*, pp. 147–152 (1895); and further, Molsdorf has published some fragments (iii. 13–iv. 4, iv. 10–14) which differ in various ways from the other Old Latin MSS. (*Z.A.T.W.*, 1904, pp. 240–250). The Syriac Version is not of much help as it is too free a translation.

VI. Literature

Grimm, *op. cit.*, iv. 3 ff. (1857).

Geiger, *Urschrift und Uebersetzungen der Bibel*, pp. 219 ff. (1857).

Wellhausen, *Die Pharisäer und Sadduzäer* (1874).

Kosters, *Theol. Tijdschrift* for 1878, pp. 491–558.

Rawlinson, in Wace, *op. cit.*, ii. 539 ff. (1888).

Willrich, *Juden und Griechen vor der makkabäischen Erhebung*, pp. 64 ff. (1895).

Willrich, *Urkundenfälschung* . . ., pp. 14–36 (1924).

Schlatter, *Jason von Kyrene, ein Beitrag zu seiner Wiederherstellung* (1891).

Weiss, *Judas Makkabäus, Ein Lebensbild* (1897).

Büchler, *Die Tobiaden und Oniaden im II Makkabäerbuche* . . ., pp. 277–398 (1899).

Niese, *Kritik der beiden Makkabäerbücher* . . . (1900).

Kamphausen, in Kautzsch, *op. cit.*, i. 81–119 (1900).

André, *op. cit.*, pp. 86 ff. (1903).

Schürer, *op. cit.*, i. 32–40 (1901), iii. 482–489 (1909).

Hochfeld, "Die Enstehung des Hanukkafestes," in the *Z.A.T.W.* for 1902, pp. 264–284.

Laqueur, *Kritische Untersuchungen zum zweiten Makkabäerbuch* (1904).

Moffatt, in Charles, *op. cit.*, i. 125–154 (1913).

Y

INDEXES

INDEX OF MODERN AUTHORS

[See also the various sections on the Literature]

INDEX OF BIBLICAL AND POST-BIBLICAL PASSAGES

[See also the sections on the " Contents of the Book "]

OLD TESTAMENT

333

APOCRYPHA

[See also the sections on the " Contents of the Book "]

NEW TESTAMENT

INDEX : GENERAL

www.ingramcontent.com/pod-product-compliance
Lightning Source LLC
Chambersburg PA
CBHW032031090426
42733CB00029B/76